Praise for *Cornered Office*

"Leaders can't afford to ignore their mental health. If they don't feel safe being open about their struggles or have the permission to figure out what they need to feel better, they won't do better for their team and organization. This book makes an undeniable case and provides a logical blueprint for supporting leadership mental health at work. A must-read."

—Kim Scott
Author of *Radical Candor*

"As someone who has confronted my own mental health as a leader, I welcome this book with gratitude. Too often, we expect leaders to be unshakable when in truth, we are humans first and leaders second. Breaking through outdated expectations of stoicism, Melissa Doman opens space for an honest, overdue conversation—and lays the groundwork for the systems and tools we need to make our organizations, and our lives, healthier."

—Alex Reid
Chief Communications Officer, Gates Foundation

"Melissa Doman's important work humanizes leaders in a way our workplaces desperately need, making a clear case for why supporting their mental health is essential for them to keep performing at the level we demand. As someone who experienced burnout firsthand, this book gives organizations the practical framework to stop expecting superhuman resilience and start creating the support systems that help leaders actually thrive."

—Jen Fisher
Bestselling Author, Founder & CEO, The Wellbeing Team

"This book flips the leadership script—finally giving leaders the tools and permission to care for their own mental health without guilt. With real-world stories, sharp research, and practical strategies, Melissa Doman delivers the support leaders have always given others—but rarely receive themselves. Must-read right here!"

—David Nurse
NBA optimization coach, former NBA player,
Wall Street Journal bestselling author, and
host of The David Nurse Show

"As a CEO who has trained and spoken to thousands of leaders globally, I understand firsthand how profoundly isolating and lonely leadership can be. Melissa's book made me feel seen. She gets "it" in a way that most authors don't. This book lays out an essential framework that helps leaders navigate the stressful, often messy, high-pressure dynamics of the modern workplace—with their own emotional survival in mind. This gem is a critical resource that every leader needs."

—**Kwame Christian, Esq., M.A.**
CEO of the American Negotiation Institute

CORNERED OFFICE

CORNERED OFFICE

Why We Need To Talk About
Leadership Mental Health

MELISSA DOMAN, MA

WILEY

Published by John Wiley & Sons, Inc., Hoboken, New Jersey.

Author disclaimer: All information contained in this book is for informational purposes and personal use only. The content in this book is not intended to be or substitute for psychological, psychiatric, medical, or other forms of professional advice. Neither the author nor the publisher of this book has any liability for the actions or inaction of any individual as a result of reading this book. If you are struggling with your mental health, please seek professional medical advice and care.

The manufacturer's authorized representative according to the EU General Product Safety Regulation is Wiley-VCH GmbH, Boschstr. 12, 69469 Weinheim, Germany, e-mail: Product_Safety@wiley.com.

For general information on our other products and services or for technical support, please contact our Customer Care Department within the United States at (800) 762-2974, outside the United States at (317) 572-3993 or fax (317) 572-4002.

Wiley also publishes its books in a variety of electronic formats. Some content that appears in print may not be available in electronic formats. For more information about Wiley products, visit our website at www.wiley.com.

Library of Congress Cataloging-in-Publication Data is Available:

ISBN 9781394350353 (Cloth)
ISBN 9781394350360 (ePub)
ISBN 9781394350377 (ePDF)

Cover Design: Wiley
Cover Image: © Biscotto Design/stock.adobe.com

Printed and bound by CPI Group (UK) Ltd, Croydon, CR0 4YY

C9781394350353_130126

To all of the leaders I've met throughout my career.

You courageously shared your truths, struggles, and showed me your humanity.

Thank you for allowing me to hear you, so I could make sure that others do, too.

Contents

Preface   *xi*

Introduction   *xix*

Part I   **Understanding the Problem: How We Got
             Here (And Why We're Still Here)**   1

Chapter 1   Leadership Mental Health: The History
             of Being Screwed   3

Chapter 2   The Dehumanization of Leaders: VPs Don't
             Have Panic Attacks . . . Right? (Wrong)   19

Chapter 3   The Impact: Leadership Well-Being, Career Path,
             and Performance   37

Chapter 4   The Leadership "Plate" Has Become a Deep
             Trough—and Leaders Are Strapped to It   55

Chapter 5   Leadership Mental Health is Also Shaped by
             Context and Identity   79

Part II	How to Create Change	123
Chapter 6	How Organizations Can Support Leadership Mental Health	125
Chapter 7	Understanding Your Internal Narrative and Leadership Mental Health Archetype	161
Chapter 8	How Leaders Can Create Change for Themselves and Their Peers	179
Chapter 9	Create Your Leadership Mental Health Self-Care Plan	209
Chapter 10	Go Action What You've Learned	229

Notes		*231*
Acknowledgments		*245*
About the Author		*247*
Index		*249*

Preface

WHEN I WANT to share an important idea, I start from a place of honesty. Being truthful is important—regardless of the feelings it may evoke. So that's what I'm going to do here: I had serious Imposter Syndrome[1] when I began writing this book. I'm talking down to my bones, and in the pit of my stomach. For several weeks before I started writing this book, I was on an oh-so-fun merry-go-round, needlessly torturing myself with lovely questions that sounded like,

"What the actual hell am I doing writing this?"

and

"Do I know about the true depths and ALL of the emotional struggles that leaders go through at work?"

Side note: for that second question, no one can know *every single* emotional struggle a group of people could have, not even some of the people in that group. Generally speaking, I'm wary of anyone who portrays themselves as a flawless-answer oracle to others on any subject, and I would encourage you to be, too. But, digressing into my principles on this would require rage-writing an entirely separate book. Okay, back to the point.

So, why did I ask myself those questions? Well, friend, let me tell you. Writing about leadership itself isn't at the center of my work. But you know what is? *People*, mental health, and the workplace. The human experience. I *know* these things, to my core. I always have.

Knowing *people* and what makes them tick means understanding their emotions, thoughts, behaviors, experiences, and mental health. The forces that govern and guide how we see ourselves, manage our struggles, interact with others, and our environment.

In my work, I've continuously said that talking about mental health at work has always been a critical workplace conversation, even if it didn't "get the press" until recent years. But here's the thing. This premise *must apply* to *every human* at work—regardless of title, tenure, or industry. As I toiled over writing the first page, this premise that I've known for years hit me again—like a ton of bricks, as if it were new. I'm writing a book about the *mental health* of leaders. Humans with job titles that carry a different meaning—and impact—at work. So, what happened to the feelings of Imposter Syndrome? I said,

"Thanks for stopping by when I didn't ask you to—and you can leave now."

In my first book, *Yes, You Can Talk About Mental Health at Work (Here's Why and How to Do It Really Well)*, I aimed to teach anyone that they can and should talk about mental health at work, through research-backed education and actionable skills. This book, however, aims to deliver a crucial message to a specific, influential, and visible group at work: leaders. A group of *humans*, who we often ask the most of. I aim to help leaders realize they have the right, and the necessity, to *also* talk about *their* mental health at work—and not always in the service of others. I aim to help them understand *why* they are often treated differently in the larger workplace mental health conversation, due to their professional position. I aim to achieve this through shattering an age-old idea of humanity:

- **That leaders must be consistently emotionally strong, stoic, and impenetrable. If they're not, or display emotional health struggles at work, they cannot lead.**

How am I going to do that?

1. Explain why this idea is unconscionably harmful, untrue, and counterproductive (despite its long-term, over millennia, global adoption).
2. Provide (what I feel) to be a healthier, more sustainable, and logical alternative approach.
3. Provide an undeniable case for all the above, and a blueprint on how to create change.

Just that, no big deal. A small feat, done in a day, with ease . . . said no one ever.

Since you're reading this book, I'm going to safely assume that you most likely have leadership responsibilities of some kind and are trying to develop yourself further in that role. Let me ask you something. From the information you usually consume about developing leadership skills, how often do you see content, material, training programs, etc., dedicated to exploring the *humanization* and *struggles* of leaders? Information centered around leadership emotional health, the thoughts and worries that keep them up at night, and the rest of the non-feel-good parts that exist concurrently with their leadership abilities.

I'll wait . . . I would have a hard time answering that, too.

Does this information exist? Of course it does. I'm one of the people who produces it. Others share my sentiments. We're a small group, often unheard, because our voices are drowned out by the loud, dominant hegemonies in a sea of 8 billion souls who feel differently (. . . or do they?). With our messaging often ignored because it seemingly goes against the grain and "natural order" of things. So, here's what we usually see, instead. Lessons and messaging that sound something like:

How to Be a (_____) Leader:
   ○ (Catchy marketing words playing on people's insecurities)
   ○ (Words implying perfection, as we often underestimate language's power)

Take "How to Be a Servant Leader" as an example. We see countless examples of literature on this topic because, in principle, it's a good method that helps develop people-focused leaders. However, this concept and all of its related content rarely, if ever, emphasize the importance of *leadership* mental health while serving others. Servant Leadership Theory[2] emphasizes being consistently in service to team members, with leaders prioritizing their team members' needs above their own. While this theory is well-intended and has demonstrable positive outcomes, when left unchecked and unmanaged, it can be unintentionally counterintuitive and dismissive of leadership mental health. This is of no disrespect to theory's creator, Robert Greenleaf, in any way. There was no way he could ever have anticipated the type and volume of pressure that leaders would be under in the twenty-first century when he wrote *The Servant as a Leader* in 1970.

What does the Madlib-like exercise above imply? Intentional or not, because I won't presume to understand or assume every professional's intention with what they put into the world, leadership development messaging is overwhelmingly and predominantly *other*-focused, *team*-focused, and *outward*-focused—with no mention of the *true* support needs of being asked to do that ad infinitum. I remember marinating on this one day in my office, and I literally (no joke) blurted out to myself, "*Oh, for f**k's sake, who is looking out for leaders?!*" Before 2018, I couldn't have answered that question myself. Until then, just like anyone else, I made the same mistake of assuming that leaders "didn't need help." I can pinpoint the day when it changed for me.

I was living in London in 2018 and working on a people and leadership development contract. I was asked to facilitate my very first leadership workshop on how to talk to teams about mental health at work. I was so proud of myself for creating a meaty three-hour workshop (which I laugh at now because you can't teach anyone a skill well in just three hours). On the day of the workshop, I walked in with confidence, thinking this session would equip these leaders and make them feel ready to use this skill. Wrong. Not even halfway into the workshop, one of the participants mentioned that, while the information I was providing was necessary and helpful, it would have been nice to be asked how they feel about doing this with their teams. They highlighted that it's a new and delicate skill set to learn and acknowledged that they have their own stressors too. As I'm sure you can imagine, I was mortified.

Like anyone else, social narratives had shaped my beliefs. At that time, I had no reason to stop and question them. It never crossed my mind that, based on who this group "was," they might feel that way or have those concerns. Nor did I consider how they would feel being expected to skillfully adopt (under organizational pressure, of course) yet another ability that their leadership predecessors weren't required to learn. Without recognizing their struggles, fears, or need for support, I overlooked their humanity. With a background in both counseling psychology and organizational psychology, I believed I knew how to work with people from all walks of life, experiences, and positions. Yet I had forgotten that the individuals sitting in front of me were people first, and leaders second. I felt so foolish for having approached it that way. I entered the process of creating and delivering this training with the sole intention of helping these leaders understand how to support their teams, and that would be enough. In reality, I was part of the problem. I'm forever thankful that this participant spoke up, because several other attendees then followed, agreeing with their sentiment. I didn't know it then, but two seeds had been planted:

- Seed 1: I need to teach the World of Work how to talk about mental health at work, as a critical professional development skill (book 1).
- Seed 2: I now need to teach the World of Work that leaders need to be part of the workplace mental health conversation for themselves, too, not just to facilitate it in service to their teams and organizations (this book).

After I wrote my first book, I was thrilled that companies were eager to read and actually use it, and I was also simultaneously shocked and frustrated. Of the companies that approached me, the overwhelming majority would say:

"We need to teach our leaders how to support their teams."

Sigh.

Yes, this is obviously a good inquiry, and better than businesses not caring to learn this at all. But it remained an incomplete picture. A foreground, without a background. So, I would often say something like,

"It's wonderful that you want to teach your leaders how to talk to their teams about mental health! AND. I would also advise you to implement support structures for your leaders, too. It's unsustainable to ask your leaders to support their teams without also supporting your leaders. Are you open to also discussing what that could look like?"

Cue seeing blank stares, hearing a disinterested-sounding vocal tone, and experiencing an awkward, quick change of subject.

While these people and companies may not realize it, I need to thank them. Without our conversations over the years through my consulting, teaching, and speaking, I wouldn't have felt inspired, compelled, and responsible to write this book to prove my point. I also need to thank the leaders I've coached throughout the years. Thank you for being honest with me about the hidden and ignored emotional struggles of being a leader. How unseen you felt, how frightened you were to be seen, and why. I've always known your truth, even if you were sadly and rightfully afraid to share it with your companies and teams. You all drove me to champion and advocate for education and narrative shifts around leadership mental health at work—and ultimately, to write this book. Because no one else was doing it, and I couldn't (and wouldn't) wait any longer.

To the leaders whose workplaces, or even teams, have ever made you feel like your mental health doesn't matter, I apologize on their behalf. I'm sorry if your basic mental health needs have been ignored or deprioritized. In this book, we'll talk about why this happens. And why it isn't okay. There's no logical excuse for this happening, and I hope it was only because they didn't know better. To the organizations that have excluded the importance of leadership mental health, intentionally or not, I won't speculate on why you've done this. I hope that you are unintentionally part of the problem, just as many of us have been. If you just haven't prioritized it yet, it's time to do better.

Since I wrote my last book, I've had a surprisingly large number of conversations that continue to reveal why I've needed to break down this wall that never should have been built in the first place. Throughout my career, I've usually been the person who raises their hand to point out why a behavior, idea, or approach might be unhelpful or wrong, and explains why. I'm used to the shock and discomfort this causes some people. And, the relief that washes over others, appreciating someone sharing what their inside voice has been screaming, when they didn't feel safe to say it themselves.

I sincerely hope that by the time you finish this book, you'll understand and feel why I felt a sense of urgency to create a comprehensive case and resource that didn't exist. To change people's minds about leadership mental health, and why we can't afford to ignore it anymore, for the mental survival of leaders at work.

Introduction

BEFORE WE PROCEED, let's pause to take stock.

I've Read the Room—I Promise

I realize that what I'm asking people to consider in this book may feel a bit unnatural, odd, or even scary. Most new, seemingly "on the fray" ideas that run counter to long-term narratives usually are, but please stick with me while you consider my case. This juice will be very much worth the squeeze.

I'm asking people to somewhat go against and reframe what we've always been taught to believe and expect of our leaders emotionally at work, and to turn care toward them when we've historically expected that care to go in one direction—away from themselves. When people are exposed to new ideas, whether for themselves or others, they can be curious, and yes, resistant, too. I'm comfortable with that, and I hope you are too. I'm asking leaders to dare to ask The World of Work, and those they lead, to see them in a humanized light and understand that they have mental health needs, too. Going against a narrative that not only doesn't account for it but actively discourages it for a variety of reasons.

It's also not lost on me that I'm writing this book at a time when many leaders are engaging in questionable behavior and when leadership is more distrusted than ever. Making headlines in the news and on social media daily. Superb timing, right? Surprising probably no one, the 2025 *Edelman* Trust Barometer Global Report on Trust and the Crisis of Grievance[1] showed that trust is at an all-time global low. I very much read the room as I wrote this book. While the world has continued to feel like it's crashing down, and in some ways it is, I've also seen great leaders do incredible things, giving us hope for the future. These leaders deserve support for the things they have to do that others don't. Not to be discarded and exempt from compassion based on the errors of others, also in a position of power. With so many people affected by bad leadership, it's hard to remember and consider "the good ones."

Despite the horrendous behavior of leaders who choose to do wrong, leadership mental health *still objectively matters*. And, this weight on leaders is *intensifying*, demonstrably (and increasingly) harming leadership mental health over time. Generally, when I bring this up to others, it elicits one of two reactions: "Um, yes please!" or "No, are you kidding me?!" The former shows intense agreement and a desperate need for acknowledgment, while the latter indicates wholehearted dismissal and dismay. I'm aware that this book may provoke similar dichotomous reactions, even among those who haven't read it and won't. That's okay. What I'm addressing touches *many* nerves, experiences, and opinions. For those who may have a trigger-like reaction, while their experiences are valid to them, it doesn't diminish the objectively valid argument that I'm presenting. I don't intend for this to seem reductionist or simplistic. Instead, I aim to highlight objective truths that have long been overlooked, even when many have resisted acknowledging them.

Phil Knight, the former CEO of Nike, is famously known for leading with one of his favorite mantras from General Douglas MacArthur, mentioned in his memoir *Shoe Dog*, and in the 2023 film *Air*—which we'll revisit in Chapter 1: *"You're remembered for the rules you break."* Of course, there are exceptions to my argument, but all exceptions require a rule, and I'm here to break that rule.

The Tone to Expect

If the Preface didn't tip you off, I like to keep things direct, funny, and no BS. It's how I conduct my life, business, and any education I deliver. This book will be the same. I've seen too many pieces of work with fantastic information and lessons get lost because the delivery was dry, hard to read, or some combination thereof. I want you to feel like you're in a candid conversation with me, learning and considering new information, while having a few chuckles along the way. Not to feel like you're being given a lecture. I will encourage you to think differently about leadership mental health in general and *your* mental health as a leader. Hopefully, it will give you a new perspective that compels you to change the conversations you have at work, for yourself, and others.

Good news—you won't find buzzwords or bumper-sticker phrases in here. I'm allergic to that disingenuous, unhelpful nonsense. If you're going to consider a new argument from me, learn a new skill, and potentially spend time applying it, then it's my responsibility to give you my best. With logic, data, a thorough and purposeful explanation, and easy-to-follow guidance you can use—and feel the effort is worth it.

You'll also notice that I have a flair for occasionally using colorful language (with asterisks blanking out certain letters, because manners, folks) to show the force of a point. I subscribe to the school of thought that these special words have several productive purposes[2], especially when emphasizing a point. It's also a fun way to apparently show intelligence (thank you, 2015 study published in *Language Sciences*[3] exploring the Controlled Oral Word Association Test [COWAT]). I do not intend to offend anyone's sensibilities, and I hope my explanation of why I've included this sparky language will lessen the potential bite for those of you who don't use this language the same way.

Leaders—This Book Is for YOU

Let's align on meaning. In my experience, when I say "leader" or "manager," people tend to think only of those at the top, who generally oversee a team of people, often with several years of experience, and other generic leadership archetypes. But this book is for *all* leaders. For *any* leader or manager, regardless of experience level—whether you're a first-timer, middle manager, senior leader, CEO, founder, or owner—across industries. My message is intended for all of you, but please don't worry—I've also considered the nuanced struggles.

Throughout this book, when I refer to individuals in leadership roles, it's regardless of their level or authority. There will also be points where I provide commentary that may be more specifically useful for individuals in roles such as leadership development, talent development, DEIB, human resources, or for owners and founders who set the tone and direction for an organization. While those I just named are also leaders, I'm conscious of their additional influence on the narrative and practices around leadership mental health in companies, so sometimes I'll be speaking directly to them, especially in Part II, in the boxes labeled like this,

> ### For Policy, Program, & Practice Shifters

Lastly, I'm also aware that some people in leadership roles are individual-contributor subject matter experts (i.e., those with a leadership title but no reporting structure). Even if you don't lead a team, you still have visibility and influence in your organization and are (most likely) treated as such. I see you, and this book is for you, too.

How the Goal Shaped the Content

Deciding what to include was a ruthless process, as I could never include every issue pertinent to leadership mental health. I didn't have it in me to write 2,000 pages—and didn't think you'd want to read that much either. I'm not trying to boil the ocean, and I encourage you to adopt a similar mindset.

As I planned the book's content, there was only one logical way to approach it: by focusing on and *honestly* examining the most significant pain points of a problematic idea, the resulting practices that followed, why we can't continue the pattern, and a few concrete, useful methods to create new outcomes. Here's how we'll keep track of those elements over the two parts of this book:

Part I: The Weight on Leadership Mental Health Equation
(How the pain points have stacked up)

Part II: The Leadership Mental Health Support Solution
(The interventions to address them)

Despite the term "equation," I promise, there's no actual math. I always joke that people go into psychology when they struggle with math. Just kidding—that's only me.

In all my work, I use the Paradox of Choice concept from Dr. Barry Schwartz's book *Paradox of Choice—Why More Is Less*.[4] A core idea from Dr. Schwartz's work that's stuck with me is this: having a lot of choice doesn't necessarily benefit us; if anything, it can act as an obstacle to action. So, I've aimed to give you the targeted, meaningful quality of less, rather than the seemingly good volume of more. Since I have your attention for only 10 chapters, each chapter will articulate the purpose of the information's inclusion and explain why it matters.

What This Book Is NOT Trying to Do

I like to address potential objectives or concerns upfront. A statement of intention is crucial when discussing mental health at work (and for many other things, to be honest) and especially when taking on an idea that has been largely unchallenged for a long time. In addition to what this book aims to do (coming up next), here are some things it's *not* trying to do (I call these the Nuh-Uhs).

I'm NOT giving a pass for bad behavior and recklessness in leadership

Generally, I don't give passes for consistently bad behavior. When people do, it makes me seethe, so trust that I will not do that here. Whether it's a boss who traumatized you or no-no behavior you've done as a leader because you know you can get away with it—no. Just no. This book explores the recognition of leadership mental health struggles that often go unsupported at work. It's not about excusing the bad behavior that may result from, or is independent of, that. A leader's mental health struggles, regardless of their source (i.e., internal or external to work), does not negate their responsibility to be accountable for their behavior and actions toward others, especially those they lead.

Not to put additional pressure on you (because leaders need more of that, right?), but your impact on your team members can be extremely potent. I know, this can be uncomfortable to think about. *The Workforce Institute* surveyed 3,400 people across 10 countries to show managers' critical role in supporting and impacting the mental health of their team members at and outside of the workplace.[5] I'm not saying this to freak you out, but rather to reiterate Uncle Ben's words from *Spiderman*, "With great power, comes great responsibility." Leaders, like any other adult, should not place their emotional baggage on others at work—especially their teams. This is even more true when they haven't tried to help themselves first. Power dynamics are real and can be very scary depending on the setup. Respect that and the power you have to influence how others feel (or don't) at work.

Yes, leadership is stressful. Life is stressful.

No, leadership mental health still doesn't get the attention it needs.

No, the proper support has not been put in place to help leaders.

And finally, no, this does not mean leaders can pass off their turmoil to others who don't deserve it.

Struggling with mental health (especially if you can do something about it but still haven't) doesn't justify treating others poorly, no matter what you're going through. Yes, we can be (and often are) a product of our environment, which influences how we feel about ourselves, others, and our actions. Like I've consistently emphasized throughout my career, having mental health struggles isn't a choice, but how we handle those struggles is—provided you have access to resources, can afford to use them, and have a modicum of social support. The fact remains, every chronologically aged adult (because mental and physical age aren't always aligned) is responsible for managing their mental health. With the responsibilities that come with leadership, you bet your butt that it includes addressing and managing your emotional health challenges, too. Being a leader *does not preclude you* from managing your mental health. If anything, for your own survival and to effectively show up for your team, it emphasizes the need to prioritize managing it *even more*.

I'm NOT making a false promise to "fix" leadership mental health or create "stress-free" leadership conditions

You would be shocked (or maybe not) at how many people I continue to encounter throughout my career who are looking to "fix" mental health at their organization. Anyone who knows me says I'm "the woman of a thousand faces," so you can imagine how difficult it is not to show my feelings with facial subtitles each time I hear people utter that sentiment. With everything we know today about mental health at work, it's not something to fix or always keep positive. It's something that exists on a spectrum. The goal is to acknowledge and discuss it constructively and helpfully. When it comes to leadership mental health, this is no different.

I'm NOT trying to give a one-size-fits-all approach

As I said earlier, no one has the answers for any single idea, problem, or practice, especially for a nuanced and deeply personal, situationally dependent topic like this. Every person is unique in their experiences and needs. This book will give concepts and suggested best practices. It's up to each reader to decide how they feel about them, whether or not they will use them, and in what way. Simply put, use what feels right for you. Leave the rest.

What This Book IS Trying to Do

Now, let's examine what this book aims to accomplish, why, and how.

Challenge Outdated Ideas & Advocate for a Perspective Shift

- *What:*
  - *The Old Idea Being Broken:* Unhealthy, unsustainable, illogical historical narratives that portray emotional struggles at work by leaders as an incapability to lead.
  - *The Encouraged Perspective:* Leaders having the self-permission to acknowledge the necessity of prioritizing their mental health at work, along with a call to action for companies to support this.

- *How:* Through logically constructed arguments, applicable theory, data, and real stories from modern-day leaders asking for this change.
- *Why:* Because leaders' mental health shouldn't be neglected based on the position they hold, let alone from what the workplace demands they accomplish. This argument should be enough, yet historically, it hasn't been. I think of Gestalt psychology here, in that we all have parts that make up the whole of who we are.[6] Make no mistake—being a leader is just *part* of who those people are—not all of who they are. Each piece has its significance. The workplace must accept this, because it's logically valid.

Share REAL Hidden Leadership Mental Health Stories

- *What:* Real-world qualitative interviews with leaders across industries, backgrounds, and walks of life.
- *How:* Through anonymous interview quotes with a few biographical details (with the interviewees' permission). Specifically, age, gender, ethnicity, leadership level, and industry. Here's an example of what these references will look like throughout the book:

> Interviewee: female, Gen X, Black, Vice President,
> non-profit industry

I did this to demonstrate how these factors influence their perspectives, experiences, and the "why" of if they feel they can talk about their mental health as leaders. It also highlights some commonalities they share, despite their differences. The identifiers I've included do not intend to represent the totality of experiences of those groups, but rather to show examples from some leaders who were willing to share. As a standard writing practice for me, these stories are anonymous because knowing the interviewees' names isn't the point. What's important is what they had to say, why they wanted to share it, and what they want others to learn from it.

- *Why:* To give a voice to and hear directly from those who can't (or won't) speak up for themselves. These stories highlighted one key truth: leadership mental health struggles are universal, even if the details vary. You need to hear directly from the people I'm speaking about, not just the vessel of information (me). To advocate for change on their behalf and do these interviews justice, I ensured that their stories were corroborated and supplemented by validated research to substantiate my argument further.

Provide Actionable Tools for Change & New Practices

- *What:* To transform how leaders and companies think about leadership mental health at work and reshape how it's supported in today's workplace.
- *How:* Through individual leadership mental health practices, creating community for leadership mental health, and shifting organizational structures and support practices.
- *Why:* It would be crappy of me to build a big case about why something doesn't work and then not give you tools for how to do things differently.

Your Responsibilities as the Reader

I'm only going to task you with three things:

Personalize the Guidance

Use what works for *you*! I won't pretend to know what that is because, hey, we don't know each other (but I hope we will someday—my sister calls me "The Friend Collector" after all). You are your own kettle of fish. Honor that, I would never tell you not to, but, at the same time, recognize the truth that changing how you think about this topic and how you behave in relation to it will be the way to produce different results. All I can do is provide my argument, best practices, and tools for you to use. How you take that information, what you choose to do with it, and when (or if) you use it is entirely up to you. Please apply this guidance to your specific job, company, industry, and life experience in a way that feels achievable, realistic, and actionable.

Dig Deep

At the risk of sounding trite, try to have an open mind, which I know can be difficult at times, especially with some ideas and concepts that we cling to for our own reasons. All I ask is that you think *very honestly* about what made you want to read this book in the first place. Identifying that motivation can be a powerful force in driving you to use what you've learned. Knowing why we want to do things can often help us do them better. Even if your reflections make you grapple with big feelings or discomfort, settle in. Discomfort is a common feeling when we acknowledge essential truths, when we need to change our minds, or realize we need to do things differently.

Do the Work

The book is divided into two parts and is structured to guide you through a deconstructed overview of long-held notions about leadership mental health, delving into specific issues, and finally, providing practical tools and strategies for implementation. Reflect, consider, and decide what you want and need to use from this book—and why. In Part I, there will be reflection questions encouraging you to ponder specific ideas you may not think about very often, so you can understand where you are now and how you got there (i.e., "inside voice" work, thinking about things privately, only for you). The results from those reflection questions are intended to drive the deeper reflection work and practical actions you'll take in Part II (i.e., "outside voice" work, speaking with others, and using your new skills).

For you recovering (or current) perfectionists out there—please take a breath and remember the goal is practice, not perfection. This will be a non-linear, slow-burning journey, and your needs may change over time. It won't be a series of milestones to achieve. Remember: any healthy growth or change is good, no matter how small the moment may be.

What Success Will Look Like

I'm usually hesitant to outline this since success can look different for each person. However, I understand it can be helpful for some people to know "what good looks like," so they can visualize the outcomes they're working toward. At a high level, if I were to define what "success" could look like after applying the education and lessons from this book, I would envision something like this:

1. Leaders *have reduced fear* of speaking up about their mental health struggles because they know it doesn't mean they're incapable of leading, weak, or untrustworthy.
2. Organizations *consistently ask leaders* what they need to feel supported at work, rather than predominantly focusing on the strategic, outcomes-focused, and efficiency-based tools they need to lead their teams.
3. The World of Work *doesn't solely emphasize outward-focused methods* of "being a good leader." Additionally, it emphasizes the importance of prioritizing mental health as a hallmark of effective leadership.

These may feel like a tall order, because in a way, they are, and we may not be able to see these successes (consistently) for a long time. Also, it's not lost on me that these successes may be more easily actualized for some people, in certain situations, companies, and industries, than others. But, with every conversation had and every idea challenged, we are one step closer to shifting what "is" to what "could be." The more examples of success that we see, the more normalized and expected they will become. It is my profound desire that every person who reads this book will be inspired to join me in creating this shift, too, because I can't do it alone.

My Accountability Promise to You

I want you to know that I, too, have faced the conflicting pressures of leadership. After years as a solo entrepreneur, I had to hire multiple team members within a year and became a leader overnight. It was one of those "building the plane while flying it" situations. I'm one of those people who practice what they preach. Even though I have helped leaders professionally through training, consulting, and coaching, experiencing leadership firsthand was something I needed to do myself to understand what it *truly* feels like. I had to build a team while applying the leadership guidance I gave to my clients, even as I wrote this book. Like any leader, I've had successes and failures. But you know where I'm always consistent? Showing my team that I prioritize my mental health as a leader, being open when I'm struggling, and, most importantly, explaining how I plan to manage it—because it's my responsibility. That includes letting my team support me when appropriate (more on this later). I follow and demonstrate the same principles and behaviors that I'm encouraging you to adopt.

So come with me, and let's get started.

PART

I

Understanding the Problem

How We Got Here (And Why We're Still Here)

1

Leadership Mental Health: The History of Being Screwed

"Leadership became a slow erasure of self. The further I rose, the less support I had, and the more I believed I had to carry it all alone. The pressure to hold things together without adequate mentorship or training eventually broke me down mentally, emotionally, and physically."

Interviewee: male, Gen X, Caucasian, Senior Leadership, construction industry

"Becoming a leader has basically destroyed my mental health. I carry the burden of my higher position, as well as that of supporting my team and their concerns, on my shoulders, all the time. I often wake up with concerns about work or how I'm going to get everything done and not sacrifice my personal life, my spouse, my children, and my health."

Interviewee: female, Millennial, Caucasian, Senior Director, health technology industry

THIS CHAPTER IS *not* meant to sound like I'm whining on behalf of leaders. When we give people visibility, impact, and influence over others, we must expect that role to bring greater accountability, responsibility, and self-awareness. However, we also need to recognize the weight that comes with a leadership position. A weight that is often overlooked, and even reinforced, through messaging, social norms, and systems that have made this clear: leadership mental health is not part of the "leadership conversation," whether that emotional distress stems from work or not.

The Broken Building Blocks of the Sociological Assignment of Power

Going back to Phil Knight for a moment, I loved the 2023 film *Air*. Great writing and acting aside, what I loved most about this film were the numerous messages about leadership, team collaboration, and trust. Set in the 1980s, a senior leader at Nike, Sonny Vaccaro, had a monologue when speaking to then-young and pre-famous basketball player Michael Jordan, who arguably went on to become one of the best basketball players in U.S. history. Sonny's message to Michael was clear in a powerful monologue in the film: that Michael's leadership in his sport, while it would be enjoyable, would also be hard, heartbreaking, and at times, feel like an impossible position.

> ". . . *People are going to build you up . . . we'll build you up into something that doesn't even exist . . . But you know what? Once they've built you as high as they possibly can, they're gonna tear you back down—it's the most predictable pattern. We build you into something that doesn't exist, and that means you have to try to be that thing all day, every day. That's how it works. And we do it again, and again, and again.*"[1]

What does Sonny's monologue show us? We need to look at and deconstruct the pattern. Addressing the ongoing, and predictable, neglect of leadership mental health means examining the figuratively cracked foundation beneath it. Examining the history reveals the building blocks upon which our current expectations and biases are based, namely "archetypes" of how we expect leaders to act, behave, and guide us. Ultimately, fueling the meaning behind the sociological assignment of power, and how we believe it should govern expectations of leadership behavior, in the hope that we've put the right people in charge, unencumbered by doubt. Unfortunately, what naturally results opposes the emotional needs of *humans* in those roles. A toxic paradox: here's what we've decided you need to be, what we expect of you, and you will not receive support in return because you shouldn't "need it." Over the years, I've observed this in my work too, seeing two main reasons why people generally don't pay attention to leadership mental health:

1. We don't think we *need* to:
   - i.e., Leaders are "fine"
     - o P.S. I once learned that "fine" stands for:
       (F)eelings (I)nside (N)ot (E)xpressed
       I know, I wasn't the same after I learned that either.
2. We don't *want* to:
   - i.e., Leaders hold power over us, so we shouldn't "have to."

How did we arrive here? Let's take a high-level trip down memory lane to see why. I'm not an anthropologist, but I want to acknowledge how our starting point often influences our current position. With a quick nod to our power dynamics as a species, I've included and focused on a few sociological and psychological theories that illustrate this point and explain how they fit into the larger idea we're trying to deconstruct, break, and replace. Thanks for indulging my sociology and psychology degrees for a moment, too.

A Brief Ode to the Unintended Toxicity of the Original Leadership Archetypes

> *"Traditionally, leaders are told to lead by example and tend to shove their struggles aside to be the inspiration that they think their team needs. It can feel like you can't be tired, emotional, or upset."*
>
> Interviewee: male, Millennial, Asian, Owner, healthcare industry

History has taught leaders not to expect to have their mental health struggles acknowledged, understood, or supported. But history alone hasn't done this; our biology has, too. Let's start there. Humans have a natural need for protection and guidance, whether from environmental factors or other members of our species, no matter how much of a #Rebel someone is (me included, by the way). Feeling the need for protection from fellow humans or having someone to follow is a deeply ingrained biological drive. We want to feel that someone will "tell us the way," provide us with proper guidance and shield us from harmful surprises in our environment. As group dynamics and social systems evolved to meet these needs, so did the expectations of both those being led and those doing the leading. From my experience working with people, I have found, as Sonny mentioned, that humans are generally predictable and tend to repeat patterns.

Spanning over time and cultures, leadership behaviors have been defined, reinforced, and reinforced again with few challenges to the traditional image. The journal *Current Biology* published a study pointing to this.[2]

> *"Leadership is arguably one of the most important themes in the social sciences, permeating all aspects of human social affairs . . . that draw our attention to the fundamental role of leadership and follower-ship . . . Converging ideas and developments in both the natural and social sciences suggest that leadership and followership share common properties across humans and other animals, pointing to ancient roots and evolutionary origins."*

In the article, they explore key findings from both the animal kingdom and our human ancestors, demonstrating how modern leadership and followership are shaped and inspired by our own evolutionary history as a species. And, how our evolutionary history contributes to our understanding, and even predicts, modern leadership behaviors today. Some popular examples we often think of include the Alpha, the King, the General, or the Elected Government Representative. Numerous contextual factors also compound and influence these evolutionarily driven archetypes, and we'll examine them more closely in Chapter 5.

Regardless of the role and its differences, each archetype shares common themes: maintaining trust, accountability, managing threats, navigating power struggles, and ensuring survival while adapting to the changing social norms within which they operate. They also share similar expectations for emotions and behaviors. There is an understood "contract" that a leader is a symbol to others and is not just an individual. The more responsibility a leader has, the higher the standards, along with the understanding that they shouldn't discuss the emotional toll it takes on them. These original archetypes have taught leaders to prioritize the needs of the group they serve and lead above their own and to demonstrate unwavering confidence and resilience, regardless of the cost. What these original leadership archetypes have done is create an image of what people *see* leaders to be and what leaders *are supposed to see themselves as*, excluding their humanity (i.e., dismissing the mental health struggles that *can* and *will* happen in life in general, and in their roles as leaders). This historical pattern has consistently placed a strain on leaders, generation after generation, to seem emotionally impenetrable, when in reality, they are not, and they never should have been expected to be.

These dynamics still exist today; they simply appear differently now. This doesn't translate well for the modern leader, who faces a more complex set of demands than ever before in history. Those original archetypes never anticipated the modern pressures of working a job, receiving endless information about multidirectional evaluation for a promotion, or the risk of being canceled online. Despite being challenged over time, social expectations have not (and sometimes seemingly won't) catch up with our current reality, seemingly locked in by these pervasive illogical myths. Ultimately, keeping leaders in systems where they're deterred from vocalizing their dissenting experiences, while maintaining emotional chlorination for show. Being expected to act seemingly error-free, with positive associations linked to their ability to do so. Error-free? One of my least favorite oxymorons and unnatural inclusions within any conversation about humanity. Why and how has this been maintained? Through the upholding of social perception and norms, influenced by the power of storytelling.

The Influence of Perception, Storytelling, and Social Norms

Storytelling shapes socially shared narratives because we find meaning through stories and experiences. Repeated stories and long-term narratives can be challenging to change, regardless of the topic. Strongly held social narratives influence how we see things, the biases we develop, the social rules we make, how we organize ourselves, and what we expect from the world—and from the people around us. We apply this to groups by creating the unwritten or unspoken rules or standards of acceptable behavior within a social group[3]—especially leaders.

And, like everything else shaped over time through storytelling, the social expectations surrounding leadership behaviors—especially those related to emotional distress—are no exception. When people share their experiences about those who have led them, these stories are ultimately categorized as either "good" or "bad." These labels are inherently binary, subjective, and limited terms that don't account for the full spectrum of behavior and experiences. However, humans rely on these mental heuristics[4] (i.e., cognitive shortcuts) to instantly categorize people's actions in the blink of an eye; therefore, I'll use those terms for simplicity. To explore the often-overlooked realm of leadership mental health and challenge the ideas that many have clung to over time, we need to examine how ongoing storytelling and narratives have shaped the image of "good" leadership behaviors and how that affects our social expectations of leaders' emotional expressions. Resulting in two types of influence:

1. What team members, organizations, and society at large perceive and expect good leadership behaviors to be (i.e., social perception); and
2. What leaders perceive and expect of themselves behaviorally in those roles (i.e., self-perception).

Navigating Social Perceptions, and Self-Perceptions, of "Good" Leadership Behaviors

> *"As a leader, there are inherently higher expectations placed on you . . . Coupled with the personal pressure of not wanting to fail, I found myself very close to rock bottom."*
>
> Interviewee: female, Millennial, Black, Senior Vice President in the C-Suite, heavy civil construction industry
>
> *"It can feel like you aren't allowed to feel your own feelings . . . Sometimes I feel embarrassed or ashamed if I feel tired, strained, injured—and try to play it down or hide it. Even knowing we're all human and feel this way sometimes."*
>
> Interviewee: male, Millennial, Asian, Owner, healthcare industry

The Social Cognitive Model of Leadership Perceptions[5] tells us that our species generally and collectively agrees that a leadership role prioritizes displaying specific behaviors. We scrutinize those in leadership roles to ensure they display the following:

Strength, decisiveness, trust, credibility, and stoicism.

When we observe others who naturally, or at least visibly, display these behaviors or traits, we tend to find it easier to attribute power to them because we've automatically assumed they are capable (i.e., this is how leaders act; thus, we believe they can handle it). We have strong mental reference points about what good leadership behaviors look like. This, in turn, influences how we evaluate current or potential leaders. Sometimes, this will even go to an extreme. A piece in *Psychology Today* citing a 2023 study published in the *Journal of Business Ethics* showed why people are even drawn to following, and I quote, "tyrannical leaders." Why would people be drawn to tyrannical leaders, especially today, with what we've seen them do? Because some people may subconsciously associate that type of leader with someone who can effectively protect them.[6] In effect, their modern ideas are driven by their original homo sapien software.

Let's consider team perceptions of leaders. In 2023, *Leadership Quarterly* highlighted a study on team cognition and its contribution to understanding leadership. When teams evaluate, judge, and interpret the behaviors of leaders,[7] this is how those team members tend to assess and cognitively organize their thoughts about leaders. I'm using "we" to describe our patterns as a species,

- *We create mental representations of leaders:* we archetype what good leaders look and act like, shaped by cultural context and previous interactions with other leaders.
  - o Ironically enough, while writing this book, I had a meeting with someone and shared my central thesis. Just by merely mentioning that leadership mental health is objectively important, I visibly triggered this person. They immediately launched into a rant about all the leaders who had failed them throughout their career and all of the horrible things "they see online," ultimately resulting in this person saying, and I quote: "I don't care how leaders are doing anymore." When I validated their experiences, which were unfortunate and unwarranted, I also explained that just because those leaders were ineffective and took negative actions, doesn't mean that all leaders are like this, and that leadership mental health is still an important topic to discuss. But it didn't matter to them, and my sentiment was dismissed. All of those leadership representatives who failed this person had robbed them of any desire to remember that leaders are still human beings, and that not all individuals and the actions they take are representative of the same group. And what this person had seen on social media and the internet cemented all those feelings, in concrete.
- *We interpret the behavior of leaders:* we do this constantly, accurately or not. We interpret why leaders do what they do based on our preexisting prototypes of what we consider a good or effective leader.
  - o Side note: Psychoanalyst and anthropologist Michael Maccoby published a fascinating piece in *Harvard Business*

Review (HBR) highlighting how people are often drawn to leaders who resemble a mental representation of important people from their past, such as a close friend, parent, sibling, or other type of caregiver (also known as transference).[8] Translation: We are drawn to leaders who we feel will protect us. Conversely, we may also naturally fight against leaders for the very same reason (which we'll unpack more in Chapter 4).

- *We attribute meaning to leaders' behavior*: we theorize what a leader's behaviors or words mean, consider the situation in which they occur, and then fill in the blanks about their potential intentions (accurate or not).
  - o We connect this to what we believe they were trying to achieve when they acted or spoke in a certain way. This phenomenon is especially evident when we encounter a new leader[9] (i.e., they are judged by all who came before them). This process can happen almost instantaneously and goes uninterrupted unless the perceiver and the one being perceived quickly compare notes.

Based on how we tend to mentally organize our views of good leaders, and knowing this, wouldn't it create a compelling push for them to predominantly display those good leadership behaviors at work? The motivation is strong to avoid creating opportunities for doubt by not veering off script into the messy realities of the human struggles they still experience behind their socially attributed power. Power dynamics are not just real and palpable to those who are led, but also to those who lead.

Cue Dr. Robert Cialdini's *The Principles of Influence*.[10] I frequently refer to his principles when I work with leaders on communication and team dynamics. Among Cialdini's seven principles, I've always felt that the Laws of Authority and Consistency unintentionally overshadow the reality that leaders can be effective while grappling with their mental health. The Law of Authority states that we view individuals favorably who can demonstrate authority and expertise. The Law of Consistency says that we favor those who are steadfast in their decisions and commentary. If we look to leaders for consistency and authority, we're not exactly preparing ourselves to be receptive to or readily accept witnessing struggles or behavioral variance from those who lead.

> "I worked for a VP who broke me emotionally and mentally . . . I never felt I was good enough. He would criticize me in front of the team that I lead. I don't remember a time that we were together when I didn't cry in front of him. It seemed that he wanted to break me. It took years of intensive therapy to heal from the trauma of this experience."
>
> Interviewee: female, Baby Boomer, Caucasian, Director, beauty industry

Not only are leaders evaluated by everyone around them, but they also put perceptual and social norm pressures on themselves. Sometimes, leaders even propagate these expectations among themselves (which we'll discuss more in Chapter 5). The toxicity of paying the wrong thing forward, if you will. People in leadership positions are part of and self-identify as part of a social group (i.e., leaders). Social Identity Theory[11] suggests that leaders compare their identity to, and are influenced by, the identities of other leaders within the same group. This informs what it means to be "good" and deemed acceptable to lead, to themselves, their peers, and by those they lead. Individuals then self-impose expectations to display those idyllic qualities to positively represent the group they're a part of (i.e., I need to fit the profile). Sociologist Erving Goffman's concept of Impression Management from his book, *The Presentation of Self in Everyday Life*, reinforces this by explaining that, "Impression management not only influences how one is treated by other people, but is an essential part of social interaction."[12] Ergo, if leaders want to be perceived in a certain way, they must constantly prioritize how they manage the impressions of onlookers, for fear of being doubted and losing credibility, or maintaining their position.

What do all these theories have in common? Society has conditioned both followers and leaders to believe that prioritizing emotional health support for leadership is not only unimportant but also signals weakness or an inability to lead. When actually, the reverse is true. Those are some crappy co-created bylaws if you ask me. Here is the wrinkle in ye olde faulty logic (please allow my teeny-tiny nihilist to come out for a moment). We have agreed upon a practice called "work." Created industries, job titles, companies, services, and products for other humans—all with (generally) agreed-upon purposes. Over millennia, this has given us purpose, meaning, and kept us busy during our time alive on this pale blue dot floating around the universe before we shuffle off this mortal coil. Now, color me crazy (no, we don't use that C word, but for the sake of the argument, I am), but the last time I checked, leaders are the same species as us. Let's follow the logic line:

→ Leaders are human beings.
→ Human beings have mental health.
→ Ergo, leaders have mental health.
→ Thus, leaders can experience the full spectrum of emotions and mental health struggles, like anyone else who doesn't hold a leadership title. (Side note: there are obviously exceptions to this, as some people, regardless of position, do not experience the full spectrum of emotion for a variety of medical and psychological reasons.)

As part of this evolution, we, as a species and a self-organizing society, have automatically assumed and acted as if leaders are immune to needing emotional support in their roles. Not to seem obnoxiously logical, but since leaders are the same species as those they lead, shouldn't leaders receive the same mental health considerations as those not in leadership roles? The biological and sociological programming nestled deep in our collective psyche has resulted in a seriously flawed belief that leaders must rid themselves of their humanity and program themselves out of showing any form of emotional struggle to be trusted as a "good" leader. A vicious cycle cemented and perpetuated by those who lead and those who are led:

→ Leaders were historically encouraged to display a certain set of behaviors that were socially approved signs of "good" leadership.
→ Leaders (generally) continued to do this.
→ Then, an assumption was created that leaders would not need support, because they are, and must be, self-sustaining.
→ Leaders are motivated not to show struggle or a need for support.
→ Leaders don't receive support, creating additional challenges to manage emotional health, potentially impacting their overall functioning, how they behave, and lead.
→ Leaders then act in ways that may damage their reputation or negatively impact those they lead. Causing others to doubt their abilities, when they were never given a net to fall onto if they fell from the pedestal people put them on.

Yes, this is as ridiculous as it sounds. Yes, it felt even more ridiculous for me to have to write it.

History Has Set Up Leadership Mental Health to Fail

"Many leaders are afraid of speaking about their mental health because of judgment, loss of authority or credibility, or other reasons that are ultimately rooted in fear. The workspace is not always a safe space for full self-expression, especially when speaking with team members who work under you. There is an implied expectation that as a manager, you 'have your sh*t together' and anything that causes wavering is kept to oneself."

Interviewee: male, Millennial, Caucasian, Director, technology industry

"Being a leader has had a profound impact on my mental health. On one hand, leadership has given me a sense of purpose, the ability to create change, and the opportunity to support others. On the other

> *hand, it has often come with immense pressure, emotional exhaustion, and the weight of constant vigilance."*
>
> Interviewee: male, Gen X, Black, first-time manager, technology industry

Leadership mental health has been set up to fail from the beginning, with struggles hidden like the bottom of an iceberg as a measure of success for professional competence and emotional strength.

The Automatic Continuation of False Correlations and Conflicting Expectations

Despite the irrefutable logic, we continue to uphold a false correlation that being a leader means one cannot, and should not, simultaneously face emotional health struggles. That's just nonsense, and we know it. Who has articulated this the best? I hope you love this as much as I did when I heard it for the first time,

> *"I have no difficulty holding both logic and feeling at the same time. And it does not diminish my powers. It expands them."*[13]
>
> **—Lawyer Barbie, from the 2023 film *Barbie***

While this commentary from the movie primarily centers on the intersection of gender and decision-making in influential positions (which we'll delve into in Chapter 5), wouldn't it be nice if this logic were generally applied to what we expect and accept around leadership displays of emotional struggle? Ironically, quotes like this and others from that movie have not been appreciated for the brilliance and truth they satirically implied; instead, they forced the certain evaluative bodies deciding whether this phenomenal movie deserved an award to feel uncomfortable with the truths they unveiled in an undeniable way. I'm going to go ahead and say that the palpable discomfort that ripped its way through the powers of Hollywood mirrors the World of

Work and how twitchy it makes people feel to even consider address-ing the mental health challenges and needs of leaders. Maybe it's too scary, like in *The Matrix*, where the decision is whether or not to take the "perception-opening" red pill because you can't go back once you've done it.

Corroborating what both Lawyer Barbie, and I, have said, *MIT Sloan Management Review* published a piece called "The Emotional Landscape of Leadership."[14] It highlighted that leaders can face various emotional health challenges and negative emotions simply because of the nature of their role and that this is part of being a leader (i.e., emo-tional challenges occur alongside their ability to lead). The piece also refers to a study published in the journal *BMJ Leader* (focusing on lead-ership in healthcare). In this study, the researchers found that ". . . about 58% of respondents confessed to experiencing anxiety when faced with critical decision-making, while almost half (49%) said they felt apprehensive about potential missteps being viewed critically by superiors." This shows that a leader *can* experience emotional distress while still maintaining their intellectual and professional capabilities. These elements are not in conflict. They co-exist. They are signs of a human and capable leader who endures their own emotional distress while simultaneously leading others, and they are not permitted to have a socially acceptable or nonjudgmental avenue to be honest about that. The leadership emotional capacity cup must just automati-cally continuously self-refill, right? Said no one.

All of the historical conditioning that has led us to where we are now has created completely unhealthy, unrealistic, and unsus-tainable conflicting expectations for our modern-day leaders. The ridiculous, continual emphasis on unwavering emotional composure discourages leaders from displaying emotional struggles or discussing their mental health at work. To top it off, as we'll look at in Chapter 4, leaders are also constantly pressured to perform, maintain, and even establish a "healthy" workplace culture while supporting their team's mental health. Yet, they aren't allowed to engage in it for themselves.

In my experience, creating change involves three stages:

1. Looking back to see where we came from and what we can learn from that.
2. Observing our current state (the relics from the past we still hold on to, the problems they may be causing, and the reasons why).
3. Focusing on our intended outcomes (the objectives we establish to create change from what we aim to avoid repeating and why).

We finished the first stage in this chapter. In the next three chapters, we'll explore the second stage. Through looking at the ongoing dehumanization of leaders, the de-prioritization and exclusion of leadership mental health in the workplace, the growing burden of leadership tasks, and the overall impact of this toxic mix that leaders are force-fed. All the while, still influenced by remnants of the past.

P.S. Look out for the start of *The Weight on Leadership Mental Health Equation* in the next chapter.

Individual Reflection Questions

- As a leader, do I feel I should talk about my mental health at work? Why or why not?
- Where do my beliefs come from? Which experiences (or people) taught me to feel this way?
- If I talk about my emotional struggles as a leader, what will this "mean"? Why do I feel this way?

Chapter Key Takeaways

- Leadership has been historically dehumanized.
- Leaders have been conditioned to internalize unrealistic expectations of themselves.
- Society perpetuates a false correlation between emotional vulnerability and leadership incapability.
- Leaders operate in a broken professional system that rewards composure and silence while penalizing the expression of struggle and a need for support.
- Leadership capacity and mental health struggles can co-exist.

2

The Dehumanization of Leaders: VPs Don't Have Panic Attacks . . . Right? (Wrong)

"Even when I'm struggling, I'm expected to be composed and unshakable. I remember showing a moment of frustration—just one difficult day—and it was held against me. A member of my own team made comments about my 'inability to self-soothe,' which was incredibly hurtful. It made it clear that, as a leader, I wasn't granted the same emotional humanity as others."

Interviewee: female, Elder Millennial, Asian, Vice President, software industry

"There's this notion or perception that you must have all the answers, be the expert, support everyone, never show signs of distress, or dare to express anything negative. A leader can succumb to this very unrealistic expectation of what it means to be successful in the workplace."

Interviewee: female, Millennial, Mexican-American, Elementary Principal, public education industry

I ONCE LED a session for leaders on the importance of mental health in leadership. Despite the session's focus, I heard numerous stories about how these leaders wanted to support their teams, even while they were overwhelmed by burnout, fatigue, self-isolation, constant hyperdrive, and feelings of failure whenever they made mistakes. I vividly remember one leader who said they didn't have access to "human ways" of letting people know they were at capacity. This leader explained how they repeatedly tried to tell others—their team members, fellow leaders, and superiors—when they couldn't take on more. Yet, when they did, it often didn't matter, as they were met with responses like "tough s**t" and ridicule. This leader had the courage to humanize themselves and admit their limits, but their disclosures were consistently ignored.

Leadership Titles Have Created Inaccurate Perceptions of Mental Health Needs

Several important studies and observations have emerged over time examining the ongoing harmful practice of stripping leaders of their humanity, often to their detriment, simply because of their roles. I know the adage "misery loves company" isn't comforting here, and some industries are clearly worse than others. In every industry, there's a relentless expectation for leaders to be unshakeable and behave consistently, as we discussed in the last chapter. No sector is immune, even if they publicly pretend otherwise on social media, because it "looks good." This doesn't even consider the additional, ongoing, and contextual pressures leaders face from their personal experiences and complex areas of personal identity, which we'll explore in Chapter 5.

Back when I worked in clinical psychology as an Employee Assistance Program (EAP) counselor, I had a phenomenal training in Motivational Interviewing (MI),[1] a modality created by clinical psychologists William R. Miller and Stephen Rollnick in the 1980s to treat people struggling with substance abuse disorders and addictive behaviors. What I appreciate about MI, in my former clinical work and the industrial–organizational work I do now, is that it taught me how to ask the right questions to understand someone's belief system, if they feel it serves them, if they think those beliefs and behaviors cause the problems they experience, and if I'm lucky—whether or not they felt motivated to see and do things differently. During one of my first MI trainings, we learned about a concept called "magical thinking." I remember thinking, "*Wait, seriously, is this a real thing?*" Yes, it was (and is), and I'll use this phrase as a golden thread throughout this chapter because it's powerful, accurate, and a necessary analogy.

"Magical Thinking" and the Dehumanization of Leaders

The EAP I worked for provided short-term counseling for employees of companies across North America and operated 13 compulsive gambling hotlines for different states. Compulsive gambling is, after all, a tough form of addiction to treat—and using MI was the most clinically efficacious thing at the time. As part of my MI training, we read Linda Berman's *Behind the 8 Ball: A Guide for Families of Gamblers*,[2] where I learned even more about magical thinking in practice. At its core, magical thinking occurs when someone develops a cognitive bias based on an unvalidated and illogical set of beliefs that support an internal narrative. This causes them to believe they can manifest or cause desired events (i.e., to create an outcome they want). How did this manifest in compulsive gamblers? Statements like, "Oh, if I do X, then I'll obviously win Y" or "Z just needs to happen, so that I can do A."

The compulsive gamblers I spoke to every week struggled with this kind of magical thinking. They often shared similar behaviors: continuing their actions, driven by faulty logic and belief systems, that they could change their luck (i.e., beating the house) by repeating destructive behaviors that had already caused them financial ruin and instability. They were still willing to face loss, heartache, and abandonment because, deep down, they believed that sticking with what they knew was the way to change their situation. The system observes them engaging in this behavior (and benefits from it), perpetuating the cycle.

While not clinical at all in nature, this magical thinking and toxic mindset mirror what the World of Work expects of leaders and what many leaders expect of themselves. All parties feed into the illogical belief system for different reasons. Remember when we talked about transference in Chapter 1? That same HBR article cemented this magical thinking concept: ". . . without a strong grounding in reality, leaders can very easily come undone by their followers' positive transferential projections. At the extreme, such followers will create a myth that bears no relation to fact."[3] Magical thinking is rampant in workplace cultures and among leaders, especially when it comes to leadership mental health. Historical influences have taught leaders to believe that hiding their emotional struggles will protect them and help them survive and "beat" the system. Just like a gambler might cling to certain behaviors in the hope of achieving a different or desired outcome, leaders are often motivated to maintain these self-sacrificing behaviors, sometimes with the false hope that their circumstances might change. Sometimes this is paired with the reasonably understandable fear, based on what they've observed around them, that if they don't stay on the same path (i.e., always keeping their proverbial s**t together to protect their reputation and professional capital), they will lose (i.e., being doubted, demoted, or even fired).

This toxic cycle prevents leaders from speaking up and seeking help, while reinforcing the belief that they shouldn't need to do so. Organizationally, whether intentionally or not, leaders are still treated as if they lack emotional health needs, supporting the larger narrative of what companies expect leaders to "be," not who they actually are. They are continuously viewed as "machines to be optimized," not people to be supported, with no plans of changing the system they operate in or how we see them. As long as the machines produce success, we're willing to have them break down along the way. Some tangible examples? I call them "leadership machine maintenance" programs. Typically, these programs focus solely on traditional leadership skills, technical skills, strategic thinking, and, more recently (thankfully), emotional intelligence. These programs usually (if not overwhelmingly frequently) neglect any mention of mental health. I've seen newsletters—no joke—telling leaders that they are expected to handle everything at work and then proceed to give leaders all the technical skills they need to deal with that, without any mention of what having that weight on their shoulders feels like. It has strong *Hunger Games* vibes with a "Here are your approved tools to use, may the odds be ever in your favor!" sentiment.

I do see the occasional "fake out" of a well-being element, which, sadly, ends up focusing solely on nutrition, exercise, or, if they're lucky, mindfulness. Remember the emotional intelligence training I mentioned earlier? I have yet to see a strong focus on managing individual mental health as a leader, despite the fact that the training content discusses self-awareness and self-regulation. These programs rarely, if ever, focus on creating a sense of psychological safety for leaders around talking about their general mental health struggles, let alone the mental health struggles that can happen in leadership.

Listen, the existence of these programs is reasonable and necessary. Leaders should be involved in these critical professional development programs. However, many of these programs are, and often remain, incomplete because of their assumptions, rooted in magical thinking, that leadership training should overwhelmingly revolve around upskilling for high capacity and, by extension, output. That's disingenuous care in its simplest form: "We will only help you in the ways we feel you need and that benefit us." Incomplete programs like this continue to fuel the harmful dehumanization of leaders and the false correlation between leadership titles and emotional impenetrability, hence the cheeky title of this chapter. But that's the gig, even though it's unnatural—and them's the breaks.

The Leader Well-Being and Mental Illness Prototypes (Yes, These Are Real)

The *Journal of Leadership & Organizational Studies* published a study called "Expectations of Leaders' Mental Health." It pointed out that even though in 2022 when the then U.S. Surgeon General released a report highlighting the critical role of organizations in promoting and protecting the mental health of employees, and the *World Health Organization (WHO)* released a set of recommendations to improve mental health at work, these research advancements and organizational initiatives do not consider whether all employees are viewed equally regarding their experience with mental health.[4] The study further emphasized how we place leaders into common prototypes (cough cough, machine analogy) for mental well-being, and especially mental illness.

One of the central theses? No joke—organizations and employees assume that leaders "enjoy" better mental health and less mental illness, based on the position they hold. The optics alone of leaders talking about mental health in general, mental illness, or even just experiencing biologically natural negative emotions from the challenges of leadership is hard enough. Now layer role-based biases on top that, which tell leaders that the virtue of their position means they already have a "mentally easier time" than others. This study also revealed why organizations often fail to implement emotional support structures for leaders. Here's how the study described these prototypes:

- Leader Well-Being Prototypes:
  - *". . . leaders are expected to be (1) sensitive, i.e., understanding, sincere, compassionate, warm, and sympathetic; (2) dynamic, i.e., bold, strong, in control, energetic, and charismatic; (3) dedicated, i.e., motivated, unrelenting, and hardworking; and (4) intelligent, i.e., clever, knowledgeable, and intellectual. We posit that the central attributes, behaviors, and characteristics . . . are more schematically consistent with the characteristics associated with higher levels of psychological well-being, and therefore, existing leader prototypes may serve as a top-down, social–cognitive framework that shapes the degree to which those in leadership roles are expected to experience psychological well-being."*

- Leader Mental Illness Prototypes:
  - *". . . general leader prototypes may additionally serve as top-down influences that determine people's expectations of leaders' experience with mental illness . . . the prototypical expectations that leaders are charismatic and optimistic (i.e., dynamism dimension), in control and determined (i.e., dedicated dimension), and express empathy and warmth (i.e., sensitivity dimension) are inconsistent with the symptoms, behaviors, and assumptions associated with depression and anxiety. Indeed, depression is characterized by symptoms of low self-worth, disinterest, and withdrawal, while anxiety is characterized by self-doubt, excessive worrying, and feelings of being out of control. Additionally, leadership roles*

are often prized and romanticized . . . and viewed as roles in which occupants wield power and control. . .Yet, internalized illnesses generate stigmatized assumptions: those with depression are often perceived as having a lack of control over emotions, while those with anxiety are viewed as having low ability to manage impulses . . . These stigmatized beliefs extend to the workplace, where mental illness is viewed as a weakness, an indication of low competencies, and a hindrance to organizational effectiveness . . . As such, cognitive schemas surrounding leadership roles on the one hand and the symptoms and stigmatized beliefs about mental illness on the other hand are conceptually incongruent and should therefore be cognitively interpreted as a mismatch. Thus . . . leadership roles will be negatively related to perceptions of mental illness."

People literally create a fantasy of what it means to serve in a leadership role. Now, I will not diminish the allure of achievement and serving in a leadership role, with some of its demonstrable, clear advantages (I'm not going to pretend they don't exist). However, when society romanticizes leadership, it simultaneously dismisses the humanity of the people serving in those roles, their emotional experiences, and any struggles they may experience independently outside of work. As a heads up, I will continue to refer to these prototypes several times throughout the book as the "Leadership Prototypes."

Returning to the "we are the same species" argument, the data doesn't lie. Leaders still experience the same stress and mental health struggles as others do.

- *Harvard Medical School* and the *Queensland Brain Institute* found in a 2023 study involving 29 countries that half of the world's population will experience a mental health disorder.[5]
- *Forbes* published the Workplace Communication & Well-Being Survey, commissioned by *FirstUp*, in 2024, showing data from 1,000 U.S. working adults, indicating that "workplace stress is pervasive, with 60% of respondents reporting their jobs as the primary source of stress. . . ."[6]

- A meta-analysis study on leadership and stress published in 2017 in *The Leadership Quarterly* showed how researchers found that ". . . In many ways, stress and leadership are inextricably linked with one another . . . it seems intuitive to link leadership with stress . . . despite the widespread acknowledgment that stress and leadership are linked, there has been no systematic attempt to organize and summarize this literature."[7]

See what I'm getting at here? History repeats itself through magical thinking and a misleading, harmful narrative that persists. We have formed biases, expecting leaders to be mentally healthy because of their position, and doubting them if they show any struggle from their socially constructed and simultaneously evaluated power perch. Leaders are effectively being acknowledged, and simultaneously deprioritized, in this data. Are there names or concepts for this pattern? You bet, they're called institutional betrayal and breaking psychological contracts. Let's discuss why these concepts are important and how, all the while, leaders are still expected to be an organization's proverbial uncrackable glue.

Breaking Psychological Contracts, Institutional Betrayal, and Being the "Uncrackable Glue"

"I have absolutely felt like I was expected to be the 'glue' holding everything together, often with little regard for the emotional toll."

Interviewee: male, Gen X, Black, first-time manager, technology industry

"We were not just sidelined but actively dismissed. The company I worked for proudly touted 'People Come First' as its leading core value. But the running joke among leadership was, 'People come first. . . just not us.' The gap between the message and the reality was staggering. It felt like a betrayal, a hypocrisy that was difficult to swallow every single day."

Interviewee: male, Gen X, Caucasian, senior leadership, construction industry

In 2008, two researchers wrote an article based on their book, *Achieving Business Excellence: Health, Well-Being and Performance*. The article discussed work stress, leadership, and organizational health,[8] focusing on the germane role of leaders in assessing, intervening when necessary, promoting, and maintaining overall organizational well-being. A necessary endeavor. They discussed the importance of preserving "psychological contracts," a concept that has been in existence since the 1960s.[9] The article described psychological safety as, "The decision by a person or group to make themselves vulnerable under the expectation that the other party will not take advantage of it is what represents the core of the relational contract." In a workplace context, it's essentially an unwritten agreement between the employee and employer. Governing the professional relationship between a worker and the company, and ensuring that its purpose, what will be exchanged, and how that relationship will be treated, will remain aligned. Employees will perform services for an organization, and in exchange, the company will compensate, respect, and look out for the general welfare of those employees (although the latter isn't done as often as it should be).

Leaders, like employees, enter into an unspoken agreement with the organization they work for—namely, that they will dedicate themselves, their time, and their energy to supporting it. In return, they hope the organization will support them as well. Although the psychological contract is a well-known concept, it is often deprioritized by organizations, despite "building trust" at work becoming a widely popular training topic in recent years. And, as you might guess, trust is the foundation of psychological contracts. Yet, trust continues to be broken. Here's a bit of irony: the same *Achieving Business Excellence* article highlighted the dangers of damaging psychological contracts for employees, warning that this can lead to feelings such as betrayal, unfairness, injustice, and a lack of reciprocity. However, it made no mention of the stress leaders face when managing these psychological contracts for others or how it feels not to have a psychological contract honored for themselves. The conflicting nature of this situation is complex to accept, especially when I read this in the same piece:

> "The supervisor-subordinate relationship has been reported as one of the most common sources of stress in organizations. A leader's behavior, when inadequate, may be abusive and taxing and become an important source of stress contributing to the emergence of negative experiences of employees and hampering their well-being."

A leader's apparent ineligibility for their own psychological contract for their emotional health at work is rarely, if ever, considered when their behavior is questioned for causing stress in organizations. Moreover, if they begin to struggle and possibly act out (again, this isn't okay, but I'm highlighting the point), they are often punished by being perceived as "inadequate" and "taxing" on their teams.

When leaders do not have a psychological contract honored for their mental health at work, but notice that their team members do, that effectively equates to being told,

> "Hey, we'll keep consistently and increasingly relying on you, pushing you beyond your limit. But don't worry, we'll reward you with professional prestige and money (if we can afford it). We'll also criticize you and probably doubt your leadership capabilities if you complain you're burnt out because you shouldn't need that help. Company resources are for your team members, not you. See you at the Q3 meeting!"

Leaders are, then, often seen as the problem. Not the collateral damage of historically unrealistic expectations, or the modern pressures that keep wearing them down to the edge of their sanity, with a touch of shattered trust.

Moving on, let's think about breaking psychological contracts and experiencing conditional trust through the lens of institutional betrayal. This concept was created and researched by psychologist Jennifer Freyd, who has dedicated her career to exploring and addressing betrayal and the resulting trauma within institutional, organizational, and societal systems. Institutional betrayal is, "when the institution you trust or depend upon mistreats you. It can be overt but also less obvious, for instance, a failure to protect you when protection is a reasonable expectation."[10] Freyd's work also talks about a concept called institutional blindness, which unpacks why betrayal-laden systems are ultimately maintained: ". . . Victims, perpetrators, and witnesses may display betrayal blindness to preserve relationships, institutions, and social systems upon which they depend." Here's why this matters.

In this situation, everyone plays a role. Just like we discussed in Chapter 1. In cases of institutional blindness, the "victims" are leaders, the perpetrators are the companies of the World of Work, and the witnesses, to some degree, are everyone. Institutional betrayal breaches psychological contracts for leaders when companies and teams expect them to act as the proverbial unbreakable glue, through unreasonable demands of constant self-sacrifice. Leaders will continue to participate in the system in the ways expected of them because they depend on that system too (like any other employee) for financial stability, professional recognition, and more.

Back to trust for a minute. If we've learned anything in the fields of leadership, employee, and organizational development over the past couple of decades, it's this: organizational, team, and individual success are all *built on shared trust*. And that should mean trust *for everyone*. Without trust, achieving much else at work becomes excruciatingly difficult. Patrick Lencioni's book, *The Five Dysfunctions of a Team: A Leadership Fable*, and his subsequent work, *The Five Behaviors*, have explicitly solidified this. Here's my quandary: Lencioni rightfully highlights that leaders, at the foundation, must unite a team through trust, and to achieve that trust, there must be shared openness.[11] He illustrates this through a nifty visual ascending pyramid, but for the sake of simplicity, I'm going to describe it through this listicle:

- Level 1: Trust (the foundation)
  - → Achieved through shared openness
- Level 2: Resolve Conflict
  - → Achieved through candid communication
- Level 3: Commit as a Team
  - → Achieved through shared clarity
- Level 4: Hold Each Other Accountable
  - → Achieved through having shared standards
- Level 5: Focus on Results (top level)
  - → Achieved through sharing collective success

As you may have noticed above, leaders must build trust through openness and honest communication within a team. However, through observable maintained social practices, those same leaders are often not allowed to show that same transparency or speak openly about their emotional health struggles at work because they worry it will cause doubt and mistrust among those they lead. It doesn't really foster trust when leaders are expected to create and maintain systemic change and success without receiving trust and support for leading that change. There is a vast chasm of a disconnect between the expectations of results and the lack of meaningful conversations and support to help those who are supposed to achieve those results. Leadership self-sacrifice is expected to be the ongoing cost in a professional system filled with institutional blindness, all in the pursuit of desired outcomes.

The Systemic Folie à Deux of Leadership Self-Sacrifice and the Illusory Truth Effect

While it pains me to say it, the magical thinking we've been discussing isn't limited to the organizations and industries where leaders operate. Sadly, society itself, social media, some leaders, and many other spheres also sustain it. When it comes to the mental health of leaders, we continue to be caught in a folie à deux[12] (i.e., a shared delusion, one of my favorite clinical diagnosis words from my counseling days) about who leaders should be and what they shouldn't need, rather than recognizing who they are and what they genuinely require. While not a clinical delusional or any form of psychosis, the absurdity of the reality that's still maintained might as well be.

As I wrote this book, I came across a post on LinkedIn about common mantras that "respected leaders" should follow. Similar to the historic idea of "good" and "bad" leadership behaviors we discussed in Chapter 1, and the unintended harm caused by well-intentioned phrases, the post aimed to be helpful and included some useful phrases about being accountable for mistakes, supporting team members, building trust, and fostering collaboration. However, every single phrase—though absolutely warranted—was other-focused. Sentiments like "How can I support you?" and "Take the time you need" were present. Not a *single phrase* was about leaders' self-disclosure or self-advocacy for what *they need* to support others. This made me feel the heat of a thousand suns, and not in a good way.

This ongoing messaging directed at leaders and the fact that prioritizing leadership mental health wasn't on that "respected" sentiments list perpetuates the toxic notion of never-ending leadership self-sacrifice and their ongoing dehumanization. I struggle to understand why phrases like the below aren't included in what "respected" (i.e., good) leaders would also say,

- *"I'm feeling stressed, so here's what I'm going to do to take care of myself to make sure I can get this project done."*
- *"Here's what's going on for me outside of work, I didn't want you to think my acting differently was because of you . . ."*
- *"So I can support you in the best way possible, it would be helpful if you could . . ."*

By the way, the person who wrote the post has a huge following with a lot of engagement. Posts like these—from prominent voices with large followings—have a significant impact. I witness this messaging constantly, everywhere I turn. And leaders do, too.

The amount of information we absorb, especially through technology, is increasing each day. Likewise, the constant "be this" messages to leaders are growing seemingly at an exponential rate. Just think about it. When someone is bombarded with similar information from multiple angles, they don't typically pause to ask, "Is this true, and does it apply to me?" Instead, they are more likely to focus on fulfilling the image of being a "good" leader as defined by the world around them. Or they might act on that information for Impression Management, aiming to maintain perceptions among those they lead through the Laws of Authority and Consistency. The Illusory Truth Effect tells us this: if you tell somebody something enough times, they will believe it—even if it's about themselves.[13]

> "My partner and I were the glue that held [our company] together . . .
> Once I sold my practice to [the parent company] and my partner
> retired, my self-defined role was continuing to be the glue for the new
> organization."
>
> Interviewee: male, Baby Boomer, Caucasian, Owner, healthcare
> industry

The paper "Knowledge Does Not Protect Against Illusory Truth" explored the power of the Illusory Truth Effect and its influence on our knowledge in general. The researchers found the following:

> "In daily life, we frequently encounter false claims . . . Repetition may
> be one way that insidious misconceptions . . . enter our knowledge
> base. Research on the illusory truth effect demonstrates that repeated
> statements are easier to process and subsequently perceived to be more
> truthful than new statements . . . Contrary to prior suppositions, illu-
> sory truth effects occurred even when participants knew bet-
> ter . . . Thus, participants demonstrated knowledge neglect, or the
> failure to rely on stored knowledge . . ."[14]

Even if leaders logically, privately, and internally acknowledge that their mental health should be a priority and that seeking support at work is healthy, this awareness often proves insufficient against the persistent messages from other sources. These messages push them to manage and reconcile their feelings privately. To illustrate this point, let's hear again from the Interviewee I quoted just a few sentences earlier, who was the self-proclaimed glue of his company.

> "Mental health issues can adversely affect leadership performance,
> productivity, and the workplace environment . . . If an individual
> leader has more profound issues, then they need private and discreet
> resources. . . We must recognize that ignoring mental health issues can
> compromise the workplace."
>
> Interviewee: male, Baby Boomer, Caucasian, Owner, physician,
> healthcare industry

This same leader, who has historically served as the glue for his organization, also privately acknowledges that leaders can experience mental health struggles, which, if left unaddressed, can lead to a variety of issues. And, even so, for understandable reasons based on being a product of the time and generation in which he came up, he encouraged that leaders receive help "privately and discreetly." What we have here is leaders logically acknowledging what silences them while continuing to operate within the system as it is designed, and only privately recognizing the damage it causes. Going back to the study from *The Journal of Leadership & Organizational Studies*, it also (not surprisingly) found that,

"... *as previous research has established, there is no clear evidence that leaders enjoy meaningfully better mental health than non-leaders. Given these inconsistencies, it is time to acknowledge that leaders' mental health matters, possibly more than people may expect.*"

Remember when I told you to keep an eye out for an equation? Well, here she is, the first iteration of the Weight on Leadership Mental Health Equation, with our first elements below:

The Influence of Toxic Historical Narratives

+

The Sociological Assignment of Power

+

When Standards of "Good" Leadership Run Counter to Displays of Emotional Struggle

+

Magical Thinking and the Dehumanization of Leaders

+

A Lack of Social Permission to Speak Up

+

Experiencing Helplessness

+

Experiencing Institutional Betrayal

+

Having Psychological Contracts Broken

+

Being Subjected to the Illusory Truth Effect

+

Being Actively Disincentivized to Speak Up About Mental Health

These factors don't quite motivate leaders to open up during tough times, no matter where their struggles originate. In fact, they actively discourage it. Take a moment now. Reread the list. Are you starting to feel the weight? What does it feel like? What emotions does it bring up in you? Notice those, because they'll make more sense as we progress further and start talking about the Atlas statue, burdened with the weight of the world on his shoulders, with the leadership "plate" becoming a trough.

The Proof Is in the Pattern

Despite strong historical patterns and the persistent reinforcement of toxic narratives, leading researchers like Brené Brown repeatedly tell us that there are clear, positive, measurable outcomes when leaders are open at work (she describes this as vulnerability). Yet, workplaces tend to repeat the same patterns. In some cases, they even show a performative acknowledgment with no real change behind it. Oh, Brené, wouldn't it be nice if more workplaces followed your guidance instead of just echoing your words?

I believe the question we need to ask isn't, "when will it change?," but rather, "*why* won't it change?" The persistent maintenance of harmful magical thinking and a systemically shared folie à deux only serves to emotionally shred an entire group of individuals that we constantly depend on. These individuals are expected to drive organizations forward, stay functional, drive profitability, and more. Yet, within a system that needs them, they are told to struggle privately (if at all recognized) and shown that it doesn't care about the toll it takes on them. Everything we covered in Chapters 1 and 2 highlights how a cycle has been created and sustained, where openness about emotional struggles in leadership is stigmatized and discouraged. For countless leaders, this has had a profoundly visible impact on their overall mental health, career paths, and even their ability to lead. That's up next.

Individual Reflection Questions

- As a leader, have I ever felt dehumanized or expected to be "the glue"? What did this look like and how did this feel?
- Have I ever felt like my mental health has been deprioritized as a leader? Either by myself or the company I work for? What did this look like and how did it feel?
- Do I think the people I lead believe I don't need mental health support as a leader? Why do I feel they think that?

Chapter Key Takeaways

- Leadership titles often distort how people perceive leaders' mental health needs.
- Biases and unrealistic expectations still dehumanize leaders.
- Leaders rarely receive psychological safety or psychological contracts—and when they do, they're often broken, while being expected to still perform.
- Traditional standards of "good" leadership often discourage emotional vulnerability, creating a harmful double bind.
- Repeated messages about how leaders should think and feel cause many to adopt unhealthy beliefs—even about their own mental health.

3

The Impact: Leadership Well-Being, Career Path, and Performance

> "My mental well-being has definitely been impacted the more senior I became. We place enormous pressure on leaders to know everything and to be all things to all people; often with very little support."
>
> Interviewee: female, Gen X, Black, Director, consulting industry
>
> "Regardless of organizational culture and the willingness to extend support for mental health struggles to non-leaders at an organization, once you reach a leadership role, the rules change."
>
> Interviewee: male, Millennial, Caucasian, Director, technology industry

CONTRARY TO POPULAR belief, many companies typically invest significant money, time, and resources in supporting their employees' mental health. Sometimes, and not as often as I would like, it's done because it's the right thing to do. In many other cases, this commitment aims to keep their workforce healthy, productive, and motivated to stay at the organization—driven by return on investment (ROI). This isn't inherently bad, but the optics can appear problematic when these initiatives convey obvious ardent capitalist vibes. While supporting employee mental health is becoming more common, leadership's emotional health often remains overlooked in these efforts. Meanwhile, data still shows the state of leadership mental health, yet organizations tend to ignore this aspect in their organizational actions. We're going to dig into that data in this chapter.

The Impact on Leadership Mental Health

"My levels of stress and anxiety have gone through the roof since my foray into leadership. . .and there is a stigma and judgment associated with mental health struggles in leadership."

Interviewee: female, Gen X, Caucasian, Senior Director, construction industry

"I wish organizations better understood that leaders are people, and you don't have to be invincible to hold a position of authority."

Interviewee: male, Millennial, Black, first-generation American, Director, legal support industry

Being Measured and Ignored: The Data

Organizations often ignore data on leadership mental health and fail to offer tailored support. This practice is illogical, especially given the dismissed importance of the obvious need. Potentially silly-sounding rhetorical question here: don't organizations want healthy, effective leaders who remain committed without risking their well-being? Of course they do! Yet, companies often overlook, or even in some cases deprioritize, the actions needed to achieve this. The data shows that mental health struggles and the need for support occur at *all* levels of a company, along with tools for understanding and caring for others' mental health. However, leaders themselves are rarely included as recipients of care in these support systems. Cue the Leadership Prototypes, again. While data clearly indicates that leaders need help, subsequently recommended action items focus primarily on how leaders can support others, enhance their skills, and maintain existing support structures. This ongoing neglect damages psychological contracts and fosters institutional betrayal and is reflected in these patterns. Let's take a look at some specific examples.

- That same *Forbes* article mentioned in Chapter 2 showed alarming levels of stress and burnout among managers, with many considering quitting their jobs.[1]

- *Mercer*[2] published a piece on the importance of self-care in leadership, which found that 33% of managers feel the stress of management responsibilities is unmanageable and overwhelming, with a third to a half of leaders struggling to cope with the challenges of leadership. What's even more disheartening, and sadly cements ongoing magical thinking, is this sentiment from the same piece: "When confronted with statistics like these, some just shrug and sigh: 'Stress is part of the job, isn't it?' Based on a growing body of research, that's a dangerously defeatist perspective."

- The 2024 State of Workforce Mental Health Report from *Lyra Health* stated, "People are facing a post-pandemic surge in serious and complex mental health conditions."[3]
  - P.S. Notice how they referred to *people*, not just employees.
  - P.P.S. Even though the rest of the data in this report discusses the general state of mental health at work, it also highlights how managers feel pressured to support employees, with no mention of support for them.

- An editorial from the *National Library of Medicine* (NLOM) shared this,

> "The workplace today is an environment where mental health issues are increasingly becoming a focus of interest and concern . . . The COVID-19 pandemic has brought mental health challenges to the forefront, exacerbating previous problems and highlighting the need for comprehensive support systems . . ."[4]

- *MIT Sloan Management Review* published an article in 2023 about the emotional experiences of leaders, which affect both the leader and their team. It revealed that leaders who lack emotional support end up burned out, make poor decisions, and ultimately harm team morale.[5]

Shocking, right? No, it's not. And the pièce de résistance: those same reports above say that managers, alone, are responsible for addressing workplace mental health struggles. With no mention of support for them. While simultaneously acknowledging that driving change around mental health at work is a systemic issue. When we discuss ecosystems in a bit, this notion may make you feel as fiery as I did. Here's what this conflicting guidance looked like:

- In a follow-up 2025 report from *Lyra*, the Workforce Mental Health Trend Forecast, it stated, "Managers hold the key to tackling mounting workplace stress—but need better tools."[6] The report then says, "the managers need support. . .through receiving better tools and resources to support mental well-being at work." The key takeaway, still, was to equip managers with tools to support others.
- The same *NLOM* editorial above also indicated:

    "Addressing this stigma warrants a comprehensive approach that encompasses a nuanced understanding of workplace dynamics, societal awareness, supportive leadership, as well as new assessment tools and innovative interventions. By integrating this knowledge into practical and actionable strategies, organizations can pave the way towards creating inclusive and supportive work environments that also care for the mental health of their employees."

Doesn't systemic change include caring for employees at all levels of a company, including leaders who play a crucial role in maintaining support for their teams at work? I found it ironic that the 2025 *Lyra* report also said: ". . . unforgiving workplaces can worsen existing mental health issues or prompt new ones." Leaders having their mental health struggles acknowledged in data but left out of recommendations on how they can be supported, aside from upskilling others, is an excellent way for them to experience an unforgiving workplace and exacerbation of or creation of new mental health struggles for them, too.

Lack of Emotional Support Structures as a Sharing Deterrent

"I believe leaders often struggle to speak openly about their mental health. . .for me. . .it was. . .the absence of meaningful support. . .Everyone in my peer group was struggling. . .There was an unspoken agreement that we had to push through, because if one of us admitted how much we were struggling, it might make things even harder for everyone else."

Interviewee: male, Gen X, Black, first-time manager, technology industry

"There was tension between mental health and leadership performance. Typically, it ended either in a person quietly retreating into their problems until they quit, or sad/angry outbursts once the frustration became unbearable."

Interviewee: male, Elder Millennial, Black, first-generation American, Director, legal support industry

Leaders continue to be painted as proverbial superheroes, and they don't even get cool outfits. Speaking of cool outfits: going back to that *HBR* article from Chapter 1, the author noted the following, sadly proving my point,

"Leaders, quite rightly, are the heroes of the corporate epic (a few leader-villains notwithstanding). They motivate us to go places that we would never otherwise go. They are needed both to change organizations and to produce results. In any business climate, good leadership is perhaps the most important competitive advantage a company can have. It's hardly surprising, therefore, that management scholars focus relentlessly on the attributes of successful leadership."[7]

Now, we face a situation where the data conflicts with itself. Some data sets clearly show that leaders are struggling, while others suggest that workplaces still expect leaders to act as if they are superhuman. This seems like the maintenance of a delusional norm at this point.

It goes beyond magical thinking; it's outright willful ignorance. Let me use some imagery to illustrate my point.

Imagine a group of people struggling to stay afloat while swimming in the ocean; some are employees, and others are leaders. A boat approaches and only allows employees to climb aboard, while those already on the boat tell the leaders they shouldn't need to get in because they should be able to keep swimming (cue Dory's voice from *Finding Nemo* . . . just keep swimming . . . swimming . . . swimming). This creates a feedback loop that looks something like this:

→ Employees, we know you need help. Here are some mental health resources.
→ Leaders, learn how to support your teams, too.
→ Leaders, we understand you're facing challenges, but you can handle them on your own. Don't alarm others with your honesty. We only want to hear about when your team members are struggling and the help they need.

Talk about showing displays of withheld care and enduring illogical double standards. The lack of emotional support systems for leaders is unsustainable and perpetuates the stigma around seeking help in leadership. What internal thoughts might this set off in leaders? Something resembling the following:

- *"I shouldn't need these resources—so I won't use them."*
- *"I feel isolated, but I can't talk about it, or I'll lose my job."*
- *"My mental health doesn't matter. If they wanted to support me, they would."*

What usually happens when people face ongoing willful ignorance and pressure to be silent about their struggles from those around them? Correct, nothing good.

I once hosted a client event for a group of leaders. One shared how exhausting it is to support her team's mental health and mentioned that she would be criticized for discussing her own struggles and fatigue, in every sense of that word, from having to operate in that capacity. The look of validation mixed with despair on her leadership colleagues' faces made my heart sink. Two of them even had tears. Their expressions spoke louder than words could.

> *"At my lowest, I checked into a motel room with a couple of bottles of whiskey, intending to disappear for a day or two. I woke up nearly 24 hours later to police entering the room during a wellness check. I was so far gone that I nearly provoked suicide by cop. I ended up being committed for 48 hours. That moment was the crash landing, but the descent had started long before. I had completely lost my self-care, joy, and identity outside of being what I thought others needed me to be."*
>
> Interviewee: male, Gen X, Caucasian, Senior Leadership, construction industry

Adding insult to injury is the rise of the "bring your whole self to work" movement. I'll be the first to admit, back in the day, I bought into this idea too. It sounded good. It felt right until that critical day. I mentioned in the Preface when a group of leaders snapped me out of it. Only after that experience did I realize how flawed that concept is, because it's only accessible to some, not all. Leaders are faced with this catchy workplace idea that they themselves are not allowed to participate in. Why? Because if they do, they risk being judged, mistrusted, or even demoted. This feel-good phrase doesn't apply to them because of the dehumanization and emotional invulnerability they are expected to maintain.

Neurodiversity in Leadership

I want to pause and acknowledge neurodiversity in leadership because this is another area within the leadership mental health realm where biased perception and assumptions do not match fact, and, as a result, can cause a negative impact. As a neurospicy person myself, who is also a team leader, this one hits close to home.

In recent years, more people, often later in life, have been diagnosed as neurodivergent (such as ADHD, autism, etc.) after being encouraged to get assessed through the dedicated efforts of those in the neurodiversity advocacy space and by witnessing a growing social conversation around neurodiversity and mental health. This has reached a point where increased diagnosis rates have even been studied by the *National Institutes of Health (NIH)*.[8] To clarify, being neurodivergent is not a mental health condition. It's a developmental difference in how the brain operates, influencing how an individual processes information and responds to environmental stimuli. *Harvard Health Publishing* reinforced this by indicating that neurodiversity is just when "People experience and interact with the world around them in many different ways; there is no one 'right' way of thinking, learning, and behaving, and differences are not viewed as deficits."[9] Yes, to all of this.

It is also important to acknowledge that neurodivergence, due to differences in how individuals process stimuli, social interactions, and some challenges they may experience, can sometimes lead to co-occurring mental health issues like anxiety or depression, influenced by a range of emotional, social, and biological factors. My ADHD decided to choose anxiety as my love language—and they have a fantastic, and sometimes irritating, relationship with one another.

Not only do neurodivergent leaders accomplish incredible things and deserve unstigmatized support, but articles exist that highlight the undeniable benefits of neurodiversity in leadership for achieving business results. I once met someone who said that ADHD stands for "attuned delicately to a higher dimension," to which I said, "100% yes, no notes." It's shown in research, too. *Forbes*[10] published a piece highlighting that,

> ". . . *Neurodivergent leaders. . .bring valuable perspectives and capabilities that enhance organizational performance. Their different ways of processing information, solving problems, and leading teams aren't just beneficial but are increasingly essential for success in a complex business environment. Organizations that recognize and support these unique capabilities will gain significant competitive advantages in innovation, efficiency, and team performance.*"

The *World Economic Forum* published a piece that I gleefully interpreted as a crucial pushback against the Leadership Prototypes, stating that neurodiverse individuals are often wrongfully overlooked for leadership roles due to the false narrative that successful neurodivergent leaders are outliers, when in fact, that's not the truth. The piece shared success stories of public leadership figures like Charles Schwab, Trevor Noah, and Richard Branson, all of whom are neurodivergent and have had careers that are truly extraordinary.[11] The piece's recommendations were a relief to see, encouraging organizations to create executive teams inclusive of neurodiverse individuals, and that people in general need to ". . .collectively shift from this perception and consider the unique cognitive abilities that neurodiverse individuals possess."

Why do I bring this up? As I'm sure you can imagine, yes, there are neurodivergent people in leadership roles. Unfortunately, some neuro-divergent individuals may feel fearful of speaking up about that fact due to outdated and incorrect social stereotypes about what that means, how it can "show up" at work, and what people may think of them. Want to hear what a common occurrence sounds like? While writing this book, I took a quick vacation to get some R&R and to clear my head. On my trip, I had an extended conversation with someone and happened to mention that I had ADHD, to which the person said, "Oh wow! I never would have guessed; you articulate yourself so clearly and your thoughts are so organized." This was just a personal social interac-tion, with zero stakes. At work? The stakes for disclosure are way higher—and we'll look at that concept very closely in Chapter 5.

The Impact on Career Trajectory and Leadership Effectiveness

"I felt undervalued, unappreciated, and unsupported. . .Especially, given that I was hired under the guise of being the 'culture keeper,' so to speak. . .we developed and communicated core values. . .I felt the workplace was toxic and unsafe. . .It affected my trust completely. . .I was planning an exit strategy, but was laid off before I could leave. . ."

Interviewee: female, Gen X, Black, Director, human resources industry

"The demand that is put on leaders is real! The 80-hour work weeks, travel on weekends away from friends and family, all the while being expected to hold it all together. It always catches up to a person. I have witnessed many leaders using alcohol as a coping mechanism that essentially exacerbates the real issue."

Interviewee: female, Baby Boomer, Caucasian, Director, beauty industry

A saddening recurring theme emerged in my interviews with leaders for this book. Many of them said they were "encouraged" to speak up about their mental health in general and that the positive side effect of this was healthy role modeling, so their teams would feel encouraged to speak up too. On the surface, big yes. But what actually happened to these leaders? Something very different. Each interviewee shared that their disclosures later came back to bite them and were used against them when the going got tough. Talk about disingenuous care, another hit to psychological contracts, and further institutional betrayal (and in some cases, holy lawsuit, Batman).

Experiencing Mental Health Shame as a Leadership Career Liability

I remember talking to a leader who told me they were trying to communicate maturely to their colleagues one day that they were struggling with anxiety, so their colleagues would understand what was going on for this person and the support they needed, enabling them to perform. Unfortunately, one of their more junior team members told this leader in the same meeting that their disclosure was "inappropriate" and that it triggered *them*. To add insult to injury, the next day, that junior team member sent an email saying they were "too distressed to work the next day," citing the leader's disclosure as the reason. This leader's mature and courageous disclosure was weaponized against them, actively discouraging them from making the same choice again, for all the reasons we discussed in Chapter 1. And another one bites the dust because of the Leadership Prototypes.

Shame is a powerful force and a formidable deterrent. Studies indicate that, especially during our formative years, excessive feelings of shame can negatively impact our brain development, affecting self-esteem, our sense of self, mood, and mental health overall. Our brains perceive shame as a threat that we must avoid, triggering fight, flight, or freeze[12] responses through our nervous system. Unfortunately, shame's impact on us is not limited by age. "Shame and Self-Esteem: A Meta-Analysis," in *Europe's Journal of Psychology,* explored this:

"... *Shame is often generated by social events in which a personal status or feeling of rejection is sensed ... When individuals experience shame, the devaluation of self is perceived, and it may lower self-esteem. The frequent feeling of shame can eventually form into a trait of shame. Trait shame, in turn, involves negative feelings that are very painful and often crippling, which involve feelings of inferiority, despair, helplessness, and the eagerness to hide personal flaws ... and it brings impact to the fluctuation of self-esteem ... Usually, feelings of shame happen due to a condition where the personal self is devalued, such as a bad performance, socially assessed. Poor performance leads to greater reactions of psychological states indicating a danger to the social self, namely a decline in social self-esteem and an increase in shame.*"[13]

Let's explore the role of shame in leadership mental health. When we consider toxic narratives, leaders who feel shame for speaking up are naturally discouraged from doing so. People usually avoid situations where they might be questioned, blamed, or made to feel "defective." Comments like, "they are unhinged," or "they're a leader—they should do better," are frustrating, harmful, and all too frequent. These remarks can make leaders ashamed of struggling at all, which often causes them to stay silent.

When leaders show emotional struggles at work, primarily if these stem from unsupported or criticized mental health issues, they are often penalized. I can't count how many times I've spoken with leaders who've said that when their emotional capacity is questioned, punitive measures, including shame, are often imposed on them. Why do we prioritize punishing these individuals over supporting them? That same *Europe's Journal of Psychology* study illustrated this:

"*Many shameful experiences can eventually crystallize into a trait-like proneness of shame. Trait shame, in turn, includes an especially painful and often disabling, adverse sensation involving a sense of inferiority, hopelessness, and helplessness, as well as a willingness to conceal private failure.*"

Organizations often see allowing those who discuss emotional health struggles to remain in leadership roles mainly as a risk, rather than an opportunity for an influential person to demonstrate healthy dialogue about what it looks like to lead while struggling. To get the support, they need to serve others without experiencing their own emotional breakdown. Creating an environment that encourages inquiry, support, and open discussions about mental health among leaders—the *same* conversations we strongly urge leaders to initiate with their teams.

Neglected Emotional Health as a Determinant of Leadership Career Trajectory

". . .if individuals don't feel that others in the workplace genuinely care or take meaningful action to address the root causes—they won't give their best at work."

Interviewee: female, Gen X, Black, Director, consulting industry

"Leaders must strike a delicate balance between modeling openness and maintaining authority. . .there's a risk that some individuals might take advantage of this, potentially undermining your respect and perceived strength as a leader."

Interviewee: female, Millennial, Black, Senior Vice President in the C-Suite, heavy civil construction industry

The ripple effect of private struggles without the ability to share them at work can negatively influence leadership performance, cognitive functions, managerial effectiveness, career growth, and the likelihood of seeking mental health support. Leaders have been made to feel that discussing their mental health at work is a professional liability rather than a sign of emotional intelligence and maturity. Discouraging leaders from talking about their mental health not only harms them but also impacts their teams and the organization as a whole. From personal and professional life to career development, team management, and mental health—the ripple effects are significant.

Let's consider it from a natural perspective for a moment and discuss ecosystems, as I mentioned earlier. I often view a company as an ecosystem, with all its workers as its constituent organisms. These organisms both manage and adapt the ecosystem while also responding to its changes. Leaders play a vital role in maintaining the stability of an ecosystem in many ways. Let's consider the homeostasis of an ecosystem and its importance in maintaining balance. It makes sense that neglecting a key element will eventually affect other parts of the ecosystem and the organisms within it. Using this analogy for the workplace, it can impact the team, the organization, and even the leader's career path. From burnout to unprofessional behavior, poor decision-making, and more, when leaders' mental health is overlooked, they not only struggle personally but can also become less effective in their roles and in managing their teams. This makes it hard to follow the "good" behavioral ideals set for them, like we discussed in Chapter 1, doesn't it? A hindered ability to prioritize mental health and functionally perform will typically have a negative impact. Then, one of two things usually happens, driven by systemic shifts beyond their control:

- Leaders may blame themselves.
- They may act out negatively toward their teams.

Let's pause to talk about burnout (i.e., "physical, emotional, or mental exhaustion, accompanied by decreased motivation, lowered performance, and negative attitudes toward oneself and others"[14]). Basically, when you reach a state of burnout, it's your body, brain, and nervous system saying something like,

> *"Okay! This is why we can't have nice things. I'm going to shut you down now, against your will, because you ignored all my signs and signals. Now you know why you're looking at a pile of laundry and crying for no reason."*

When it comes to burnout, it's not surprising that leaders are also measured in the data but are also expected to "solve for burnout" in their organizations. Considering the demonstrable impact of leaders' mental health invisibility, it's logical to conclude that reaching a burn-out state is entirely possible and potentially correlated. Translation?

"Solve burnout for others, but shut up about your own, please."

Let's look at the data again: the cleverly titled "Burnout of Command,"[15] also published in *Forbes*, examined how leaders can recognize and prevent burnout not only in their teams but also in themselves. As I'm sure you can imagine, I was elated when I saw that burnout in leadership was also being recognized. At the same time, I noticed something that made my heart sink again, highlighting how this double standard persists: leaders are encouraged to manage their well-being in a system that doesn't support them, yet criticizes them when they are running on fumes to show up for others. Let's see if you can spot the irony within this piece:

- "The Development Dimensions International's Global Leadership Forecast 2021 showed that nearly 60% of leaders have reported experiencing feelings of exhaustion at the end of their workday."
- "A 2022 Microsoft Work Trend Index showed that over 53% of managers feel burned out. . .If leaders of people are experiencing higher degrees of burnout, it is obvious that so are their teams, especially if the leader does not prioritize their ability to manage stress."

The article continues by offering more advice on identifying and addressing burnout in teams and not for the leader. The most that leaders got from this article for themselves was to, and I'm not joking, "look in the mirror" and "get it done." The message remains clear: shut up about your own burnout, manage it privately, and welcome to the Thunderdome of Shame if you don't. I have mental whiplash. I understand the person who wrote this article was trying to help; people who write about these topics generally are. But if you continue to offer advice and guidance in a system with a broken narrative, is that advice actually realistic or actionable? This doesn't exactly give positive reinforcement to feasibly function within leadership or remain within it. The same *Lyra Health* "2024 State of Workforce Mental Health Report" from earlier showed that 27% of managers reported their mental health had a significant or severe impact on their ability to perform their job in 2023, up from 18% in 2022. That's a big jump in just a year. What can this mean? Having a "Sophie's Choice" of potentially having to choose between prioritizing mental health survival over professional growth.

Younger Generations See the Warning Signs—and Don't Want the Leadership Gig

While writing this book, I saw a TV segment[16] on why some Millennials and Gen Zer's are avoiding taking leadership roles because they don't want to sacrifice their mental health. It discussed a concept called "conscious unbossing," where these generations aren't pursuing leadership roles not from a lack of interest, but to protect their mental health. *Business Insider* also published a piece on this topic in 2025, corroborating that the workforce is seeing a trend toward avoiding management roles to preserve mental well-being.[17] Frustratingly, this article focuses on the key takeaway of how businesses need to work harder on a culture of work–life integration so that newer generations *want* to become leaders, without mentioning supporting those who are flailing *right now*.

Here's the mixed bag I've observed. Younger generations have noticed the toll on the leaders of previous generations. They're choosing not to follow that pattern, and I don't blame them. They want career growth but not at the expense of their mental health. While I understand this and I'm not pointing fingers, it seems that even though workplaces are recognizing that up-and-coming generations of leaders are saying "no thanks," companies are not using this as a dire signal to care for those who are currently in leadership roles. They're keeping flailing leaders in the ocean. We'll look more at this further in Chapter 4.

A Brief Note on the Impact on Team Culture

> *"When you aren't heard, seen, or supported, resentment and resistance grow. When it gets to the point of resentment and resistance, it becomes detrimental to an organization."*
>
> Interviewee: female, Millennial, Mexican-American, Elementary Principal, public education industry

I won't spend too much time on this, as I covered specific chapters in my first book about how leaders can (and should) foster a culture of mental health for their teams and the ways to do so. While this book is aimed at leaders, we must also recognize the impact that unmanaged leadership mental health has on team members' mental health as well. We expect leaders to continuously develop an ever-growing list of skills that will make them—and their teams—successful in their positions within the organization, as well as how they support their teams. All the while, without acknowledging the importance of supporting their mental health so they can function to meet those expectations. In Chapter 4, we'll discuss this in depth, focusing on the additional pressures leaders face in supporting their team's mental health at work, often while managing their own in silence.

When leaders face relentless stress in an organization or industry that pressures them to push through without expressing dissent, the personal and professional damage that occurs can have widespread effects. If that situation goes wrong, teams won't see a leader whose mental health is overlooked; they'll see a leader who is diminishing morale, potentially harming the rapport and well-being of the team, without considering all the factors that may have contributed to the leader's behavior. There are also other unintended ripple effects on team members' mental health. For instance, if an unintentional tone of silence and white knuckling your way through things has been set as the norm by a leader, it may cause some team members to wonder:

- *"If they aren't talking about their mental health, can I?"*
- *"Will they think I'm incapable of doing my job if I talk about my struggles?"*

Hmmm, that last second sounds familiar, doesn't it . . .

All of the theory, data, and the Leadership Prototypes have demonstrated that negatively perceived variations in leadership displays of emotional struggle are not met with curiosity or empathy but rather with criticism. If a leader's behavior goes off the rails, for any reason, the initial response is often not a calm, logical form of self-disclosure about what led them to that point. Instead, because they're already panicked and burned out—sometimes, they become destructive. Their reputation is damaged, trust with others erodes, and their abilities are doubted. Additionally, their teams miss opportunities to understand what their leader is experiencing and, when appropriate, to offer support. We will explore this further in Part II, along with the Leadership Mental Health Archetypes, which will help individual leaders understand why they might end up in those states in the first place.

Let's revisit our growing Weight on Leadership Mental Health Equation, with the new elements below:

Experiencing Worsening Mental Health Through Data Invisibility & Support Neglect

+

Experiencing Mental Health Struggles as a Career Liability

+

A Lack of Emotional Support Structures as a Sharing Deterrent

+

Having to Choose Between Emotional Survival vs. Career Progression

+

An Impaired Ability to Lead Effectively

+

Creating an Unintentional Negative Impact on Team Culture Around Mental Health

I realize this chapter and the ones before it may have felt heavy. I'm with you, really. Here's the thing: to break apart a big idea that needs to be challenged, especially for the sake of those it harms, the pain points must be highlighted, logically explained, and beyond reproach to make a case for change (which is what we're doing here in Part I). Think about everything we've covered so far. These are *just* the active deterrents that prevent leaders from discussing their mental health in general, and they don't even include the additional pressures of being a leader *today*, or the individual circumstances, identities, and personal factors they bring into work. We'll explore that further in Chapters 4 and 5.

Individual Reflection Questions

- Have you ever felt that discussing your mental health as a leader might hurt your career? Why do you feel this way? What are you worried might happen if you speak up?
- Have the mental health challenges of leadership, or facing mental health challenges while also being a leader, caused you to reconsider your career path? Why or why not?
- Have your mental health struggles affected your leadership at work? If so, what has that looked like?

Chapter Key Takeaways

- Leadership mental health challenges are quantified in data, yet they are often overlooked in recommendations.
- Some leaders feel they can't speak up about their mental health because it could threaten their career.
- Some leaders do not share about their mental health because they fear being shamed due to their position.
- Unrecognized and unmanaged mental health issues can harm leadership effectiveness.
- Neglecting mental health in leadership can impact how leaders manage their teams.

4

The Leadership "Plate" Has Become a Deep Trough—and Leaders Are Strapped to It

"I was leading one of the most high-pressure projects in the world, with over 7,000 workers and 35 million man-hours. People were in crisis constantly. I was holding space for thousands of workers in crisis, and no one was holding space for me. That's what it means to be a leader in a system that hasn't evolved."

Interviewee: male, Gen X, Caucasian, Senior Leadership, construction industry

"We are supposed to figure out how to do more with less and at the same time be the best. The expectations continue to increase, and the support decreases."

Interviewee: female, Millennial, Mexican-American, Elementary Principal, public education industry

I'M GOING TO use some uncomfortable imagery as a metaphor throughout this chapter to emphasize the gravity of what I'm trying to convey. You will quickly understand why I have done this.

From Plate to Trough

When discussing everything we typically need to manage at work, we often describe ourselves as having a "full plate." When it comes to leadership, it's more than that. Picture this: instead of "cleaning off" a plate, imagine that you're chained to a trough, with heavy iron shackles wrapped around your body. Then, you're told to use every ounce of your energy to claw out everything you can to empty the trough, but it just keeps refilling, and somehow—getting deeper. You never seem to "get ahead" and always feel behind or like you're failing. When you tell others that you're tired and feel like you're stuck with an impossible, never-ending task, you're criticized, and your struggles are dismissed. Doesn't sound pleasant, does it? It's not meant to. It's meant to feel overwhelming, to show the weight that today's leaders carry at work, and the mental toll it takes on them compared to their predecessors.

If this metaphor doesn't resonate with you, try thinking of the Atlas statue. You know, the muscular guy with the globe on his shoulders. Visualize the concrete cracking beneath Atlas' feet, sinking farther and farther, while he's expected to keep holding up the world. As a leader, have you ever felt that way? If so, what emotions or thoughts came up for you just now? I would be surprised if they were anything positive.

The Intensifying Weight and Burden of Leadership

"As the leader at the top of an organization, there are not a lot of people whom you can open up to. Particularly in my role, I would not want to share with my staff. . .So, while I do have a small group of peers in a similar role, there just aren't a lot of outlets that are appropriate."

Interviewee: male, Millennial, Caucasian, CEO, nonprofit trade association industry

"I would like for companies to recognize that leaders are human beings too—fallible and prone to mistakes; and that where the stakes and

> *risks are higher—the greater the mental health support on offer should be."*
>
> Interviewee: female, Gen X, Black, Director, consulting industry

There's no way I could cover *every* pressure, expectation, and responsibility leaders face in today's workplace in just one book. It wouldn't be useful to you either. Remember the Paradox of Choice. I'm offering targeted quality rather than overwhelming quantity. So, I've decided to focus on three key areas:

1. The overall intensifying demands and burdens of leadership
2. How leaders "burn" when the world burns
3. The court of digital public opinion

Think about the factors we've explored so far in our Weight on Leadership Mental Health Equation. Now add these three areas on top. We ask more of leaders now than ever before. The world and the World of Work are evolving. Even though the tasks (i.e., the demand) are growing, changing, and becoming more challenging to accomplish, the emotional support (i.e., the supply) for leaders to succeed isn't increasing enough. It never has. It's almost like putting a virtual reality headset on leaders who are tied to the trough, with visuals of "how to perform," while asking them to ignore the overwhelming distress they're experiencing at the same time. All while they scream, saying it's too much. Does that sound like effective leadership development or genuine concern for leadership mental health? No, not to me, either.

Our Asks of Leaders Are Intensifying and Multiplying

To grasp how increasing demands impact leaders' mental health, we need to examine what is generally expected of leaders today. Many of these expectations are very important, while some, although considered significant, can actually be harmful. All leaders are generally expected to meet these standards with the same level of proficiency. I liken this to the following: having to be a strategic visionary, an emotional janitor for others, while simultaneously whiteboarding Q1 organizational goals and suppressing a potential nervous breakdown so you don't get accused of not having a Growth Mindset.[1] What exactly is on leaders' shoulders now? Let's break down some common leadership tasks; I'll refer to them as Base Leadership Tasks (Base Tasks, for short) and Bonus-Added Leadership Tasks (Bonus Tasks, for short).

"Leaders are cautious. . .personal emotional needs are always secondary to the company's performance . . . I remember more than one occasion expressing that I was reaching the end of my rope and being told to simply push through it."

Interviewee: male, Millennial, Black, first-generation American, Director, legal support industry

---

Base Leadership Tasks: Base Tasks are the essential requirements and cornerstones of leadership roles. They include responsibilities that are *generally* accepted across industries, companies, and locations; though there are always exceptions for various reasons, which we'll explore in the next chapter. Base Tasks cannot be outsourced. While challenging, these tasks demonstrate a person's ability to manage leadership fundamentals and are generally expected to be manageable and learnable. These tasks often include, but are not limited to, managing employee output, project management, strategic decision-making, performance reviews, setting team direction, creating and maintaining goals and objectives, resource management, inspiring commitment, promoting innovation, encouraging accountability, and more.

However, these Base Tasks are increasing in volume, becoming more complex, and the time to become proficient at them is decreasing, along with organizational and team member patience. So, while these essential tasks must be completed, more tasks are being added with growing pressure and higher stakes, coupled with less forgiveness, understanding, and grace if those expectations aren't met. Now, let's talk about the Bonus Tasks.

Bonus-Added Leadership Tasks: Depending on the industry, company, team, and situation, Bonus Tasks are often regarded as part of Base Tasks, even though we recognize that Bonus Tasks demand even more time, effort, and experience to develop. These Bonus Tasks are positive and useful, but they can be challenging to perform *well* due to task volume and high expectations. I see these Bonus Tasks in two categories:

1. Healthy, important, and necessary:
   o Representing the evolving leadership responsibilities in a modern workplace, designed to meet contemporary needs. Leaders must also adapt their skills accordingly. Simply put, when we learn to do better, we need to actually do better.
2. Unhealthy, toxic, and unreasonable:
   o Representing the vessel of expectations in which the healthy Bonus Tasks reside.

When the distinction between the two isn't recognized, it becomes a slippery slope for leadership mental health and leaders' overall sanity. Imagine being told to bite down on a jawbreaker candy to reach the bubble gum center faster—and being criticized if your teeth break. In our effort to better equip leaders, we often overlook the extremely steep learning and adaptation curve they face, criticizing them when they fall short. While these leadership tasks are important, they add stress, complexity, and weight to the roles that leaders are responsible for.

What do the healthy, important, and necessary Bonus Tasks look like? While not exhaustive, this list shows the most common ones for leaders:

- *Have emotional intelligence (EQ):* Understand its value and develop the ability to engage in self-awareness, self-management, social awareness, and relationship management.[2]
- *Understand team dynamics and communication:* Learn how to navigate the complexities of team interactions, conflicts, communication, trust-building, and collaboration.

- *Create psychological safety at work:* Understand the importance of fostering a healthy work environment based on the principles of psychological safety, so that team members feel comfortable sharing their thoughts, ideas, feedback, and engaging in conflict without fear of unwarranted retaliation. Hopefully, leading to a healthy and positive team culture.[3]
- *Get feedback right:* Give feedback effectively in a way that's healthy, respectful, and useful to team members, not just in a way that "feels good to say." Side note: all hail Kim Scott, author of *Radical Candor*, whom I fan-girlingly refer to as the Queen of Feedback because she's taught us the importance of using the Radical Candor approach when delivering feedback. Simply put: giving feedback through Radical Candor is when you care enough about someone to give them honest, direct feedback—with care.[4]
- *Support team mental health and overall well-being:* Be aware of the team's general well-being, offer appropriate support, and guide individuals to the right resources when needed. The purpose of this skill, its boundaries, and how to do it right as a leader are all explained in detail in my first book.
- *Be literate in diversity, equity, inclusion, and belonging (DEIB):* Understand key principles such as access, social marginalization, and identity. Show genuine allyship, not just claim it, and demonstrate these values within your team.
- *Be adaptable to digital transformation:* Stay current with evolving technology trends and how they influence team communication, teamwork, and organizational output.
- *Manage a remote or hybrid team:* Adapt management styles when leading and overseeing teams in a distributed workforce, as this can affect everything a leader would handle in person—such as creating psychological safety, building trust, checking on employee mental health, task delegation, handling miscommunications, and being aware of and inclusive toward work accommodations needed for individual disabilities based on best practices and guidelines for supporting various ways of working.

All of the above are essential, modern-day functions of leadership. Yes, they are vital. Leaders must recognize the importance of understanding and applying these skills. And. . .there is still a dark side to that process.

The Darker Side of Bonus Tasks

". . . more and more is being expected of leaders . . . we're expected to do more with less, amid volatile external market conditions. Boards and investors set unrealistic expectations with little concern for the well-being of the leader being expected to deliver such ambitious targets, and a delivery at all costs mindset prevails."

Interviewee: female, Gen X, Black, Director, consulting industry

"The pressure was relentless, and acknowledging burnout or emotional exhaustion felt risky. There was an expectation to always be 'on,' to keep delivering no matter what, and admitting that the load was too heavy could have been seen as a red flag rather than a sign that structural support was needed. The result was a culture where struggles were silently endured rather than addressed. Without time to process or access to meaningful support, the stress compounded."

Interviewee: male, Gen X, Black, first-time manager, technology industry

Now, let's look at the darker side of Bonus Tasks—the unhealthy, toxic, and unreasonable vessel of expectations in which the healthy Bonus Tasks sit. For short: Servant Leadership *on steroids*. The result? It negatively affects a leader's ability to be effective in their roles and their overall well-being, making it more difficult to succeed at the healthy Bonus Tasks they are also expected to handle. Let's explore this further by looking at three common areas where this can show up daily for leaders.

- *Output demands are endlessly increasing:* There is now a demand for leaders to push themselves and their teams to breakneck speeds to deliver more faster, and in higher volumes. The worst part? When leaders are asked to do this despite fundamentally disagreeing with the process, they are pressured to enforce it just to keep their jobs. This is the darker side of innovation—pushing boundaries too far sometimes. Pressure for innovation, if left unchecked, can lead to excessive abuse at the expense of reason-ability and well-being.

- *Controlling the uncontrollable:* Human error is increasingly not tolerated and is seen as an oxymoron. Leaders appear to be held responsible for things they sometimes can't control, no matter how much effort they put in. Some common issues? Employee engagement (people disengage from work for various reasons that are beyond mitigation) or being caught between employee frustration or organizational decisions they can't influence. What this can look like: return-to-office orders, employee dissatisfaction with pay bands, and budget cuts. Changes in market conditions that impact the company's ser-vices or products. Turnover and employee retention—people leave jobs for many reasons, despite the common adage that people leave managers, not companies. Customer satisfac-tion—no matter how good you are to clients and customers, someone will always be unhappy for reasons beyond anyone else's control. Employee performance. And too many other factors to name. And if things go wrong on a leader's watch? It's considered the leader's fault.

- *Being a shapeshifter who must accommodate everyone's needs:* Yes, flexibility, empathy, and adaptability are essential leadership traits. Leaders need to have these qualities, plain and simple; however, reasonable limits must be set. When leaders try to establish those boundaries (when warranted, not when it results from laziness, ignorance, neglect of leadership duties, unfair favoritism, nepotism, and other workplace issues), they are often villainized for not being everything to everyone all the time. Yes, each team member's personal life circumstances matter. Yes, everyone has challenges. Leaders should be aware of this and try to accommodate them when possible. No, ask-ing exhausted leaders to go above and beyond while mentally contorting themselves is neither reasonable nor healthy. It's mental gymnastics that even the most experienced leaders can't sustain.

■ *Being "volun-told" to act as emotional support figures (unintentionally resulting in workplace caregivership):* Please take a deep breath as you read this. I tell leaders that they can and should know how to discuss mental health with their teams, but there must be limits to this approach. Being skilled in a particular area doesn't mean that skill should be abused, taken advantage of, or change a leader's role in an organization to an inappropriate one. I've lost count of the number of stories I've heard from leaders where the reasonable guidance, empathy, and support they're expected to give employees are pushed far beyond reasonable limits, resulting in an approach that kid-gloves people's situations so much that it resembles clinical case management. That's not caring for team wellbeing; that's just inappropriate and enables people not to take individual responsibility for managing their mental health distress.

■ *Maintaining a limitless capacity for emotional labor:* The term "emotional labor" was first developed and explored by sociologist Arlie Hochschild in her 1983 book *The Managed Heart.* It was initially intended to describe the type of emotional effort needed to work in the service industry.[5] Now, the term implies much more. Emotional Labor is more than just being there for people these days. In many cases, leaders are expected to serve as emotional anchors for their teams, supporting them as they navigate uncertainty, ambiguity, and work-related stress. Should leaders support their team's overall mental well-being? Absolutely. Should that be an endless process with no limits or awareness of a leader's capacity? No. On top of that, leaders must do this at a time when there is active intergenerational disagreement about what supporting mental health at work *means*, what it looks like, and whether it is even acceptable.

"My role wasn't just about overseeing tasks; it was about making sure people felt valued, understood, and supported. The real glue work was building trust—showing my team that I cared about them so that they, in turn, would care about the success of the team. But this emotional labor was largely invisible . . . They didn't see the time and energy it

(continued)

(continued)
took to maintain that balance, to make sure people felt seen, heard, and motivated. Over time, this took a toll on my well-being. I carried the responsibility of keeping everything running smoothly while also ensuring that people didn't feel like just another cog in the machine. The pressure to be both a supportive leader and a high-performing manager meant that my own needs often came last. The experience made me realize that organizations need to recognize and support the emotional labor that leaders put into their teams—not just the operational outcomes they produce."

Interviewee: male, Gen X, Black, first-time manager, technology industry

A 2023 *Frontiers in Psychology* paper did a fantastic job at gathering qualitative data from leaders, focusing on the impact on leadership mental health from heightened demands since the onset of the COVID-19 pandemic. There was an emphasis on how this work intensification increases the emotional impact on leaders from enduring these growing demands.[6] Here's what they found:

- Increased work demands with unrealistic expectations:
  o "Higher amount of work and higher speed of work, fewer breaks."
  o "Generally, a higher need for planning, reorganizing, and consultations under highly uncertain conditions."
  o "A feeling of being responsible for everything caused by a blurring of responsibilities; new responsibilities without more time, resources, and higher needs for decision-making."

- Being caught in the middle:
  o "Atmosphere of annoyance that could lead to overreactions on both sides; even more difficult in a virtual leadership setting due to loss of emotional ties."
  o "Contradictions between . . . attitude of organization's management on the one hand [(no) sense of the seriousness of the

situation] and the followers' needs on the other hand at expectation of loyalty on all sides; this led to a takeover of organization's responsibilities regarding crisis management due to a lack of clear rules."

■ Managing employee mental health with not enough training or support for themselves:
  o "Dealing with . . . problems, worries, fears while partly being confronted with the same challenges themselves."
  o "Time and effort needed for supporting employees, dealing with individual problems, and finding individual solutions."

Did your heart race while reading this? Did any feelings or memories surface about your current or past job? That's understandable if it did. That list can be overwhelming, even for the most experienced leader. To act as if they can perform miracles, be oracles, and be facilitators of the forces of nature.

When the World Burns—Leaders Burn Too

Remember from the Introduction when I mentioned that I read the room while writing this book? Well, the world was burning, again. Many visible leaders were doing terrible things that hurt people and caused other problems as well. The president of South Korea, Yoon Suk Yeol, abused his power and declared martial law[7] for funsies. The UK Supreme Court (wrongfully) ruled that the definition of a woman is only based on biological sex and does not include trans women.[8] The now former CEO of Boeing, David Calhoun, received a multi-million-dollar bonus, while some planes in their fleet endangered people's lives, and while whistleblowers were being harmed.[9] That's just barely scratching the surface. Layoffs multiplied, global stock markets tanked (with intermittent recessions manipulated by peek-a-boo tariff wars for the financial benefit of those wanting to buy low), cost of living rose, trade wars erupted, fascism rose internationally, xenophobia heightened, extremist far-right governments flourished, immigrants were mistreated and imprisoned, and women, BIPOC, and LGBTQ+IA communities were targeted.

Leaders Are Stress Targets During Times of Turmoil, Chaos, and Crisis

It doesn't matter if or how much the world is burning; leaders are still expected to lead, period. Humans naturally struggle with nuance; it's something we have to work at consciously. When organisms are overwhelmed by stressful or threatening stimuli, they seek a way to release the negative energy that has built up inside. They don't naturally pause to reflect and think, *"Okay, so A, B, and C are stressing me out. I don't have a healthy outlet for this. Let me make sure I don't take it out on those who don't deserve it, even if it would be easier."* In reality, and for those who are easy targets when emotions explode, the stressed organism is essentially calling for help—but often does so through blame and attack.

Let's look at layoffs. In recent years, they happened one after another, many of which were very poorly and inhumanely executed. I'm talking about automated emails and a blatant disregard for employment laws. Then came the social media comments, like, "Employers have lost all humanity." Is what happened to those people wrong? Yes! Are all employers like this? No. Yet, those who aren't are still perceived as if they are, especially during times of increased stress, chaos, and uncertainty. At the time of writing this book, the odds were stacked against leaders, even more than usual, for speaking up about their struggles.

Just like any individual contributor, leaders *also* worry about paying their mortgage, keeping their job, supporting a family or partner, fearing for their emotional or physical safety, and any other "life" concerns you can feasibly think of. The "good" leaders, however, are considered rare because of the toxic dominant narratives and stories that draw our attention. These leaders, these decent human beings, often work for the same employers who have "lost their humanity." But because of the leaders who cavalierly break (intentionally or not) psychological contracts with countless employees, their actions undermine any emotional regard for the leaders who don't.

Despite the additional burden of unpredictable stressors, leaders' emotional experiences are often forgotten and dismissed during times of chaos and crisis. They are further dehumanized, the depths of their struggles deepen, and their VR headset is strapped on even tighter. They are expected to ease the suffering of those they lead, with a target on their back if they fail to do so.

Leading through crises and uncertainty is a key part of leadership, and it is both demanding and exhausting. In today's world of instant information, a 24/7 news cycle, and Cancel Culture on social media, leading through a crisis is like walking a tightrope above a bed of fire while being yelled at by the crowd if you say your feet are burning. Leaders are still expected to act decisively, handle adversity, influence others, and hide the emotional toll these crises take on them. If they don't, they're labeled "bad" leaders and accused of "lacking the resilience to lead." Sadly, societal chaos and uncertainty are often caused by poor, and sometimes objectively negative, leadership failures. Remember how taking situational nuance into account isn't in our nature? Well, it's even harder to do when people face crises and turmoil caused by ineffective leadership. Chaos doesn't encourage people to pause their prototyping of leaders. It often leads to the vilification of them.

Even as far back as 2020, during a once-in-a-century pandemic, SAP published an article reaffirming the expectation that leaders must "assume responsibility for employee well-being" to "buffer stress for employees" and that employee mental well-being is part of a core company strategy they must carry out.[10] The message was clear: lead and adapt through crisis and focus on others, not yourself. When researching this idea, every source that appeared offered advice to leaders on how to effectively lead during times of social tribalism, unrest, and other challenges. I had to change my search terms multiple times to find literally one source that focused on the mental health impact on leaders during times of crisis. The ironic thing? The *Frontiers of Psychology* leadership mental health study from earlier in this chapter highlighted the critical components missing from articles like this *SAP* piece, just like so many other pieces dedicated to leading through crisis. What did the *Frontiers of Psychology* study declare?

". . . leadership research tends to neglect leaders' own health . . . and their specific constellation of demands and resources . . . This is a critical shortcoming as leaders' health status . . . While leaders are important for organizational functioning, particularly in times of crisis, they are also confronted with crisis-related demands with likely consequences for their own health . . . Crisis leadership means guiding while

being guided by contingencies . . . Overall, work intensification and emotional demands yielded significant positive relations with negative mental health outcomes."

This study clearly demonstrated that the pandemic taught us valuable lessons. Future crises will occur, leaders will have increased responsibilities during those times of turmoil, and as a result, they are a mentally vulnerable group. Last, but not least, (shocker—not) leaders will need tailored mental health support from the organization to match those demands. This critical assessment and recommendation, which could have helped so many leaders, was buried in the annals of the internet. Want to know the part of the study that made me giggle? They proved, through data, that telling leaders to "believe in themselves" didn't help with their exhaustion, irritability, and adverse mental health outcomes while leading, unsupported, through a crisis. Who would have thought?

Leading Through Social Tribalism, Polarization-Driven Unrest, and Systemic Volatility

"You're there to support everyone else, maintain stability, and set the tone—regardless of what's happening in your own life. Especially in times like these, when our country is facing so much turmoil, it's been incredibly difficult. The anxiety of just living day to day is real, and my family and I have been personally impacted by these broader changes. I once spoke up against what I saw as performative DEI decisions that excluded the voices of impacted employees and myself as the HR executive. Instead of being engaged in dialogue or respected for raising a concern, I was penalized. . .based on false, unfounded claims. That experience was one of the most damaging of my entire career. I was working 12–15-hour days for months to build out the parts of the HR function from the ground up . . . Yet when I advocated for employees and called out inauthentic behavior, I was made to feel like the problem."

Interviewee: female, Elder Millennial, Asian, Vice President, software industry

While I know this is not a new behavior, we're now in a time, seemingly again, where team and organizational management have to include how leaders deal with people's most common verbal weapon of choice: a pitchfork often aimed at each other, sometimes with reckless abandon. Leadership models aside, leading through increased social tribalism, persistent values polarization, and the echo chambers of social media has been profoundly soul-crushing for so many leaders.

Being expected to lead, guide, adapt, and thrive, even as trust erodes and social divisions widen into what seems like an insurmountable chasm, they are told to "keep calm and carry on" without regard for the emotional toll they endure during this time. The VUCA model, a leadership methodology, was first coined by economists and university professors Warren Bennis and Burt Nanus in their book *Leaders: The Strategies for Taking Charge*, and later adopted by the U.S. Army War College in the 1990s in response to the collapse of the USSR.[11] It's become a crowd favorite in leadership development, teaching leaders how to navigate volatility, uncertainty, complexity, and ambiguity. Not to sound cavalier, but these days, with the seemingly limitless depths people will sink to when attacking each other, no model on the planet can emotionally save the leaders who need to lead through that gauntlet.

Navigating complex societal changes, challenges, and systemic inflation isn't easy for anyone. Much less those responsible for the output of others and ensuring everything is handled correctly, while experiencing those systemic changes themselves underneath what feels like society's descent into a real-life version of the film *Civil War* or TV shows like *The Handmaid's Tale, Years and Years,* and *Extrapolations*. Through it all, leaders are expected to bridge the gap within the teams they manage while simultaneously upholding some semblance of group cohesion when they cannot control other adults and what they say. Furthermore, they face challenges if those adults work within an organization that takes public and/or internal political or social stances with which they may disagree. Leaders cannot completely control the conversations they are expected to mitigate in the workplace. Conversations fueled by intensifying, emotionally driven levels of polarized social identity, group loyalty to those who are similar to us, and frightening levels of hostility toward those who are not.

Unfortunately, the steadily growing trend of social tribalism feels like a thought infection that's spreading to minds faster than we can treat it. Political encouragement, a lack of constructive public discourse, and people auto-dividing themselves into what seems like increasingly polarized groups isn't helping anything and just continues to fan the flames. While human beings are naturally tribal, the global society in which we are in is not a healthy depiction of that. This is not "*we stick with the familiar and protect our own.*" It's turned into, "*You are wrong and dangerous, and I hate you because you are not like me because you don't agree with everything I think.*" These sentiments extend to the workplace, whether it's virtual or in a brick-and-mortar building. Leaders are expected to manage the occurrences and even the fallout around them. Some examples based on the Base and Bonus Tasks from earlier?

- Maintain trust, cooperation, and psychological safety
- Walk the line of compliance, legality, and Cancel Culture
- Survive their own impending burnout while fostering inclusive environments
- Manage employee rage and disengagement caused by anti-women and anti-DEIB sentiments spreading through companies (more on this in Chapter 5), with rapid reversals of programs that took years and decades to build, all while feeling disheartened by these changes and unable to influence organizational decisions against them
- When a fellow leader (or even a team member) expresses offensive sentiments in their organization, or publicly on social media, resembling hate speech, which then becomes a "work issue" for that leader and potentially HR to manage
- And they have to "deal with it," despite the fact that none of the above is even remotely in their control

Remember, when the world burns, leaders burn, and the organization at large, or even team members, may feel compelled to shoot their arrows of stress at the targets on leaders' backs, warranted or not. It all takes a toll on the people who must manage this sharp fragmentation.

The Unending Pressure to Take a Public Stand—Even at Your Own Expense

In recent years, leaders have also faced the expectation to make a public statement about almost every social occurrence, be overt about all affiliations, "pick a side," or face the wrath of unimaginable consequences. And depending on their walk of life, they may feel terrified, enraged, and hopeless themselves. Let me be clear: taking a stand in the face of oppression, harm, and inhumanity is something that every person should do, and leaders even more so. However, to expect leaders to do this consistently, ad nauseam, and with zero regard for becoming collateral damage in this process, is something anyone not in a leadership position would be potentially resentful or shocked to be asked to do if they weren't comfortable or didn't want to. Remember the *2025 Edelman* Trust Barometer Global Report on Trust and the Crisis of Grievance[12] I mentioned in the Introduction? It provided a crystal-clear depiction of the direction the world is going, sampling 33,000 people in 28 countries, and three highlights stood out:

- "Fear of being discriminated against surges to an all-time high"
- "Fear that leaders lie to us at an all-time high"
- "Grievance demands more action from business, not less"
  - This last one is completely warranted. But what happens to the leaders who must manage employee discontent and those who cannot effect this change in businesses? Or those who try to, but are met with insurmountable pushback?

Again, much of the above is also caused by poor leadership, so those numerous bad apples taint the perception of any good ones. I don't blame people for being pissed at leaders; it's completely warranted in many respects. The world is heading in a frightening direction, but countless individuals are trying to combat what feels like an irreparable decline of society. In contrast, others seem to be actively promoting its demise. The former doesn't get as much attention as the latter—because they don't make for good eye-catching headlines or social media clickbait.

I was watching the television show *The Pitt*, starring Noah Wyle (i.e., the heartthrob from the television show *ER*) when I wrote this book. *The Pitt* is a seriously realistic portrayal of what it's like to work in healthcare today. The show conveys numerous messages about mental health in the workplace, particularly for leadership mental health. In one episode, Wyle's character (the lead Attending Physician in the ER) said something profound. When speaking to a colleague temporarily deemed the Head Charge Nurse on the floor, he said, "One must imagine Sisyphus happy."[13] This philosophically implies that leaders need to envision the impossible—that Sisyphus could ever feel happy. Context: Sisyphus, a king in Greek mythology, was sentenced by the gods to push a boulder up a hill daily, only for it to roll back down every day, starting all over again.

Wyle's line was, in fact, from the 1942 essay "The Myth of Sisyphus" by the philosopher, author, and journalist Albert Camus. In a paper published by the *University of Hawai'i*,[14] the paper explained that Camus' writings on Sisyphus served as a commentary on the concept of absurdity in the world and the pressing need to find meaning within it, resulting in Sisyphus' ultimately attempting to find, and choosing to find, joy by consciously embracing his inescapable fate. The paper went on to explain the following,

> "The absurd comes with the realization that the world is not rational: 'At this point of his effort, man stands face to face with the irrational. He feels within him his longing for happiness and for reason. The absurd is born of this confrontation between the human need and the unreasonable silence of the world'."

With the aim of this book, and an immense amount of respect for Camus and all he stood for, we must, in some respects, endeavor to acknowledge and simultaneously push against Camus' notion. To fight against irrationality and the unreasonable silence of the world in order to change leaders' fate. Unlike Sisyphus, we can't continuously "sentence" leaders to push boulders up the hill, daily, with no help, ad infinitum.

Fearing the Digital Court of Public Opinion and Inked-on-the-Internet Social Scrutiny

I will admit this: social media and the internet have some very positive elements. Often, these platforms serve as powerful tools that highlight fundamental issues, including exposing horrible workplace experiences that should not and cannot stay hidden from the public. These online spaces can offer opportunities for individuals who might otherwise go unheard. Whether being bullied at work, discriminated against, harassed, or facing other unconscionable situations, social media and various internet platforms can create a space for individuals to be recognized and rally others around these crucial causes to create change. To demand accountability from wrongdoers and those in power who may enable such acts. However, the passion and intensity of these conversations and movements have a complex, darker side.

These movements are, rightly so, often driven by deep-seated emotions and feelings of abuse, betrayal, pain, and hurt. What happens when a large group connects over these intense, triggering feelings and ideas? Things can and often do escalate rapidly. What often begins as a genuine plea for equity, acknowledgment, and justice can spiral into a whirlwind of anger, outrage, and blame directed at the representative groups from which the offenders originate, overshadowing individual situations and circumstances.

Returning to Social Identity Theory from Chapter 1, a therapy practice group wrote an article about the intersection of Social Identity Theory and Cancel Culture,[15] as well as the impact of Cancel Culture on mental health. They highlighted,

> *"In Cancel Culture, this could lead to 'us versus them' dynamics, where individuals align strongly with the opinions and actions of their group, often to the detriment of understanding and empathy for the 'out-group.' This polarization can have profound effects on mental health, as it fosters environments of conflict and alienation."*

The rush to condemn those in the wrong often leads to the swift decapitation not only of the offenders being rightfully canceled, but also of those associated with similar positions of power and authority (in the workplace, managers, leaders, etc.). This occurs because leaders are, and continue to remain, symbols of all the things that are unjust and wrong at work, with a seemingly total disregard for who they are as individuals.

When these waves kick off, social media and the internet are not places for understanding, nuance, or patience. In many cases, situational nuance is not only not considered, but it's discouraged. Those advocating for moments of critical thinking are frequently attacked because the conflict mode of an internet mob is triggered, shutting down the cognitive skills that we as a species still struggle to practice (i.e., patience, creating space between stimulus and response, and simply breathing through anger). The result? Good leaders are often vilified alongside bad ones, despite the movement originally being meant to foster desperately needed positive change. Calling out poor leadership is crucial. Accountability helps ensure those in power do the right thing, but criticism, in some cases, can sometimes become excessive. Being in a position of power doesn't automatically mean someone is malicious or undeserving of care. The internet and social media are full of opportunities for public scrutiny, especially for those who make decisions that affect workers' lives, as everything they do can potentially become fodder for internet commentary and real-time judgments. Here is an example.

I'll never forget the infamous 2022 LinkedIn post of "the crying CEO,"[16] who uploaded a photo of himself visibly crying after having to lay off employees from his company. As you can imagine, this garnered a significant amount of attention, with over 57,000 tap backs, 10,280 comments, and 1,050 reposts. I read this post several times and went through all the comments. I never make excuses for bad behavior, disingenuous messaging, or anything similar; however, I will say that his post seemed genuine. He explained that having to engage in layoffs like this, based on mistakes he had admitted to and wished he had not made, was a gut-wrenching feeling. He explained that it's a horrible feeling to be forced to wield this professional axe, resulting in people losing their jobs. His point was objectively true, as were the tears on his face, unless he doused himself in Visine just for a photo op; however, the online mobs of the interwebs did not agree.

The internet came for him, and hard. The comments implied that this CEO was seeking sympathy, despite still having a job, suggesting that this leader was a narcissist, an attention seeker, and a virtue signaler. That his pain had no business being mentioned when people had lost their incomes without certainty of where their next paychecks would come from. People did not hold back, posting endless mock photos of themselves fake-crying over "manufactured problems" that didn't actually affect them. It was a public execution. I was impressed that this CEO did not back down from the social scrutiny, even after the media literally came to his doorstep. In an article, he said, "People have no idea what has actually gone on, what actions we have taken, what conversations we have had with these employees."[9] The article went on to explain that this CEO defended his actions by explaining that he did not take a salary for the first 18 months of the company's existence, and even at the time of the article, he was still only receiving a paycheck of $250 per week.

Am I going to say that this CEO handled this situation perfectly? No, because perfect is a social construct, made up by humans, that often does more harm than good. But what he wrote was honest, brave, and reasonable—humanizing himself to those who refused to see him that way. Nonetheless, his explanations went largely unrecognized because, as a CEO, he represented everything that makes people twitch with anger about power and authority. This leader attempted to engage in a constructive dialogue about this topic transparently, while working through difficult decisions, only to be met with criticism, hate, and vitriol. This happened because of the group he represents.

Remember from Chapter 1 how we discussed the mental representation we create of leaders based on our experiences with other leaders? Good leaders are torn down because of countless stories of those in power who crush the financial stability, emotional well-being, and careers of countless workers, some of whom even financially benefit from potentially nefarious actions they take, while publicly saying awful things resembling Satan incarnate. I've had leaders literally hyperventilate during coaching sessions, expressing how extraordinarily anxious, obsessive, and depressed they've become because their best intentions are being misunderstood. Fearing that anything they do could end up online and that they will not only lose their job, but also have their careers ruined. And these were good leaders, kind humans, and decent people. Think of the stress, fear, and dread of navigating leadership in a digital environment where every action, no matter how minor, is eligible to be subjected to public scrutiny that lasts indefinitely through online search terms, with minimal and rare opportunities for recovery. And leaders are supposed to talk about their mental health, without fear, in that kind of environment? Yeah, right.

Verywell Mind did a fantastic piece on how Cancel Culture often prevails over Call-Out Culture, where the former occurs even though people claim it's the latter,[17] highlighting that, "These terms are often used interchangeably, but there is a difference. Call-out culture is about calling attention to someone's wrongdoing and giving them a chance to learn from and correct the issue. Cancel Culture does not give this opportunity and, instead, immediately labels them as bad." This piece also highlighted a 2020 *Pew Research Center* study that showed 38% of people feel that calling someone out on social media ends up punishing those who don't deserve it, yet this is outweighed by 58% of people who believe it holds individuals accountable for their actions. What is the mental health impact of being canceled? It's just as you might expect. The *Verywell Mind* article went on to describe it as,

"Canceling often turns into bullying. Like bullying, if you've been canceled, you may feel ostracized, socially isolated, and lonely. And research shows that loneliness is associated with higher anxiety, depression, and suicide rates. If you are canceled, it can also feel as if everyone is giving up on you before you've even had the chance to apologize (let alone change your behavior). Instead of creating a dialogue to help you understand how your actions hurt others, the cancelers shut off all communication, essentially robbing you of the opportunity to learn and grow from your mistakes."

The article also addresses the hyperventilating leaders I mentioned earlier,

"Cancel culture doesn't just affect the canceled and the cancelers. It can also wreak havoc on onlookers' mental health. After seeing so many people being canceled, some bystanders are plagued with fear. They become overwhelmed with anxiety that people will turn on them if they fully express themselves. Bystanders might also worry that others will find something in their pasts to use against them. Or they may fear that every word they say or write is going to be examined under a microscope and construed as offensive, even if it wasn't meant to be."

When the intention of balancing power through public social scrutiny goes awry, we lose sight of the accountability these online movements aim for. Those who take leadership seriously and generally try to do the right thing are simultaneously distracted and worried about how (or if) they can manage the digital court of public opinion for one misstep and the virtual firing squad that may come after them. One must wonder if these experiences sometimes lead to poor behavior within leadership, potentially resulting from emotional fatigue, burnout, and the feeling like *"It doesn't matter what I do, I'll always be seen as the enemy."* Just some food for thought.

Let's revisit our growing Weight on Leadership Mental Health equation, with the added new elements below:

The Leadership Plate Morphing Into an Endlessly Refilling Trough

+

The Intensifying Weight and Burden of Leadership

+

The Intensification and Multiplication of Leadership Tasks

+

Enduring the Darker Side of Leadership Development

+

Being a Stress Target During Times of Turmoil, Chaos, and Crisis

+

Leading Through Social Tribalism, Polarization-Driven Unrest, and Systemic Volatility

+

Fearing the Digital Court of Public Opinion and Internet Social Scrutiny

The stack is getting heavier. We've covered a lot in the last few chapters. Now, we're on the verge of tackling the crucial question:

what do we do about this? Before that, there's one more topic to cover to complete the picture: understanding how systemic factors and individual identity influence leadership mental health, shaping whether leaders feel permitted—either by themselves or through life experiences—to discuss the critical themes we've explored so far. Then, we'll discuss how to create change. Through shifting the narrative, adjusting organizational practices, and what individual leaders can do—starting with you.

Individual Reflection Questions

■ Based on what you've read in this chapter, what are some of the toughest experiences you've had to lead through in recent years? How did they affect your mental health?

■ During these times, did you feel comfortable talking about your own mental health struggles and experiences? Why or why not?

■ If you had to choose one thing your team or organization should understand about the mental health challenges of leading through chaos, what would it be and why?

Chapter Key Takeaways

• Leaders are stress targets in times of chaos and crisis.

• The weight, burden, and expectations placed on leaders are growing and intensifying, often unbalanced due to a lack of extra support or patience for that learning curve.

• Some of the evolved expectations of leaders go beyond what is reasonable, which can place them in uncomfortable, toxic, and unhealthy positions with their teams and companies.

• Leaders must persist in leading through times of turmoil, social unrest, and volatility often without permission or space to share their own experiences of having to do this.

• Leadership mental health is increasingly harmed by the fear of Cancel Culture.

5

Leadership Mental Health is Also Shaped by Context and Identity

THE SYSTEMS IN WHICH WE LIVE, OUR IDENTITIES, and their interactions shape how we see ourselves, relate to others, and understand the world. Like Russian nesting dolls, each layer reveals a different influence within us. I wrote about this extensively in my first book because it helps us understand what people bring to the conversation when we're trying to bridge potential differences through discussions about mental health, regardless of someone's role. This framework applies to perceptions of mental health, leadership, and the intersection of these two areas. Here's why this matters: a leader's identity exists outside of, and is brought into, the workplace. We need to examine how these layers and systems influence beliefs, stigma, and expectations on a leader's comfort level, willingness, and permission to discuss their mental health at work. For a deeper dive into how these layers and systems influence perceptions of mental health in general, check out my first book.

As discussed in Chapter 4, just as leaders should understand intersectionality among those they lead, we must also consider how their own intersectional identities influence their mental health at work and whether they feel comfortable discussing it. This is especially important as different communities can experience mental health struggles for a variety of reasons and often lack equitable support, even at work. An example? *Calm* published a 2023 Workplace Mental Health Trends Report: The Future of Work, showing that "mental health is not equal: neurodivergent, LGBTQ+, Hispanic, and low-income employees feel unsupported."[1]

How We'll Approach This Chapter

The influences we will cover are by no means exhaustive. That would require multiple books. I have made a deliberate effort to gather a broad range of data and lived experiences to provide as balanced a view as possible, highlighting specific areas to make a point. The stories shared in this chapter do not encompass *every* perspective and may, in some cases, differ from norms and models seen elsewhere in the world. All of these perspectives are valid and exist simultaneously. We will focus on these four areas and how they influence perceptions of leadership mental health:

- Culture and ethnicity
- Gender
- Age and generation, with a nod to leadership rank
- Specific industry challenges

We'll explore these intersections by drawing on the lived experiences of my interviewees and research data to gain a deeper understanding of how leaders from various backgrounds and identities experience and navigate the often-invisible terrain of identity, mental health, and expectations around leadership mental health. I am not, and would never aim to, represent the opinions of entire groups of people. There is a broad spectrum of experiences that cannot be fully captured here, and different views exist within groups as well. My highlighting of these factors is *not* meant to reinforce stereotypes; instead, it aims to help you consider the nuances of how these factors influence perceptions and experiences of mental health in leadership. And, consequently, how they affect the permission (or lack thereof) to discuss it.

As you go through each section, remember that while focusing on specific elements, other elements are often still active in the background. No matter your background or circumstances, I hope you gain valuable lessons from this chapter that can deepen your understanding of the influences surrounding leadership and mental health, hopefully sparking meaningful conversations about it, too. I hope you find things that resonate with you. Pay attention to what those lessons are, what they mean, and what they might be trying to tell you.

I also want to acknowledge that my own lived experiences have inevitably shaped my perspective. Despite popular belief, the world doesn't need more ultracrepidarians. So, I encourage you, beyond this book, to continue learning by exploring additional resources and listening to other subject matter experts who can offer a more profound understanding of leadership intersectionality from a global perspective than I ever could.

Understanding Contextual Influences on Perceptions of Leadership Mental Health

Leadership mental health is not an isolated concept. Society's perspective and how leaders view this topic, like any other issue, are influenced by the systems around them and the people involved. Every part of a person's identity and the environments where that identity exists can shape the narrative about whether leaders feel psychologically safe enough to discuss their mental health at work.

The Compounded Effects of Intersectionality on Leadership Mental Health

Let's discuss intersectionality, the interconnectedness of different personal and social categories that shape an individual's experiences and opportunities.[2] Individuals possess multiple identities, which form an intersectional identity. This can create unique perspectives, experiences—and yes—, challenges. The term intersectionality was initially coined by Professor Kimberlé Crenshaw, an American civil rights advocate and law professor. She has made critical contributions to the public discourse on discussing how factors such as gender, sexuality, immigration status, socioeconomic background, and ethnicity influence one's perspective on the "stakes of disclosure" when it comes to speaking up about experiences of encountering personal and social challenges.[3] Here's the key point from her work in relation to what we're discussing: depending on a person's identity and location, they must weigh the number of risk layers they will have to accept to discuss their mental health as a leader at work.

Going further, intersectionality can influence the Leadership Prototypes, with endless variations in how those prototypes are assigned to leaders. The main takeaway? This isn't a one-size-fits-all, or even one-size-fits-most, conversation. It's about the leaders who have already had to claw their way to earn a proverbial seat at the leadership table based on their identities. Yes, this still happens, all the time. The number of leaders who shared this in their interview questionnaires made my stomach sink. It's disheartening that, despite everything we know about human potential, regardless of identity, we continue to subject certain groups to this in the workplace and in leadership roles.

Thankfully, in recent years, we've seen perceptions of intersectionality, leadership, and mental health shift from static to dynamic. Through the incredible global connections built by various means, traditional norms and expectations are gradually changing. Leaders from a variety of backgrounds are speaking out more often. We see a brave few who aim to inspire (and unmuzzle) the many. They're working to reshape the conversation by emphasizing that regardless of your background, you can (and should) speak up to seek help for your mental health as a leader. However, there is still a lot of work to do, such as recognizing the specific impact of intersectionality on leadership mental health in the first place.

How Culture, Ethnicity, & Social Norms Shape Perceptions of Mental Health in Leadership

"My ethnicity has absolutely influenced how I felt I should act as a leader when it comes to emotional vulnerability and mental health."

Interviewee: female, Elder Millennial, Asian, Vice President, software industry

"My cultural background included a lot of shame in showing vulnerability as a leader. You are supposed to be an infallible model for others

and a mentor to those in more junior roles. When I took a leave of absence for my mental health, this was seen, in part, as culturally taboo and not broadly shared outside of 'need to know' individuals."

Interviewee: male, Millennial, Caucasian, Director, technology industry

"The culture that shaped my mental health priorities is that of a first-generation American, the child of two immigrant parents. As an immigrant, the focus was always on academic performance and social standing, not mental health."

Interviewee: male, Millennial, Black, first-generation American, Director, legal support industry

"My ethnicity has a profound influence on me. It shapes not only how I should act as a leader, but also how I should act in general. There is added pressure I place on myself to avoid showing vulnerability because I represent an entire race of people who have never held this position in my organization. As the first person of my ethnicity in this role, I strive to set a positive precedent for those who will follow. This means I am very guarded and limit my discussions on vulnerability and mental health. Often, it means saying nothing that could give anyone a reason to doubt my presence here."

Interviewee: female, Millennial, Black, Senior Vice President in the C-Suite, heavy civil construction industry

Culture, Ethnic Identity, & Mental Health in Leadership

First, let's align on meaning. When I refer to ethnicity, I mean a group of people who share and identify with a common culture and history, which may sometimes correlate with national origin,[4] and have perceived shared attributes that distinguish them from other groups. When I say culture, I'm referring to a general way of life, including ideas, beliefs, behaviors, and social norms that one group shares, passed down from generation to generation, even though these may adapt over time.[5] Culture often overlaps with ethnicity, and both inform perception. This varies from culture to culture and from one ethnic group to another. The same applies to expectations and perceptions around leaders' expressions of showing emotional distress at work.

> *"Mental health is often considered a taboo subject. The expectation is to work hard, push through whatever you're feeling, suppress it, and keep moving forward. Mental health is seen as 'those other people's issues,' the ones who have the privilege of not worrying about their reputation, livelihood, or other consequences."*
>
> Interviewee: female, Millennial, Black, Senior Vice President in the C-Suite, heavy civil construction industry
>
> *"Mental health in Hispanic culture is not really acknowledged. You don't tell people your problems, you don't tell people your family drama or issues; it is expected to stay in the family. Bringing up your own mental health in the workplace is not safe and will make you seem weak. Keep your head down, do your job, don't give anyone any other reason to think you are incapable or not the one for the job."*
>
> Interviewee: female, Millennial, Mexican-American, Elementary Principal, public education industry
>
> *"In the Black community, going to see a therapist is not common. We were told to just pray about it and GOD will handle it."*
>
> Interviewee: male, Black, Gen X, Director, entertainment industry

When we consider ethnic identity, our perspectives on, experiences of, and feelings toward expressing emotional challenges are highly personal but also heavily shaped by social influences, mainly when expressed—or not—by someone in a leadership position. A leader's ethnic identity can play a role in how leadership behavior is perceived overall, and therefore, how the expression of mental health struggles in leadership positions is viewed by those they lead, and by leaders themselves. Reflect on what we discussed in Chapters 1 and 2, particularly the Leadership Prototypes. Those expectations can be deeply influenced by an individual's ethnic identity and the cultural context in which they operate.

Social stigmas surrounding mental health, cultural norms, and other factors create an even more complex landscape for leaders to navigate. This includes whether a leader feels they should seek help or even if they should need it. In many cultures, visiting a mental health professional is considered a last resort. Remember the power of shame in Chapter 3? In some cultures and certain ethnic identities, there can be a strong presence of shame around mental health. Within families, social circles, and especially in professional settings—and particularly for leaders—these influences are significant. Consider the conditioning, norms, social messages, and potential deterrents involved. While researching this chapter, I read "Stigma: Barrier to Mental Health Care Among Ethnic Minorities," which highlighted these challenges, especially for those from collectivistic cultures (i.e., the group matters more than the individual), those with a sense of duty in leadership roles, and those navigating specific religious beliefs.[6]

If there's a lack of psychological safety around mental health in a leader's culture or ethnic group, pressures to emote or behave in a certain way, or if they face expectations from others in their work environment influenced by similar (or even different) cultural or ethnic rules and practices, it becomes an uphill battle to feel like they can speak up at all. Not only because they may be expected not to, but also because they don't want to risk reprimand, judgment, punishment, or jeopardizing their career—even at the expense of their mental health.

Regardless of whether these leaders reside in their country of origin, have emigrated, or identify within a minority group within their company, Professor Crenshaw tells us that when people remain in environments where messaging is consistently reinforced over time, it often becomes unsafe for them to speak up. The stakes of disclosure often seem too high. What can this lead to? Leadership self-sacrifice, at the cost of their mental health, due to the compounded challenges of their identity, the systems they operate within, and the people they work with. Let's look at two examples.

Asian and Pacific Islander (API) cultures are often characterized by collectivism. The social norms surrounding leadership behavior and displays of emotion are frequently centered on composure, restraint, stoicism, and mindfulness, emphasizing the importance of considering one's actions to avoid disturbing the group's stability. Even if that means enduring unrelenting pressure and potential emotional isolation. *UCLA Health* shared in 2023[7] that,

". . . In some Asian cultures, mental health challenges are viewed as an individual problem or weakness and talking openly about sadness, disappointment or depression is rarely encouraged . . . We know that within the Asian American populations, the stigma around mental health is really significant . . . They worry about it affecting their jobs or their ability to maintain employment, and also the perception among their peers."

Hogan, the talent development assessment provider, found that in Japanese corporate culture,

"Japanese leaders . . . are supportive, team-oriented, and have a flexible agenda to accommodate team, peer, and superior opinions. . . . In line with the concept of wa, Japanese leaders are expected to promote group harmony . . . Japanese leaders . . . will prefer to use only what will help them get their work done."[8]

As I mentioned earlier, we need to have more conversations about the lens of individual identity when it comes to mental health and how support needs need to be tailored depending on the community. Thankfully, conversations like this are now happening. Ascend Global Leaders, a non-profit organization working to advance Asian and Pacific Islander equity at work, is working on precisely that. They shared the following in 2024:

"While mental health is part of the national discourse and many companies are comfortable promoting how they support their workers, the discussion rarely addresses the unique socio-cultural issues that impact API identity, such as the influence of collectivist cultures, stigma and

shame, and stereotypes of Asians as the 'Model Minority' and 'Perpetual Foreigners' . . . Effective mental health support goes hand-in-hand with a deep understanding of cultural differences and nuances."[9]

"*Mental health is definitely taboo in AAPI culture.*"

Interviewee: female, Gen Z, Asian, Senior Manager, entertainment nonprofit industry

"*In my Indian culture, mental health is often seen as a weakness, something to be hidden or dealt with quietly. For a long time, I internalized that—believing I had to be strong, composed, and never let anyone see the cracks. Being a woman made it even more complicated. There's a cultural expectation to be nurturing but also resilient, to hold everything together without asking for help. It took me years to unlearn that.*"

Interviewee: female, Elder Millennial, Asian, Vice President, software industry

---

Let's also look at the Latinx community, bringing in intersectionality again for a moment, where the intersection of ethnicity, culture, and gender significantly influences the display of emotions in leadership. For example, to show how early this conditioning can occur, a group of researchers from several universities collaborated to gain a deeper understanding of how Latino male college students perceive and find meaning in their masculinity in 2021—specifically looking at how these beliefs shape their perceptions of "expected" behavior in leadership roles.[10] The researchers found that for Latino men who participated in the study, their understanding of leadership was based on the relationship between cultural expectations of masculinity, strength, and familismo—a shared sense of responsibility, solidarity, and loyalty. There is an added pressure to be seen as strong, steady, and dependable, while being caught in a double bind. Latino men are often expected to be strong, while simultaneously being unfairly labeled for exhibiting machismo (i.e., exaggerated strength and masculinity), and silently struggling. We also tend to see double binds like this for men from so many other communities—and it's sadly not a rare occurrence.

For Latina women in leadership, it's no easier. Latina women often face a tough triple whammy of intersectionality for gender, ethnicity, and cultural expectations. DePaul University published a paper on the leadership experiences of Latina women illustrating this point,[11]

> ". . . Latinas may look to satisfy . . . group needs before they even attempt to take care of their own needs . . . Servant Leadership . . . This leadership style is often adopted by Latinas because of the cultural significance it has for them . . . Characteristics of servant leadership include listening, healing, empathy, and stewardship."

"There's this stereotype placed on women, that if you show emotion and try to speak up, you are 'emotional, sensitive, difficult, unstable' . . . We learn how to suppress and minimize everything in order to belong or be liked. However, all this does over time is build up anger, resentment. . .when you don't feel seen or heard. Throughout my career, I have always been confident and vocal, because being silent was not something I was willing to do a second longer and it never benefited anyone. However, I was labeled 'troublemaker, firestarter, difficult, and tough,' which I'm sure I've also been labeled or called some other not so nice ones."

Interviewee: female, Millennial, Mexican-American, Elementary Principal, public education industry

---

Latina female leaders are also often expected to be both authoritative and nurturing in their roles, with conflicting expectations surrounding these qualities. While Latino men are influenced by familismo and caught in a double bind related to machismo, Latina women are often influenced by personalismo[12], emphasizing the importance of building personal and trusting relationships through caring for others. *Forbes* published a piece exploring the leadership experiences of Latina women.[13] In this piece, each one of these women shared about the challenges and complexities they encounter as a Latina woman in leadership. From feeling pressured to stay silent so they don't proverbially rock the boat, to reframing asking for help as a strength instead of a weakness for not being able to "hold everything" for everyone, to monitoring their capacity levels so they're not unhealthfully self-sacrificing, to sharing struggles with others so they aren't experienced in isolation. Similarly to the complex and sometimes conflicting pressures of other collectivistic communities and communities of color, Latina female leaders encounter unique ongoing challenges related to stereotypes and microaggressions, such as cultural expectations to be consistently nurturing and supportive, while they are unfairly labeled as "bossy" if they are assertive.

The Pressure to Conform, and Perform, When You're Outnumbered and Already Marginalized

"As someone from a marginalized group, I have always felt that I had to be perfect or mentally strong for fear of judgment or fear of not being viewed as a good or credible leader."

Interviewee: female, Gen X, Black, Director, consulting industry

"As a Black leader in tech, I've always been aware that I don't have the same margin for error or the same freedom to express vulnerability as some of my peers. There's an unspoken expectation that I need to be twice as competent, twice as composed, and twice as resilient just to be seen as equally capable. Because of this, I've often felt pressure to suppress my struggles rather than openly discuss them. There's a historical and cultural expectation—both external and internal—that Black professionals, especially in leadership, need to be strong at all times. Any admission of stress, exhaustion, or mental health challenges can be misinterpreted as a weakness rather than a reality of the job. I've seen how vulnerability can be weaponized against people who look like me, so I've been cautious about how much I share and with whom."

Interviewee: male, Gen X, Black, first-time manager, technology industry

Good leadership can come from anywhere; we know this. And yet, leaders from communities of color and those who have emigrated to other cultures or countries are forced into adapting behaviors and wearing a metaphorical mask to prove their "worth" as leaders, continually. They feel compelled to do this through silence and self-sacrifice, often at the expense of their mental health, out of fear of being unreasonably further doubted or not being allowed to "keep their seat at the table" that they never should've been forced to vie for in the first place. It's morally reprehensible bu*lsh*t. To have to endure all of this to avoid unjust, biased situations, and microaggressions.

Let's look at leaders from the Black community as an example. This community is often profoundly impacted by the shared history they carry of systemic discrimination, various forms of racism, marginalization, and oppression. Additionally, countless professionals in the Black community are already underrepresented in leadership roles. The *Human Resources Professional Association* published a piece in 2024, noting that "In Canada, less than 1% of corporate leaders are black . . . one crucial factor often overlooked is workplace psychological safety. It's important to recognize that even leaders are not immune to mental health challenges."[14]

Black leaders wrongfully continue to face ignorant stereotypes, heightened criticism, excessive scrutiny, and unfair evaluation—with demonstrably horrendous consequences. While continuously being expected to prove their worth in ways that their Caucasian colleagues, and even other communities of color, do not. The risks of disclosure for their career if they share about their mental health struggles as a leader are far too high. The acknowledgment of their continued unwarranted struggle? Basically zero. A 2024 *Forbes* piece explained this well,[15]

"The unfortunate and sobering truth is that Black leaders in the workplace experience microaggressions at an alarming rate. Despite the 'racial awakening' of 2020, which led to widespread marches and protests worldwide and increased spending on workplace diversity and inclusion initiatives, the data doesn't show a decline in these experiences . . . The data presented exposes the mental health toll that microaggressions have on Black leaders. It highlights the gross disconnect

between the values and emphasis on diversity that many workplaces claim to possess versus the actual lived experiences of disrespect, invalidation, and mistreatment that these individuals have daily."

"My ethnicity has absolutely influenced how I feel I 'should act' as a leader, especially when it comes to emotional vulnerability and mental health discussions."

Interviewee: male, Gen X, Black, first-time manager, technology industry

---

Like many other marginalized groups, these leaders carry this burden, potentially negatively impacting their mental health, while feeling forced to wear a metaphorical mask to be seen as "capable" leaders. . .when they already are. They face a challenging duality in their work environments. They bear the additional weight of representing their communities, cultures, and ethnicities—while simultaneously performing well and rebuking stereotypes—all while carefully weighing the stakes of disclosing how or if they speak up about their emotional health struggles.

Corroborating this, *The Hartford*, a large insurance provider, released a 2022 report based on research conducted in collaboration with the *National Alliance on Mental Illness (NAMI)*, specifically surveying over 2,300 people about mental health at work for Black Americans.[16] Here's what they found: "Black and white U.S. workers reported different mental health experiences—from their mental health status to stigma in the workplace. . .White workers were more likely than Black workers to agree that their company has an open, inclusive company culture." The report also indicated that:

- Only 33% of Black workers felt their work environments had an open work environment to have dialogue about mental health, in comparison to 43% of Caucasian workers.
- Only 27% of Black workers felt comfortable speaking to their managers, and 29% talking to their co-workers about their mental health. With their Caucasian colleagues ranking at 49% and 48%, respectively.

- And that, "Black workers were more likely to note barriers to speaking out about mental health in the workplace," citing that 32% of Black workers felt that "Aspects of my identity make it/would make it hard for me to discuss mental health in my workplace."

When Gender Norms, Mental Health, and Leadership Collide

> *"In my role, which is traditionally female-dominated, there are certain expectations that come with being a woman in HR. One notable influence is the greater acceptance and expectation for women to show vulnerability . . . While I recognize this expectation, I consciously strive to balance vulnerability without being overly so."*
>
> Interviewee: female, Millennial, Black, Senior Vice President in the C-Suite, heavy civil construction industry
>
> *"Being a 'man' comes with certain unspoken, yet undeniable, expectations especially in the construction industry. It's not a role. It's a mask, a posture, a performance we're taught to wear from the time we're boys. We're told that strength means silence. That showing pain makes you weak. That to lead, you have to harden . . . Masculinity becomes identity, and armor used to justify and protect the toxic culture we've all inherited. We wear it like a badge, but really, it's a weight. That version of manhood is soaked in generations of abuse, neglect, and stigma. And we've been trained to pass it down, unexamined, like a family heirloom made of rusted steel."*
>
> Interviewee: male, Gen X, Caucasian, senior leadership, construction industry

Gender can play a significant role in shaping expectations about leadership behaviors, particularly in terms of emotional expression. When we impose the crushing weight of gender-based rules on mental health in general and emotional expression in leadership, leaders are expected to perform in a maddeningly exhausting way based on their gender identity. This requires extraordinary levels of vulnerability, suppression, constant self-monitoring, and hyper-awareness of what may or may not be perceived as tolerable, respectable, or "appropriate." My brain hurt just from attempting to describe those mental gymnastics. It's no surprise that this often leads to quiet despair, exhaustion, anger, potential disconnection, and burnout. Gender norms put relentless, dichotomous, conflicting, and unattainable pressure on people, and especially leaders, regardless of the gender they identify as.

How Gender Norms & Stigma Can Influence Leadership Mental Health Disclosures

"Technology, like most industries, values stoicism in male leaders, especially senior leaders. There are, of course, exceptions to this rule, but generally, male leaders are often expected to be a lighthouse in the storm. Societally, we have a lot to change before that expectation can evolve."

Interviewee: male, Millennial, Caucasian, Director, technology industry

"As a female leader, I do feel that there is an expectation for me to show and model empathy beyond what's expected from my male counterparts. Earlier in my career, I was met with a lot of judgment when I showed vulnerability, kindness, or empathy."

Interviewee: female, Gen X, Black, Director, consulting industry

I'm about to do something that was never on my career bingo card: cite myself, and a concept I created. I'm doing this because this concept from my first book is, sadly, still relevant when it comes to the intersection of leadership, mental health, and gender: Gender-Based Emotion Shaming.[17] This concept means that, regardless of the gender you identify as, there are arbitrary social rules, expectations, and norms imposed on individuals regarding how they express emotions. This becomes even more intense, especially during times of struggle or stress, and if you serve in a leadership role. No matter where someone sits on the gender identity spectrum, there are societal pressures to conform to a large amount of subjective nonsense. Here's what this looks like, with two examples based on the historical binary assignments of gender, which have thankfully been expanded in the evolution of the gender identity conversation.

- *Toward women:*
  - "Historically, women have been labeled as the 'emotional' gender. . .that our *biology* is always to blame . . . This couldn't be further from the truth. Being emotional, empathetic, and in touch with one's emotions and mental wellbeing is a massive strength, particularly in leadership . . . Sadly, for many women, speaking about their mental health at work still comes with a costly price tag: their professional reputation. It would be easy (and careless) to assume that it is solely men that make women feel this way. That's not the case . . . Women are just as capable of unfairly labeling, disparaging, and criticizing other women's vocalizations around mental health—in particular, if they don't share the same feelings and perceptions. I've always called this 'girl on girl crime.'"
- *Toward men:*
  - ". . . men have historically had an expectation placed on them that 'masculinity' means being strong, stoic, dominant and in control . . . some men go so far as to taunt other men for talking about mental health struggles and use cruel derogatory language while they do it . . . And some women do this to men too, because they were raised to believe that narrative. . . . These very real socially constructed mental barriers have horrible consequences . . . There are many men I've spoken to that still don't feel comfortable to speak up about mental health in a work setting, even with initiatives that encourage them to. Why? Because the private beliefs they hold about mental health . . . don't give them the 'permission' to do so, in *any* setting. The most common fear I've heard in my work is that they're worried they'll be seen as weak or incapable. And the *last* place they want to be seen that way is *at work.*"

Even though I coined the term Gender-Based Emotion Shaming in 2020, Greta Gerwig, the Director of the 2023 film, *Barbie*, was able to articulate what I was trying to say in a way that I never had the creativity, insight, and perhaps even the strength to do. Whether it's the female archetype of Barbie herself, navigating unimaginable expectations of femininity while trying to lead with accompanying pressures, or the male archetype of Ken, desperately attempting to appear impenetrable while emotionally crumbling inside, the toll is real. And no one escapes that payment. America Ferrara's character had a monologue in the film that was nothing short of phenomenal. Making endless women and those who identify as female feel seen and understood with incredible totality. Thanks to the editorial efforts of *Elle* magazine, here's part of the monologue, with some areas highly relevant to women's leadership at work,[18]

> *"It is literally impossible to be a woman . . . we have to always be extraordinary, but somehow, we're always doing it wrong . . . You have to be a boss, but you can't be mean. You have to lead, but you can't squash other people's ideas . . . You have to be a career woman but also always be looking out for other people . . . But always stand out and always be grateful. But never forget that the system is rigged. So, find a way to acknowledge that, but also always be grateful. You have to . . . never be rude, never show off, never be selfish, never fall, never fail, never show fear, never get out of line . . . It's too hard! It's too contradictory, and nobody gives you a medal or says thank you! And it turns out in fact that not only are you doing everything wrong, but also everything is your fault . . . I'm just so tired of watching myself and every single other woman tie herself into knots so that people will like us."*

Pop culture references aside, let's look at the data, too.

Myers-Briggs published a study in 2020 that examined stress, gender, and leadership, investigating which factors may increase or decrease stress among leaders. The study found that ". . . stress levels for women were more extreme."[19] In 2024, the *World Economic Forum* published a piece[20] stating that research from the *McKinsey Health Institute*, which surveyed 30,000 employees from 30 countries on their mental and other forms of health, found that female employees reported more exhaustion and worse mental health, comparatively, to men, putting them at higher risk for burnout. While simultaneously "facing the challenges of societal expectations, gender biases, and organizational structures, which increase demands on their overall well-being." This was global, by the way, where:

"42% of participants reported symptoms of exhaustion. However, women experience exhaustion at a higher rate than men, 46% vs. 38%, respectively. When we fold culture into the mix, the biggest gaps on exhaustion between men and women were found in France, India, Japan, the Netherlands, Nigeria, Saudi Arabia, and South Korea, with a difference of more than 10%."

Okay, back to *Barbie*.

Besides highlighting the emotional contortionism women face, Gerwig also nailed the toxic masculinity that continues to seep into the male psyche, despite society's efforts to stop this damaging rhetoric. This narrative has harmed men's mental health and contributed to the rising rates of mental illness, substance abuse, and suicide worldwide. The resurgence of hyper-masculine traditional gender norms and values in recent years, which have reached extreme levels in particular. . .cough cough. . .sociopolitical circles definitely doesn't help. Here's why this is harmful: when certain groups promote extreme and regressive gender stereotypes, it rarely (if ever) leads to anything positive—and often causes harm. What does this mean for men and those who identify as male, especially leaders at work? More voices may tell you to silence your own.

The *Frontiers in Sociology Journal* even published a piece on this, showing how the "he is just Ken" mentality from *Barbie* is a deconstruction of hegemonic masculinity and a discourse on masculinity, gender conflicts, and the systemic challenges that influence all genders.[21] The article described how the film highlights the same mental gender acrobatics I mentioned earlier,

". . . traditional gender performances . . . points to the patriarchal structures as the narrative's true antagonist . . . it underscores that the issue lies . . . in the patriarchal system itself . . . The film, with its

humor and satire, deconstructs the established symbols of masculinity within patriarchy, highlighting the complex and often absurd nature of these constructs."

Gerwig's creative commentary and the sociological academic lens above highlight a critically important moment in the discourse on gender identity and the archaic system that upholds these ideals. Both infiltrate the workplace through expectations around leadership and mental health. While different in medium and intention, these pieces and countless others portray a simple and essential truth: gender norms, especially when applied to expectations around leadership emotional expression, are a complete freaking trap that leaders get caught in.

How the War on DEIB and Gender Identity Influences Leadership Mental Health

Long before I began writing this book, a noticeable global pushback against workplace diversity, equity, inclusion, and belonging (DEIB) initiatives had emerged. It occurred and continues to appear alongside increasing politicization and scrutiny of the gender identity spectrum itself. Apparently, the overwhelming amount of lived experience, data insights, and moral calls to do the right thing was too much for some people, leading to their ignorant, misguided, hate-driven fears. In addition to the significant emotional suffering and the erosion of psychological safety for those targeted by this societal regression, it created a great deal of emotional turbulence in the World of Work. This outright assault on gender identity and DEIB forced leaders—especially those who lead with social consciousness, integrity, empathy, and genuine allyship—to adapt to a new level of stress they could never have anticipated. In the United States, for example, this has ranged from debates in schools about gender-neutral bathrooms to even the mere mention of anything related to DEIB or gender equity on government websites (including pressure on private entities and organizations to remove such initiatives and job titles if they wanted to keep receiving federal funding).

The painfully ironic part? You read about it in Chapter 4. Leaders, rightfully, had to learn and apply their understanding of intersectionality and DEIB, only to be threatened later for doing so—in certain circles. Then, poof, yet another example of conflicting expectations placed on leaders to navigate in front of the professional firing squad, with no room for their own experiences. They must be chameleon-like, constantly adapting their moral compass depending on who they're talking to, swiveling 360 degrees to please everyone, even if their necks feel like they're breaking. Caught between media narratives, shifting government policies, evolving corporate rules, money-hungry stakeholders, and managing angry (or excited) team members. All while trying to handle their own burnout, conflicts, fears, and even potential moral injuries. And just like that, the bar has been raised yet again with dissonant expectations, with Emotional Labor reaching new heights. It remains a no-win scenario—leaving many leaders exhausted, cynical, resentful, and disengaged. But don't worry. Throughout it all, leaders generally received some training on how to lead through hostility and prevent workplace fractures without breaking the law. With no acknowledgment of how their mental health was silently breaking.

The Intergenerational Tug-of-War of Mental Health and Leadership

"It's a generational mindset peppered with ignorance and shame. I remember the days when people would whisper that 'So-and-so has cancer.' Seriously. We have to be able to talk out loud without judgment about the human condition and the associated trauma."

Interviewee: female, Baby Boomer, Caucasian, Senior Director, association management construction industry

"I have felt dismissed in the past when talking about my mental health, as others have seen it as a 'product of my generation' rather than something they should practice and adopt as leaders themselves. I feel that my generation is generally more open about mental health than older generations."

Interviewee: female, Gen Z, Asian, Senior Manager, entertainment nonprofit industry

"Sometimes being a Millennial (and the often-negative stereotypes that come with it) can make certain discussions/situations uncomfortable."

Interviewee: male, Millennial, Caucasian, CEO, nonprofit trade association industry

"As a Gen Xer who was raised in a generation where children are seen and not heard, I am motivated to be heard as an adult. To some degree, I am intentional about prioritizing my mental health because I know the generation before me did not."

Interviewee: female, Gen X, Black, Director, human resources industry

"When I was coming up in the working world, especially under the influence of older generations, speaking about mental health was seen as completely off-limits. Admitting to anxiety, burnout, or emotional struggles was often equated with being weak, unreliable, or incapable of handling the demands of leadership. There was this unspoken rule that if you wanted to be taken seriously, you had to push through—no matter what. Sharing anything personal or emotional could damage your credibility or . . . question your work ethic. That mindset was deeply ingrained, and it made it hard to ask for support or even acknowledge your own limits."

Interviewee: female, Millennial, Asian, Vice President, software industry

I'm calling this one "The Age Ingredient." Generational beliefs about mental health are *strong*. Each generation has been generally conditioned about what to hide or reveal, resulting in different lessons, rules, and norms about what is "acceptable" to express, especially in a professional setting, and particularly for leaders. What people tend to forget is that each person merely reflects their position along the space-time continuum and the social narrative, beliefs, and values of that time. Still, there's endless finger-pointing about who is wrong or right. We (hopefully) understand that browbeating others into agreement usually doesn't work, but this approach persists. The intergenerational divide causes ongoing friction as each generation of leaders advances in their careers and navigates internal and external expectations about how they do or don't express their emotional struggles at work.

"The Age Ingredient": Generational Identity, Mental Health Disclosures, and Navigating Judgment

Generational identity and age can significantly influence a leader's perceptions of the psychological safety, appropriateness, permission, and even necessity of discussing their mental health at work. While there are exceptions, a generally accepted set of values, practices, and expectations tends to exist within each generation. Regardless of a leader's age, I firmly believe that discussing and managing one's mental health, especially as a leader, shows maturity, self-awareness, and personal responsibility. Does that make it easy for people to do when they've grown up in a time when they've been discouraged from doing so? No. However, that doesn't make the argument any less valid.

WebMD did a helpful piece about intergenerational narratives about mental health experiences and the importance of generation-specific, tailored mental health support.[22] While I loved the article's recommendations, the call to action was solely focused on how managers should support these generations in the workplace, with no mention of managerial support from those same generations. Below is a summary of the article's *italicized* key takeaways, along with my application of these takeaways to leaders in those same generations:

- Baby Boomers and Generation X:
    - Birth years:
        - Baby Boomers: 1946–1964
        - Gen X: 1965–1980

    - The Common Practice & Internal Narrative:
        - Baby Boomers:
            - Practice: private
            - Likely internal narrative: "Leave it at the door, obviously. Do I really need to explain why? Two words: career risk."

- Gen X:
  - o Practice: private, with a hint of hesitant openness if nudged
  - o Likely internal narrative: "I want to, but can you blame me for being afraid to?"
- o What research shows us:
  - Baby Boomers: *"The Baby Boomer generation is not particularly comfortable discussing mental health in general, and even less comfortable bringing it up in a workplace setting. This generation grew up talking about mental health mostly in relation to mental illness or as the result of something traumatic, like fighting in a war or being involved in a devastating accident. They were taught to persevere through challenges and keep their emotions to themselves."*
  - Gen X: *"Like members of the Baby Boom generation, Gen Xers were also taught not to discuss emotions, or else they might be viewed as weak, especially in the workplace. This generation prizes their independence and resilience, having grown up during numerous periods of inflation and recession. They were also the original 'latchkey kids' who may have had two working parents, creating an 'I can do it myself' mentality. They can be among the most stressed generations in the workforce."*
  - o Applying the leadership mental health lens: Baby Boomers and Gen Xers are products of their time. Focused on emotional survival, they were rewarded for emotional consistency, and perceived fragility was punished. These leaders may see younger generations of leaders as "asking for too much" because they themselves didn't have the opportunity to prioritize their emotional health during their careers, let alone as leaders. These leaders are also pressured to adopt new workplace mental health trends, even though they may have mixed—and sometimes resistant—feelings about it. This can leave them feeling misunderstood, judged, or pushed aside—when all they've tried to do throughout their careers is emotionally survive, in private, in the only way they knew to feel safe.

- Millennials:
  - Birth Years: 1980–1996
  - The Common Practice & Internal Narrative:
    - Practice: willing, but still cautious
    - Likely internal narrative: "My mood disorders take five therapeutic interventions to manage, so like hell if I'm going to keep up this superhuman expectation nonsense that keeps my therapist employed. But I'm going to be careful about who I open up to, because I hate being labeled a Snowflake."

  - What research shows us: "*Millennials are often termed the 'anxious generation,' some say resulting from the rise of 'helicopter,' or overly involved parenting. They are also the first generation to grow up with access to the internet and technology, including social media, making them vulnerable to the pressure to be perfect and project a certain image. But they are also the pioneers when it comes to mental health. They were the first to talk openly about having a therapist or going to therapy. In the workplace, this generation values transparency, openness, and authenticity. They also prioritize their well-being, and they're not afraid to advocate for it.*"
  - Applying the leadership mental health lens: Millennials grew up exposed to a developing social discourse around therapy, mental health, mental illness, and the normalization and expansion of the terminology surrounding these topics. They may see emotional transparency as a leadership strength rather than a weakness but still have concerns about the potential liabilities this may bring for those who disagree or are willfully ignorant. They often find themselves caught between managing their mental health and the perceptions of their elder leadership counterparts, and those they manage, who may recognize the importance of discussing mental health. In some cases, they may worry about their willingness to discuss the subject being exploited by team members or younger leadership colleagues, who

may weaponize therapeutic and mental health language at work to avoid their own discomfort (yes, this does happen, remember the story from earlier?).

- Gen Z:
  - Birth years: 1997–2012
  - The Common Practice & Internal Narrative:
    - Practice: open and proactive
    - Likely internal narrative: "How could we not be honest about this? It's ridiculous not to be. You know better. Why aren't you talking about it?"

  - What research shows us: *"This generation has experienced a considerable amount of turmoil already in their young lives—the 2008 recession, political discord at home, geopolitical events abroad, climate change, and school shootings. True 'digital natives,' social media has been their forum for talking about mental health, which has helped break down the stigma. . .Gen Zers lived through a pandemic at a particularly vulnerable stage of life, contributing to the skyrocketing rates of mental health concerns, particularly anxiety, that we are now seeing. Fortunately, Gen Zers are the most comfortable of all the generations discussing mental health and will be the first to say we should be prioritizing it as much as we do our physical health. At work, they're seeking a sense of belonging, connection, inclusion, and purpose, and they value boundaries between work and life. Of all the generations, they also feel the most strongly that employers should provide support for mental health."*
  - Applying the leadership mental health lens: Despite the widespread normalization of discussing mental health, mental illness, stress, and burnout, Gen Z leaders may worry that leaders or team members they manage who are older than themselves might label them as "too sensitive." Just for being honest about their emotional capacity and for striving to work to live rather than live to work. Conversely, they might also criticize their older leadership colleagues for resisting

conversations about mental health without asking how to make them feel heard. Ironically enough, similarly to their older leadership peers, Gen Z leaders may also feel misunderstood, pressured to conform, or judged for wanting to present themselves in a way that feels authentic to them.

Every generation is caught in this multidirectional riptide, navigating invisible, arbitrary rules and uncertainty about which version of themselves will be judged the least critically. They all feel the weight of their mental health experiences, grappling with mixed feelings, fears, and concerns about naming them to others. Here's the thing: each generation of leaders needs mental health at work support, period. What does it come down to? Building intergenerational fluency, permission, and support structures on how to talk to one another—without finger-pointing as to who's right or wrong. Continuing to try to prove "rightness" is a fruitless and damaging competition that's ultimately shaped by their own birth time and social conditioning.

Research Showed That. . .No One Agrees If Leadership Mental Health Experiences Differ Based on Seniority

The amount of conflicting research I found here was shocking. It seemed like no one could agree on what was most common. While I was deeply appreciative to see several articles and studies on managerial burnout and leadership mental health, and each of these writers and study authors shared the same goal of drawing attention to leadership stress and burnout, I had significant trouble finding alignment among researchers and their conclusions. I then realized it's scenario-dependent, on a variety of influential factors, and measuring managerial stress is a HUGE undertaking with too many levels of leadership to account for. Ultimately (and understandably), this results in a lack of consistent findings based on seniority. Let me give you a snapshot to show you what I mean:

- *Forbes* noted in a 2023 article about the severe stress of "top-level" executives,[23] citing a *Harvard Business Review (HBR)* study, that "50% of top-level executives experience significant levels of stress, with one in five executives experiencing levels of stress that are considered high or extreme." However, upon examining the *HBR* study,[24] the reference became more generalized, stating that "50% of managers report feeling burned out." Then, digging even further, I saw that the *HBR* data was pulled from *Microsoft's 2022 Work Trend Index*[25], which also referenced managers in general. Referring to "managers" in general is far too broad when there are so many levels of seniority within that professional designation.

- *Mass General Brigham McLean Hospital* published an article in 2025 about the silent strain "at the top,"[26] specific to mental health struggles in executive-level leadership being demonstrably worse than other areas of an organization. Citing the *Journal of Occupational Health Psychology* stating that, "26% of executives report symptoms consistent with clinical depression, compared to 18% in the general workforce. A Harvard Business Review study found that nearly half of CEOs report feelings of loneliness and isolation, and 61% of them believe this affects their performance." Side note—while I recognize that CEOs are part of executive leadership, not all executive leaders are at the C-suite level, so this isn't a clear depiction of the data.

Conversely, I found conflicting research to the above. I even found a study, no joke, titled "Leadership is associated with lower levels of stress,"[27] where the researchers went so far as even to measure cortisol readings in leaders, as well as self-reported anxiety levels. Here's what they found:

- *"In two studies, we found clear evidence that leadership is associated with lower levels of stress. . .leaders had lower levels of the stress hormone cortisol and lower reports of anxiety (study 1). In study 2, leaders holding more powerful positions exhibited lower cortisol levels and less anxiety than leaders holding less powerful positions, a relationship explained significantly by their greater sense of control . . . these findings reveal a clear relationship between leadership and stress, with leadership level being inversely related to stress."*

- The study also indicated, and very importantly, the role that social support plays in relation to leadership stress levels: ". . .other factors, such as social support. . .also play a part in buffering against the negative effects of job strain. . ."

Remember the *Myers-Briggs* study from earlier? The same study corroborated the above: that middle managers experience the highest levels of stress, while CEOs report lower stress levels due to their greater sense of control at work.

Here's what it comes down to. When it comes to discussing mental health, some researchers say it's harder for C-suite executives, while others argue it's middle managers. Some sources state that the higher leaders climb, the more freedom and flexibility they have to be open about their mental health struggles because they objectively hold more power and (sometimes) certainty in their roles. Conversely, other sources claim that as leaders ascend the professional ranks, they feel less psychological safety to discuss their mental health because they have more to prove and maintain as leaders, regardless of other identity factors. Some sources suggest that middle managers have the greatest sense of flexibility to open up due to their proximity to team management but are also caught in an in-between "squeeze" of their positions and lower authority than those above them, making the stakes of disclosure seem too high.

Every leader's situation, regardless of their leadership rank, wholly depends on their unique circumstances, the company they work in or lead, whether there is a culture of support, their industry, individual identity, cultural context, and more. Regardless of leadership level, the stakes of discussing mental health are layered, nuanced, and complex, with varying implications based on leadership seniority.

Industry-Specific Challenges

Not all industries are equal when it comes to discussing mental health at work, especially within leadership. Specific sectors and roles don't naturally lend themselves to talking about mental health struggles or even types of mental illness based on their scope. That's just how the world works, and I understand that. If I said that discussing mental health in leadership is the same across all industries, I would be lying— and delusional.

Along with all the factors we have discussed so far in this book, the nuances in each industry can create challenges and obstacles that affect how (or if) leaders feel they have permission or even the right to talk about their mental health at work. Some specific roles are designed so that what is required of those leaders closely resembles that of an AI robot, with a 0.02% margin of error, that appears externally as a human. This is an uncomfortable but truthful reality. When leaders in those roles and industries find themselves in situations where there is seemingly always too much at stake, the leaders who serve in those positions are unfortunately pressured to maintain (or at least outwardly show) either consistent mental health and emotional expression patterns or a level of resilience that most people cannot maintain. Some examples:

- Government work with security clearance: individuals actively don't share about mental health struggles because, in some cases, they can be stripped of the security clearance required to perform their roles.
- Air traffic controllers: In 2025, *Last Week Tonight with John Oliver* did an episode about the stringent screening and application process to become an air traffic controller.[28] The episode highlighted the extreme stress levels in the industry, which went largely unrecognized and unaddressed until recent years. This exhausted population, who are overworked, undersupported, and have to claw their way into these roles with a less than 10% acceptance rate of applications, is expected to perform tasks that only a tiny fraction of our world's population could ever do. Get this: if there is any record of them having previous mental health problems or treatment, they will likely be denied entry into the training program.

In some sectors, open conversations occur more frequently, and mental health (at all organizational levels) is easier to address and sometimes even encouraged. Meanwhile, in other industries, expecting sincere discussions about mental health is like hoping a snake will fly (without hitching a ride clutched in a falcon's talons as that afternoon's snack).

Looking at Leadership Mental Health Through the Industry Lens

Specific industries can, and often do, determine the stakes of disclosure that leaders are aware of and cautious about. I've selected a few different industries—just brief snapshots—to illustrate their unique challenges, knowing that exceptions always exist. These examples reflect leadership experiences within those industries, highlighting the themes that influence their comfort level in discussing mental health. I have focused on three different forms of industry: white-collar client and patient-based sectors, Human Resources (a people-centered function that spans across industries), and blue-collar industries such as construction and manufacturing. Despite their differences, these industries share similar themes, practices, and pressures. A common theme I've noticed? Leaders are expected to normalize mental health conversations for others—if and when they're encouraged—even though it's still not entirely safe for them to open up themselves (hello again, Chapter 4).

Medicine, Finance, & Law: When Client and Patient Care Means Silencing the Self

> *"Mental health is simply not a topic of conversation in the industry. . . . There are plenty of people talking amongst themselves about their struggles, but mostly as a way of coping, not so much with any expectation of help. Perform, perform, perform. The biggest challenge in this industry is unforgiving deadlines, and lots of them. . .with no time for considering mental health."*
>
> Interviewee: male, Millennial, Black, first-generation American, Director, legal support industry

> *"When I worked for an organization that set unrealistic expectations and disregarded my feelings with words from mentors that said things like 'I'm not asking you to do anything that I didn't do,' I felt resentment. My loyalty to my position in the organization started to wander, and it wasn't long before I left."*
>
> Interviewee: male, Millennial, Asian, Owner, healthcare industry

I've come to a sad realization over the years. When you need licensure in a specific industry to provide services to other humans that can impact their lives, health, financial stability, and other high-stakes scenarios, emotional inconsistency is generally not tolerated. This is because displaying negative emotions is wrongly predominantly seen as a likely risk for mistakes. Whether it's medicine, law, or finance, the pressure for accuracy, attention to detail, maintaining control, and following procedures, at the risk of jeopardizing a license or credential, is intense. In high-stakes fields like these, leaders are expected to be even more emotionally unshakeable anchors for their teams. Should high levels of safety-based, ethics-based, and fit-to-practice-based scrutiny exist in these professions? Absolutely! Should it exclude the likelihood and spectrum of common human struggles? No. Yet, it happens. Let's look at the data:

- Finance:
    - In 2023, the *Journal of Epidemiology and Health* published a study examining the impact of performance pressure on the mental health of individuals working in the finance industry in South Korea.[29] It showed that this pressure has negatively impacted mental health, manifesting through anxiety, depression, and suicide.
    - The same report from *Calm* at the start of this chapter stated employers need to provide more preventative mental health support in the banking industry, showing that "36% of workers in the finance industry are feeling stressed and anxious

more than half the days or nearly all the time. Forty-four percent of banking employees say being overworked negatively affects their mental health, and 34% say being too busy does the same."

- Healthcare:
  o In 2024, the *U.S. Centers for Disease Control and Prevention (CDC)* published an article through the National Institute for Occupational Safety and Health (NIOSH) saying that healthcare workers face "challenging working conditions and high stress levels that can lead to poor mental and physical health."[30]

- Law:
  o In 2023, the *National Association for Law Placement* published an article about the importance of addressing burnout in the legal profession,[31] showing "Law.com's midlevel associate survey from August 2019 revealed that burnout was a growing concern even pre-pandemic. More recently, the Bloomberg Law Workload and Hours Survey showed that lawyers reported feeling burned out an average of 44–52%."

Maintaining emotional composure and professionalism is paramount for leaders in these fields. If those qualities are questioned, you risk losing credibility from other leaders or your team, the trust needed to handle high-stakes situations, and possibly even your license or certification, depending on what people observe. Leaders who witness their leadership colleagues have a professional downfall after opening up don't exactly feel they will be greeted with open arms or psychological safety if they show their struggles.

The work cultures in these industries can be, unfortunately, unforgiving. In finance and law, whether it's meeting billable hours or following the rules of being a registered fiduciary, the margin for error is almost nonexistent, especially in leadership roles. If your clients or firm don't trust you, or see you as a liability, in many cases, you're finished. Additionally, these fields have traditionally been male-led, and many still are, often influenced by toxic masculinity. This adds more complex pressures on leaders, regardless of their gender.

> *"Male-dominated corporate leadership has historically suppressed addressing emotional issues. I've seen many leaders, reluctant to seek help, self-medicate with drugs and alcohol."*
>
> Interviewee: male, Baby Boomer, Caucasian, Owner, health-care industry

Let's look at healthcare. As a former mental health therapist who worked in healthcare, specifically behavioral health, and had to obtain multiple levels of licensure to provide services to clients, I can state this very confidently: it doesn't matter if you work in a care-based profession that serves others where care, empathy, and health are essential. If you are a practitioner, you must follow strict standards to practice in that role, and even more so in a leadership capacity (i.e., people practice under your license in a provisional capacity). When that stability is questioned, it can cause doubt about your abilities to supervise, practice, and ensure client safety. And in many cases, rightfully so, as client and patient outcomes take priority over individual mental health (i.e., do no harm). However, it is logical to concurrently focus on maintaining practitioner mental health so they can perform optimally when delivering care in high-stakes professions. Say, for example, a brain surgeon. Wouldn't that be a no-brainer? Sorry, I love a good pun.

Fortunately, some progress has been made in healthcare regarding discussions on mental health for healthcare professionals. I've seen it first-hand, having been hired by organizations to address this myself. In May 2020, at the start of the pandemic, I hosted a virtual event for a room full of socially distanced doctors and nurses on the brink of burnout. I've also worked with community mental health organizations and other healthcare companies. Progress is happening, slowly but surely, but it's often met with resistance due to lingering stigma and outdated expectations.

Going back to *The Pitt* for a moment, I took extensive notes on the quandaries of leadership mental health in healthcare across multiple episodes. The show created a fantastic depiction of this, likely based on the input of ER physicians who consulted on the show's scripts.

Noah Wyle's character privately struggled with anxiety and panic attacks after failing to save his mentor, who died from insurmountable complications from COVID-19 during the pandemic. Throughout the series, each episode highlighted the complex and often contradictory expectations faced by Wyle's character. Some characters acknowledged his impressive abilities as both a leader and a surgeon, recognizing that he's also a human dealing with struggles. Others, however, didn't hesitate to weaponize his vulnerabilities against him, questioning his credibility.

Human Resources—The Humanity Cost of Working in the People Function

> *"As an HR executive, there's often an unspoken expectation that your emotional needs come last. . .There's this expectation that because I'm in a leadership role. . .I should always be composed, available, and emotionally steady—no matter what I might be going through personally."*
>
> Interviewee: female, Elder Millennial, Asian, Vice President, software industry
>
> *"There's no HR for HR. No one inside my organization checked on my own well-being for most of my time there because I looked like I had it all together. I didn't."*
>
> Interviewee: female, Gen X, Caucasian, C-Suite, human resources industry

The Human Resources (HR) industry is one of the most paradoxical fields to work in. My heart goes out to HR professionals, especially HR leaders. Remember in Chapter 4 when I discussed how leaders are easy targets when people get upset? That's even more true for HR leaders. I've lost count of the number of conversations I've had with HR leaders who have shared some truly terrible things said to them, and some of the situations they have had to endure. Visceral attacks on their character, assumptions that they lack humanity because of their role, and mandates they have to enforce that are often outside their control, dictated by "higher-ups." When you're an HR leader, people outside the department frequently try to knock you down or push you aside.

SelectSoftware Reviews published a piece on mental health in HR in 2023, citing numerous reasons why working as an HR leader is challenging for one's mental health.[32] Here's what they shared:

> *"HR leaders are tasked with supporting the mental and emotional health of employees across business units. However, finding the space and resources to tend to their own emotional wellness is challenging . . . When HR professionals are experiencing burnout, they are not getting the support they need and are not in the space to help other employees do their jobs effectively."*

Here's what's expected of HR leaders daily: be human-centered and deliver people-focused initiatives. Support others and prioritize their well-being. Keep quiet about organizational decisions you may disagree with ethically. Handle difficult layoffs, lead investigations into sensitive issues that can easily go sideways, and manage confidential employee data to prevent lawsuits. Facilitate mental health conversations across the organization, even if you're unable to join them, to avoid making employees uncomfortable or feel like they can't rely on you. Make employees feel safe and at ease. Stabilize the chaos after a traumatic event. Always remain composed, calm, and trustworthy. If something goes wrong, you'll be blamed because, historically, your industry makes you an easy target. You won't be seen as human. And none of the caring you'll do will be returned to you, because you're considered "the people person," so you shouldn't need it—and no one else can do it. In HR—you're "the other."

HRDive did a piece in 2022 on HR burnout[33] showing that "a staggering 98% of HR professionals have felt burned out at work in the last six months, according to a survey of 524 HR and internal communications specialists . . . Nearly 4 in 5 (79%) are open to leaving their jobs." HR leaders face pressure from all directions, from all levels of leadership, and from employees. The only support they can sometimes find is among their peers within their industry because, no matter how much they try to humanize themselves, people in other functions seem resist-ant to accepting that. The amount of compassion fatigue that HR pro-fessionals experience is alarming and honestly sometimes resembles what is seen in frontline workers, clinical mental healthcare providers, and other fields where these issues are common.

Construction, Manufacturing, and Toxic "Toughness"

"I do not believe our industry promotes regular conversations . . . Contributing factors to mental health struggles within construction include high stress levels, substance abuse, and gender norms. While stressors may vary at different levels, mental health remains a significant issue across all levels of the industry."

Interviewee: female, Millennial, Black, Senior Vice President in the C-Suite, heavy civil construction industry

Historically, blue-collar and "rough-and-tumble" sectors have often emphasized hard work, long hours, requiring strength, endurance, dependability, and self-reliance. They also have alarmingly high rates of suicide, substance abuse, and mental illness. In 2024, a *National Academy of Engineering* article focused on suicide and mental health in the construction industry articulated this point,[34]

". . .A survey conducted in 2020 revealed that 83% of construction workers had struggled with mental health issues. As Adrienne Selko reported in EHS Today, according to the Centers for Disease Control and Prevention, 'construction occupations have the highest rate of sui-cide, as well as the highest number of suicides across all occupational groups' . . . These statistics represent astounding critical problems in the construction industry that need to be resolved."

Spring Health also did a piece on how the manufacturing industry is trying to reduce mental health stigma in the industry, specifically cit-ing data from the *Manufacturers Alliance* that 41% of manufacturing employers say that mental health challenges have negatively impacted employee retention efforts, and 54% of manufacturing workers know a co-worker affected by a substance abuse disorder.[35]

Adding the complexity of intersectionality, norms in these industries are reinforced by generational attitudes and gender expectations around emotional health, too. Historically, these sectors have been very male-dominated, with many "lifers" acting as de facto mentors and cultural gatekeepers. Many of them continue to follow the norms based on when they entered the industry. When people were rewarded for silence rather than honesty—despite the fact that many were devastated upon learning that some of those who remained silent developed mental health issues, substance abuse problems, or took their own lives—it's clear that the system is flawed. Paradoxically, men are bullied or teased if they open up, while women are also ridiculed when they speak up among their male peers. Both are screwed based on Gender-Based Emotion Shaming, especially in visible leadership roles. When we add culture and ethnic identity, or even the family that raised you, it creates additional layers of rules and biases for these leaders to navigate.

When you're in a leadership role in these industries, whether you're a crew lead, plant manager, site supervisor, or foreman, it's expected that you are even more resilient than those you oversee in high-stakes, sometimes physically dangerous, and ironically, safety-focused environments. I facilitated a session for a manufacturing company on the importance of stress management. When I talked about the value of taking a few minutes each day for mental well-being, one male leader joked in front of the group, saying, "Oh, *like going outside to stand in a yoga pose while humming 'ohm'?*" The group laughed. Unfortunately for him, I (gently) responded, "*Your joke, while funny, just shows why people are afraid to talk about mental health in your industry—especially if leaders make jokes like that.*" He went quiet.

These trends and data mentioned above, sadly and thankfully, led to the creation of multiple organizations focused on providing education and changing these mental health statistics. There is a reason why there are noticeably strong efforts happening these days around mental health and suicide prevention in these industries: the data we're seeing is alarming at best and catastrophic at worst. I know several mental health advocates in these industries, and let me tell you, people are finally listening to the message because they don't want to lose anyone else. Yet, despite ongoing intense efforts within these industries, the stigma around mental health still runs deep.

It's Time to Total up the Weight on Leadership Mental Health Equation

While we've just touched the surface exploring the different identities, systems, and contextual factors that influence leadership mental health, we must recognize this: it is vast and complex. Countless influences shape the experience of leadership mental health, how leaders perceive their ability to discuss their mental health at work, or whether they should (or even hope to) talk about it within the organizations they lead.

It's time. We've reached the end of building our Weight on Leadership Mental Health Equation. Let's total up all of the elements we've covered in Part I, with the final pieces added in **bold**:

The Influence of Toxic Historical Narratives

+

The Sociological Assignment of Power

+

When Standards of "Good" Leadership Run Counter to Displays of Emotional Struggle

+

Magical Thinking and the Dehumanization of Leaders

+

A Lack of Social Permission to Speak Up

+

Experiencing Helplessness

+

Experiencing Institutional Betrayal

+

Having Psychological Contracts Broken

+

Being Subjected to the Illusory Truth Effect

+

Being Actively Disincentivized to Speak Up About Mental Health

+

Experiencing Worsening Mental Health Through Data Invisibility & Support Neglect

+

Experiencing Mental Health Struggles as a Career Liability

+

The Emotional Deterrent of a Lack of Emotional Support Structures

+

Having to Choose Between Emotional Survival vs. Career Progression

+

An Impaired Ability to Lead Effectively

+

Creating an Unintentional Negative Impact on Team Culture Around Mental Health

+

The Leadership Plate Morphing Into an Endlessly Refilling Trough

+

The Intensifying Weight and Burden of Leadership

+

The Intensification and Multiplication of Leadership Tasks

+

Enduring the Darker Side of Leadership Development

+

Being a Stress Target During Times of Turmoil, Chaos, and Crisis

+

Leading Through Social Tribalism, Polarization-Driven Unrest, and Systemic Volatility

+

Fearing the Digital Court of Public Opinion and Internet Social Scrutiny

+

Navigating Leadership Mental Health Rules in Different Systems and Identities

+

Enduring the Compounded Effects of Intersectionality

+

Managing Leadership Mental Health Within the Contexts (and Confines) of

Culture, Ethnicity, Gender, Industry, Age, and Countless Other Factors

That is a crushing weight on leaders' shoulders and a never-ending supply filling the trough they're tied to. Isn't it? Any of these factors can be challenging to manage independently. When they're all added together? It seems colossal, because it is.

So . . . What Can We Do?

When we name things and why they're hurting people, we can work to create change. Let's start doing that, now.

In Season 2 of the TV show *The Last of Us*, I heard a sentiment that perfectly summed up a practice that we need to rally against and is how I'd like to take you into Part II, the action-oriented part of this book: that some people have their certainty masquerading as knowledge.[36] We have the knowledge, so we can't cling to biased-driven certainty that isn't based on logical truth. We can no longer observe and unintentionally contribute to the problem. Leaders should never have been, and can no longer be, asked to choose between their emotional survival and their careers. As a leader, do you want to keep making that choice? I'm not just asking you to reflect on what you've read. I'm asking you to join me at a pivotal moment to act and create change.

The last five chapters have helped us reach a crucial goal: recognizing and understanding the problem and the barriers that often stop leaders from discussing their mental health at work. These aren't just simple challenges—they reflect a deeply complex reality that shapes the emotional experience of leadership today. Part II is where we move from understanding the problem to taking action through tangible solutions—so that each leader, organization, and industry can work, one step at a time, to break down those barriers. How do we do that? Who does what, and when? This won't just take a village; it will take as many villages as possible—and lots of people in them.

In Part II, we'll explore what it takes to actually normalize conversations about leadership mental health at the organizational level, peer-to-peer, and what realistic, constructive leadership mental health self-care can look like. We'll also discuss creating practices and systems to support that. There are numerous ways to approach this, so I'm sharing my perspective. And let's remember, we can't boil the ocean; it's not a realistic goal. Yes, we'll discuss some broader ways that organizations and industries can contribute to moving the needle, but change is a slow process, considering the numerous individual circumstances, opinions, and levels of willingness involved.

When it comes to you, you're just *one person*. Depending on where you sit, all I ask is that you focus on what you can do, whether that's for yourself or your fellow leaders. I won't make you feel responsible for more than you already do. All you can do is decide the change you want to make, with your voice, in your organization, and in your industry. Remember the answers to your reflection questions throughout Part I? In Part II, it's time to act on them.

I'll show you how. Let's get it done, together.

PART I: INDIVIDUAL REFLECTION EXERCISE

Create Your Leadership Mental Health Map

Purpose

This exercise will help you identify and integrate the insights from your reflections in Part I, clarifying the changes you want to pursue in Part II. I've suggested names for each part of your map, but if you'd like to have some fun with naming, feel free to come up with creative names for each section that feel right to you. I also recommend going old school with a pen and pencil on paper, but you can also do this digitally if you prefer.

Step 1: Map Out Your Influences

Get two pieces of paper. Take the first piece of paper, lay it down horizontally, and draw a small circle in the center. Inside the circle, write "My Leadership Mental Health." Then, around and connected to that circle, draw four larger circles, with one side of each touching the center circle. Inside each of those outer circles, write the following labels:

- Identity, systemic, and intersectionality influences
- Company norms for leadership behaviors
- Personal leadership values and beliefs
- Concerns about perceptions from others
- Create additional circles with other relevant influences as needed

Fill in each circle with the pressures, influences, and messages that resonate in each area, which have impacted and affected your mental health as a leader throughout your career. If thinking about your entire career feels too overwhelming, you're welcome to do this exercise based on a specific leadership role or organization you worked (or currently work) for that feels relevant to this exercise.

Step 2: Highlight the Double Binds

As we've discussed in Part I, what's often expected of leaders contains conflicting expectations. From the content you've written in the circles, highlight those that may conflict with messages in other circles (i.e., "be honest, but don't show struggle"). Next, on the second sheet of paper, write down,

- How do these conflicting pressures make you feel? (i.e., *"These conflicting pressures make me feel resentful and exhausted."*)
- Why are they unreasonable? (i.e., *"This is unreasonable because I can't effectively perform my role or take care of myself."*)

Step 3: Identify Pressure Points and Support Gaps

Also on the second sheet of paper, write down the support gaps for your mental health, regardless of where they come from (i.e., yourself, your peers, or company). Include some examples of how this manifests (i.e., "I don't let myself take breaks…," or "My boss expects me to work 14-hour days….")

(Note: Identifying what the deprioritization or neglect looks like will help you understand the support you need, how, and when. It will also help inform the strategies you choose in Part II to meet those needs, while considering your individual circumstances.)

Step 4: Write Your Statement of Intention & Declaration to Yourself

Describe the current state of your mental health and why you want to shift your perspective and behaviors to improve it. (i.e., *"I'm so stressed I can't sleep at night, and I'm not getting the support I need from my company. I haven't spoken up about this. As I head into Part II, I will open my mind to new ways of getting support for my mental health as a leader."*)

Part I: Key Takeaways

- **Leaders are humans first**, their titles second.
- **The expectations and "rules" surrounding leadership mental health** are harmful and outdated.
- **Leaders are professionally responsible for accomplishing and managing more in the workplace than ever before**, while expectations have increased—and support has not.
- **Silence has a cost for everyone.** When leaders are silent about their mental health, the ripple effects extend to them, their teams, and the companies they lead.
- **Social narratives and systems shape and reinforce leadership mental health behaviors**, affecting leaders' psychological safety, willingness, and ability to speak up.

PART

II

How to Create Change

6

How Organizations Can Support
Leadership Mental Health

"Organizations need to be more honest with themselves about the pressures that leaders face. While sometimes it is the nature of the beast and cannot be eliminated, the stress and mental health challenges that come with being a leader need to be acknowledged. Organizations need to allow leaders to deal with the challenges they face and offer them the support they need to get through these challenges."

Interviewee: female, Black, Generation X, Vice President, sports and entertainment industry

"To create a more supportive environment, organizations need to extend the same compassion and flexibility to leaders that they do to employees. That means normalizing mental health struggles at all levels, creating psychologically safe cultures, and ensuring leaders have access to support, not just responsibility. When leaders feel safe and supported, they're better equipped to support everyone else."

Interviewee: female, Asian, Millennial, Vice President, SaaS industry

> "*Companies can foster a safe environment for speaking about mental health by implementing key changes in their culture, policies, and leadership approach. It starts with the organization investing in a 360 approach to their investment of support they will offer.*"
>
> Interviewee: female, Baby Boomer, Caucasian, Director, beauty industry
>
> "*We need to show that having mental health struggles doesn't threaten your job security and promotion prospects.*"
>
> Interviewee: male, Millennial, Black, first-generation American, Director, legal support industry

IN PART I, WE discussed a harsh but necessary truth: why and how leadership mental health isn't prioritized in the workplace mental health conversation. Now, we're going to discuss how to change that. We've made our case. Now we need the collective courage of our convictions to act (I love a good alliteration, don't you?). This chapter will emphasize the organizational role and responsibility of supporting leadership mental health at work. As a heads-up, unlike Part I, the chapters throughout Part II have the reflection questions and action planning boxes throughout the chapters, rather than at the end of each chapter.

What's the "Answer" to the Weight on Leadership Mental Health Equation?

In Chapter 2, we discussed the three steps involved in creating change. We are now on Step 3: focusing on our intended outcome, which includes setting objectives, based on what we aim to avoid repeating and the reasons behind it. We will define our goals and the paths to achieve them.

Numerous heavy elements contributed to the Weight on Leadership Mental Health Equation. What could we possibly add to the other side of that equation to "balance" it out? Can a complete "solve" for this exist? Of course not. This isn't a linear problem with a simple fix. It's a complex, multidirectional issue with a range of long-term suggestions, not all of which every company would be open to or could be logistically (or even financially) feasible based on their setup. However, when it comes to the willingness piece, some industries, companies, and leaders will continue to ignore mental health at work. They will continue to promote (overtly or not) the notion that leadership mental health doesn't matter. We can't control that. The goal is to reduce the number of industries, companies, and leaders who act this way. Making them the weird ones in the corner, so to speak. We're going to do our best with what we can, when we can, with what we've got, through as many willing people as possible. To balance the Weight on Leadership Mental Health Equation, I've labeled what sits on the other side of the equals sign as this. . . drumroll please. . .

Leadership Mental Health Support Solution

Just as in Part I, watch out for the newly added elements in **bold** starting at the end of this chapter.

Shifting from Observation to Action Through Collective Efforts

This kind of change—the seismic shift we're aiming for—isn't just a typical top-down or bottom-up process; it's multidirectional. Each organization will influence and reflect this change based on the people who lead it. It's also not lost on me that those who can drive the most visible change around this will be leaders themselves—the ones who need it the most. With everything else leaders are responsible for, it can feel unfair—it's yet another thing to do. In this case, the adage "be the change you want to see" is not just a bumper sticker quoting Gandhi you see on a car in front of you. Its a valid, necessary principle. We can't ask people to lead the charge who don't understand why, can't relate to it, or even—resist. This is a call to action and an invitation to build a better future for leadership mental health, for those who are willing to lead the charge when others won't or don't know how. For those who have the ability and responsibility to. These leaders, struggling in the ocean, will need to claw their way into the boat so they can turn around and pull other leaders up with them.

Achieving transformation will require a collaborative effort, encompassing the C-suite, Human Resources, learning and development, health and safety, talent development, and leaders across business units. If we want to shift the leadership trough back to a manageable plate, this is what's required. If we want to rebalance the ecosystem, we need to shift it so the organisms can healthfully adapt. If you're a leader capable of driving change within your organization, depending on your specific situation and where you sit, you have the opportunity to help rewrite the narrative and shape new outcomes.

How do we accomplish this? By understanding who's responsible for what, being strategic, and adopting a methodical approach to facilitate change. We'll examine the individual leaders' responsibilities in later chapters. In this chapter, we'll focus on the organization's role and responsibilities, and how companies can create change by reshaping organizational narratives, normalizing resource usage, providing education, and developing community support for leaders.

An Organizational Imperative to Support Leadership Mental Health

> "I want organizations to understand that right, wrong, or indifferent, they are both the problem and the solution. Leaders aren't burning out in a vacuum. They're burning out inside systems that reward self-abandonment and punish vulnerability. We have to stop creating environments where showing emotion is seen as a liability. . .Until that happens, leaders like me will keep burning out."
>
> Interviewee: male, Gen X, Caucasian, Senior Leadership, construction industry

Effective, sustainable change is driven by ongoing, clear motivation, purpose, and value. And having a solid case, which we established throughout Part I. We've highlighted the illogical, unsustainable, and unhealthy. To counteract that, we will take a logical approach, building on valid arguments, methods, and reasoning, with references to where it's already being done successfully. Let's start with three non-negotiable reasons why organizations must actively support leadership mental health moving forward:

1. The moral case of Duty of Care
2. The logical strategic case for sustainable leadership
3. The normalization case to add "managing struggle" to the list of leadership strengths

Additionally, some of the suggestions I have in this chapter are methods that you may have seen suggested elsewhere in the "information overload superhighway". The reason I've included them is this: they work, and are more likely to succeed when done well, in conjunction with each other, and consistently. Lastly, their proof of success has been demonstrated when applied to general employee mental health. Ergo, we need to consider the same application for leaders. Not to check a box or appear to do it just because it looks good. Pick what is feasible for your organization. All I will say is this: the more you do, and the more often you do it, the more you increase the likelihood of having better outcomes.

The Moral Case: Organizational Duty of Care

When I lived in the United Kingdom (UK), I was inspired by the fact that the UK government had a legal mandate to ensure that companies acted on their moral and legal responsibilities for the well-being of their entire workforce. This was called Duty of Care. *Indeed.com* even did a piece on it in 2025, by explaining that,

> ". . .*Employers have certain legal duty and moral obligation to maintain minimum working standards and a healthy work environment for their staff. These obligations fall within employment law and form the employer's duty of care. They include things like health and safety. . .and employee wellbeing. Professionals in human resources and related roles require an understanding of this duty of care, to ensure it is applied across the workplace.*"[1]

Notice how it said across the workplace—this includes leaders. The *National Health Service (NHS)* healthcare system in the United Kingdom hammered this point home; that Duty of Care is not a "nice to have," but a must, with crystal clear language saying,

> ". . . *This means promoting wellbeing and making sure that people are kept safe from harm, abuse and injury. Duty of care is a legal requirement; you cannot choose whether to accept it.*"[2]

A similar concept, federally mandated in Canada, known as the Duty to Inquire, holds organizations responsible for checking on employees' well-being, especially if they believe an employee may require some form of accommodation related to mental health.[3]

These ideas seem pretty reasonable, logical, and valid to me. They are about caring for everyone's well-being in your organization. I believe this should be a basic requirement, no matter where a company, its workers, or leaders are located. Based on this argument, we can deduce that supporting leadership mental health through prioritizing a form of Duty of Care isn't just the legal, moral, and compassionate thing to do—it's a clear sign of a company's integrity and dedication to doing the humane, logical, and smart thing. While laws like the Duty of Care are undervalued and underrepresented in various regions and countries, their absence doesn't diminish their importance.

The Logical Strategic Case: Ensuring Sustainable Leadership (with Existing Proof of Success)

While I wish the moral case would be enough, it usually doesn't seem to be. So, let's focus now on the business aspect—it's good for the bottom line. The business case is obvious. Mentally supported leaders can become healthier leaders capable of driving results. We've established that the expectations for leaders today are astronomically high. If workplaces want "good" leadership behavior, performance, and results, then companies need to provide emotional health support and social permission to discuss mental health in a matching manner. As I often tell clients, discussing mental health at work isn't an optional wellness activity; it's a critical workplace conversation. And when it comes to leaders, it must be a core strategic priority.

Supporting the emotional well-being of key individuals in the workplace ecosystem should be a no-brainer.

Studies and data have shown that prioritizing mental health in leadership is essential for sustainable leadership. The research clearly indicates that leadership mental health contributes to the foundation of organizational culture and effective leadership behaviors. Supporting leadership mental health leads to more effective leadership actions, which in turn enhance capability and increase the likelihood of supporting their teams. What's the intended outcome?

Supported leaders < > Supported organization

In addition to promoting sustainable leadership, let's also consider the importance of the impact on employee mental health. Studies have shown that supporting mental health for leaders—shocker—increases the chances that employee mental health, job satisfaction, and retention will improve.[4] If leadership mental health is not managed, where do you think the resulting issues can cascade to? Employees and the rest of the organization. Leaders are influential and need a support system to help build their capacity to demonstrate the stability, credibility, and reliable support that their teams need. Here are the studies and data to support that case:

- A 2023 article in *Frontiers in Psychology* highlighted the non-negotiable need to support leadership mental health, demonstrating how this aspect is often overlooked or invisible when fostering a healthy organizational culture, effective leadership behaviors, and positive effects on employees.[5]
- The *Ginger* 2021 Workforce Attitudes Toward Mental Health Report showed that "88% of employees appreciate when their company's leaders talk about their own mental health . . . Of the CEOs who do talk about their mental health, more than half report that doing so makes them a better leader."[6]
- CEOs are speaking up about their mental health struggles and why we need to talk about leadership mental health in general, like when Emma McIlroy, the CEO of the sensationally successful clothing brand, WildFang, shared about her depression and the importance of talking about entrepreneurial and CEO mental health.[7]

- *Fortune* published a piece on the importance of talking about "board burnout."[8]
- A 2023 *Forbes* article confirmed that managing leadership stress is associated with improved overall mental health in the workplace.[9] The article explained it clearly,

> *"Managers are at the center of the storm. . .A Deloitte study found that one-third of executives are constantly struggling with fatigue, stress, and feelings of being overwhelmed, lonely, or depressed. The result, record numbers of CEO resignations. . .The stress felt by managers can cascade to employees, impacting wellbeing, retention, and performance. Harvard Business Review finds managers can trigger anxiety in their employees through unusual or erratic actions, emotional volatility, excessive pessimism, and ignoring people's emotions . . . stress management is actually a key leadership skill. Managers who do it effectively can see improved relationships with their team, better conflict resolution, and enhanced project management skills. . .Managers who enact strategies to reduce their own stress will be better equipped not just to lead, but to be the greatest advocate for employee mental health and wellbeing."*

These benefits are not abstract. They are specific, reasonable, and logical. We even see examples on much larger scales, from government leaders to popular mainstream television shows and movies depicting leaders, speaking up about why they need to prioritize their mental health so they can survive their roles, and even in some cases, when it's become too much just by virtue of their positions:

- In government:
    - o Using support, in order to keep leading:
        - Senator John Fetterman's open admission of needing inpatient care support for his clinical depression and entering a treatment facility,[10] later returning to his position, unapologetically, despite public scrutiny from those who tried to stigmatize him.
    - o Leaving leadership when the stress is too high:
        - New Zealand's former Prime Minister Jacinda Ardern stepped down from her role, citing burnout,[11] where she

bravely chose to prioritize her mental health and put an end to what felt like an unsustainable career path that was at the expense of her well-being.

- In entertainment:
  - o Highlighting industry-specific stress with concurrent needs for support:
    - Following those gold star examples from *The Pitt,* another show called *The Studio,* starring Seth Rogen, is equally poignant in its accuracy regarding specific industry levels of stress for leaders. Seth Rogen plays a Hollywood executive of a major movie studio. The character unapologetically demonstrates the depth of his commitment to his leadership position, as well as the simultaneously challenging and stressful nature of it. *AP News* literally referred to the show as "the defining portrait of modern Hollywood"[12] for its accuracy. In the *AP News* piece, the journalist interviewed Bryan Cranston, an actor on the show who portrays the studio's CEO, who went as far as to say, "The conflict that my character lives and breathes every second of his life is one a lot of people with his job are facing in real life." In the same piece, the journalist also interviewed a former editor of *The Hollywood Reporter,* who appeared in the show as himself, who also shared, "There's truth underlying almost every scene in 'The Studio,' for better and mostly worse." In one episode, Seth Rogen's character uses voice note journaling to cope with recent stressors. One of his team members approaches him while he's doing this and mocks him, to which Rogen replies, "Don't mock my therapy." The team member responds by encouraging his boss to do whatever works for him. While this may seem like a fleeting exchange, it isn't. It highlights how Rogen's character normalizes mental health challenges related to leadership and shows what he's doing about them. He's not hiding it; he's humanizing himself.

Whether in the public sphere or in entertainment, stories about the importance of mental health in leadership are present—we just need to notice them. They're not on the fringe; they're revealing the truth and the trend toward desperately needed change.

For Policy, Program, & Practice Shifters

Reflection – Will Your Company Prioritize Leadership Mental Health Strategically?

- Is your organization open to strategically supporting the mental health of its leaders? Why or why not?
- Who can you engage to help drive strategic change for supporting leadership mental health?
- Based on your organization's current resources, what is one initial practical way that your organization can better support leadership mental health?

The Normalization Case: Adding "Managing Struggle" to the List of Leadership Strengths

---

"Redefine leadership 'strength'. . .We need this to be a constant conversation. . .."

Interviewee: female, Baby Boomer, Caucasian, Director, beauty industry

---

In my first book, I wrote that people who choose to talk about their mental health struggles and how they manage them demonstrate incredible courage, openness, and strength. This is where we challenge the dysfunctional narrative from Part I and replace it with the actual truth. That leaders who struggle with their mental health, are aware of it, and actively manage it show leadership strength—not weakness or incapability—essentially, blowing up the Leadership Prototypes with reason and logic. We'll get deeper into narrative shifting shortly, but part of that means encouraging leaders to see talking about their mental health struggles as a leadership strength. Remember the power of storytelling from Chapter 1? Organizations can use that for good, to shift the ecosystem further for their view of "good" leadership behaviors. Let me give you some examples.

While writing this second book, I was deeply moved by a LinkedIn post I saw from Dr. Eric Arzubi, a psychiatrist I follow, who shared a story about President Abraham Lincoln's lifelong battle with severe clinical depression. This is especially meaningful because Lincoln faced his struggles at a time when mental health support was nearly nonexistent, especially for men and those in visible leadership roles. Here's why Dr. Arzubi's words inspired me and helped me express my view on the importance of redefining mental health struggles in leadership as a strength. Below is part of what Dr. Arzubi shared, as relevant to leadership mental health,

> *"Our greatest president battled severe depression his entire life. And it made him a better leader. . .What Lincoln's struggle teaches us:*
>
> *1. Depression doesn't disqualify greatness*
> *⌊ His suffering deepened his empathy*
> *⌊ His darkness sharpened his resilience*
> *⌊ His pain connected him to others' struggles*
>
> *2. He never 'overcame' depression*
> *⌊ He developed coping mechanisms*
> *⌊ He found purpose within his pain*
>
> *3. His mental health shaped his leadership*
> *⌊ More patience during setbacks*
> *⌊ Deeper understanding of suffering*
>
> *. . .The most powerful mind of his generation was a mind that struggled. His greatness wasn't despite his depression. It was, in part, because of it."*[13]

I realize that we live in a very different world than when Lincoln was President. But the point is still valid. Look at what President Lincoln accomplished, and at a time when there was even less understanding, more stigma, and less help for mental health. Look at what that man achieved, the leadership challenges he faced, all while struggling. He garnered admiration for his remarkable ability to broker some of the most important changes in U.S. history. Shouldn't examples like this, from 160 years ago, inspire us to redefine what leadership strengths look like today? We've gained an even deeper understanding of mental health, mental illness, and stress, and have clear examples of leaders who struggle *and* accomplish incredible things simultaneously. Why aren't the successes that we keep seeing enough?

These days, leaders have been encouraged even more to incorporate storytelling into their leadership toolkit for how they inspire their teams, create change, and produce outcomes. Talking about mental health struggles is within that same vein. Harvard Professor Marshall Ganz, a recognized expert on narrative training for leaders, was interviewed in 2023 for a piece on the importance of leaders humanizing themselves by sharing their struggles as part of their "story."[14] The piece shared that,

> *"Ganz's coaching emphasizes that leaders who can effectively convey their experiences can captivate audiences, instill a sense of purpose, and foster genuine connections to shareholders and within their teams. . .Your story becomes a source of motivation, offering insights into resilience and the human experience. Ganz's approach to public narrative training encourages leaders to not only communicate their triumphs but also to reveal the lessons learned from struggles, creating a narrative that is authentic, relatable, and ultimately empowering."*

I'm pretty sure that Lincoln did that pretty damn well. He captivated audiences, instilled a sense of purpose, and didn't hide that he struggled while doing it. Lincoln's struggle was part of his story, and he demonstrated strength in acknowledging it, normalizing it as a concurrent human experience alongside his other leadership strengths. While Lincoln didn't shout his struggles from the rooftops to the general public, he didn't hide them from his friends and close colleagues, the people he knew would understand. This is why community within leadership is so crucial, and we'll discuss that shortly.

Academia backs us up here, again. Sharing struggles in leadership not only makes leaders more relatable but also increases the chances that team members will feel more connected and motivated to follow them. Those seem like pretty essential and already demanded leadership strengths to me (ahem, Chapter 4). Back to Brené Brown. Yes, she's famous, but remember, she is also a PhD-level researcher who has taught us a lot about the human condition. The woman knows things. The *Association of Talent Development* published a piece about vulnerability as a leadership strength, citing Brené's work, in particular—her research work on uncertainty, risk, and emotional exposure—through acts of vulnerability.[15] The article shared this, "For leaders. . .it includes sharing your challenges. . .Vulnerability fosters trust, encourages open communication, and builds stronger relationships within teams. Long story short, it makes you seem more human and much more relatable." In 2025, *Psychology Today* published a piece from two Industrial–Organizational Psychologists who focus their work on leadership well-being for positive organizational impact.[16] They explained why historical precedents for leadership behaviors are irrelevant in modern leadership. In fact, those old expectations are counterproductive given the advantages of modern storytelling, where leaders are often asked to do that as a Bonus Task because of its demonstrable benefits. Here's what the article said:

> *"Leaders have been idealized as stoic characters who always know the answers, never falter, and who have a plethora of strengths with no weaknesses in sight. But there's a big problem with this concept of what makes leaders great. Not only is this an impossible vision for leaders to achieve—it's also incorrect. . .Sharing your struggles is a strength. . .This seems counterintuitive to many. Shouldn't leaders hide their struggles from their team members, so that it seems that they have everything under control at all times? In fact, the opposite is true. . . sharing your struggles builds trust with your team because they know you're willing to be honest about your shortcomings. . .Great leaders develop and inspire other leaders. But it's hard to do that when your team thinks that leaders never struggle on the job."*

Practical Ways Organizations Can Support Leadership Mental Health

> *"Leaders should be encouraged to utilize resources without shame or economic repercussions. Regular peer group meetings provide an outlet for emotional release and problem-solving."*
>
> Interviewee: male, Baby Boomer, Caucasian, Owner, healthcare industry
>
> *"We have a bi-weekly supervisors meeting at our organization, and it has been really great in providing a peer space where we can talk about our challenges...It's nice to find commonalities."*
>
> Interviewee: female, Gen Z, Asian, Senior Manager, entertainment non-profit industry

Prioritizing leadership mental health at work and teaching leaders how to discuss it constructively must be viewed as a core business priority and a fundamental value, not just "another initiative." This involves starting from the ground level and building a solid foundation before constructing the house. If your house is already built, you might need to assess and repair a cracked foundation. Yes, it can be costly, time-consuming, and somewhat intimidating, but which would you prefer: investing in rebuilding a sturdy foundation that endures or leaving things as they are and hoping they hold? Despite the challenge, I would choose the first option. All I ask is that you treat this investment as equally important as all other investments in your organization, because it is. If you want leaders to feel supported and capable of performing effectively, then embed leadership mental health support into your company's practices and organizational culture.

How to Begin: Be Strategic

It's one thing to say that something is important; it's another to explain why and how you plan to implement change to recognize its long-term significance. Keep your intended outcomes in mind. Being clear about your purpose and ultimate goals is one of the most helpful ways to facilitate intentional action, change, and participation. What does this look like at a high level? Beyond the willingness and readiness to adopt my suggestions, I understand that each company faces its own financial challenges, with simultaneous pressures to balance investment in leadership mental health with other critical core business initiatives. While I will outline some practical ways to start and sustain an investment in supporting leadership mental health, choose what works best (and is feasible) for your company.

Build Human Behavior into Your Approach

Before we delve into the specific actions you can take, let's examine a couple of psychological models that can guide your mindset for creating change effectively. Additionally, we know that intention isn't always equivalent to impact. These two models will help you narrow the potential gap between the two:

- The SCARF Model[17] from Dr. David Rock, a neuroscience expert, author, and the co-founder of NeuroLeadership Institute.
- The EAST Model[18] from The Behavioural Insights Team, a UK-based organization dedicated to embedding a deeper understanding of human behavior into public programs, policies, and products to ensure that people use the helpful things that are available to them.

When evolving the organizational narrative through various methods and aiming to influence organizational behavior and discussions, using these models will support your strategy, messaging, and mindset around promoting leadership mental health at work. If you build it, you want people to come, and people will if they believe there's something valuable for them, regardless of their motivation.

The SCARF Model: Pre-Emptively Addressing Perceived Threats

This model highlights five domains that influence human behavior in common social situations, all of which can also occur in the workplace.

Each of these is a deeply innate driver that everyone possesses, to varying degrees, at different times, and for diverse reasons. When these key needs are perceived as threatened, depending on our motivations and surroundings, we tend to react. When I work with teams, I tell them to "rank" their SCARF because each is important to some extent, and some more than others. Understanding what our needs are, and their order of importance to us, can help us better meet them. Those needs must be met somewhere, somehow, and in some way. Below, I've included the motivation for each of these domains from Dr. Rock's model and added what it means for you as a change maker to validate and recognize these need domains related to leaders' mental health in your company.

- **Status**: the drive we feel to stand out from the crowd, to feel important, and valued.
  - o *What you may need to validate and recognize:* Some leaders may feel threatened that discussing their mental health struggles could harm their professional status. These leaders may need reassurance that their positions won't be at risk if they are open about their emotional challenges.
- **Certainty**: the drive to know what's going on in our surroundings and have the ability to predict outcomes.
  - o *What you may need to validate and recognize:* Some leaders who seek predictability and certainty may need clear communication about why this change is happening, what to expect, what their options for involvement could be, and what the desired outcomes of "good" look like.
- **Autonomy**: the driver to feel a sense of control over the work we do and the decisions we make.
  - o *What you may need to validate and recognize:* Some, likely many, of your leaders will want flexibility and choice in how they participate in these efforts. You want it to feel like an option without obligation, while also emphasizing the clear benefits of those options if they choose to use them. It's important to let them know they are needed for this change, but equally vital to let them decide how they want to contribute.

- **Relatedness**: the drive to feel like we belong to an in-group.
  - o *What you may need to validate and recognize*: Some of your leaders will benefit from a strong sense of peer-to-peer community. Help ensure they understand the importance of community and actively participating in it. The organization will need to work to create those spaces for leaders. More on this shortly about the creation of leadership peer groups.
- **Fairness**: the drive to feel a sense of equity and explainable justness in social situations.
  - o *What you may need to validate and recognize*: Some of your leaders, if not many, will also value this. Fairness, or rather unfairness, can be triggering for people for a variety of reasons stemming from their life experiences. Ensure you have transparent programs, policies, and measurement methods (to indicate success and highlight areas where the organization can improve their efforts).

By proactively addressing these perceived threats through considering your leaders' internal narratives, motivations, and social behaviors, you're more likely to help your leaders feel capable of participating in this change in a way that's right for them, by establishing the psychological safety they need to do so.

The EAST Model: Making Behavioral Change Easier

I love this model. Not only does it truly account for human nature, but it also structures the change process to reflect it. When we want people to engage in change, because yes, humans are naturally resistant to it, we want that change to seem Easy, Attractive, Social, and Timely (EAST). When considering how to create organizational change related to leadership mental health, here are some examples of how to apply the model in that context.

- **Easy**: make it simple and destigmatized for leaders to access mental health support, conversations, and resources.
- **Attractive**: explain the mental, cognitive, professional, and social benefits of prioritizing leadership mental health, and talking about it, too.

- **Social**: emphasize the value of shared experiences, community, and peer support among leaders; a space solely for them, with no one else involved, and not for the benefit of others.
- **Timely**: aim for good timing. Remind leaders to prioritize their mental health, and let others know that their mental health matters, along with the support they need when it's most critical (i.e., during high stress and change).

For Policy, Program, & Practice Shifters

Reflection—Using These Frameworks for Transformation in Your Company

Think about how your company tends to generally approach organizational transformation. How could using these models help your organizational transformation approach to leadership mental health in your company?

Methods of Impact

"A peer group is the best way for any leader to be able to discuss mental health. I see it most in the stresses of our industry, when leaders of companies can recognize that others are in the same boat as they are when it comes to the day-to-day stresses. Recognizing they are not alone is a HUGE step in dealing with some of those issues, that can pile up if not addressed."

Interviewee: male, Millennial, Caucasian, C-Suite, non-profit trade association industry

"To create a more supportive environment, organizations should support regular discussions about mental health at all levels, offer access to mental health resources and support, and create a safe space where leaders can seek help without fear of judgment or repercussions."

Interviewee: female, Millennial, Black, C-Suite, heavy civil construction industry

---

If you already support employee mental health at your company, I'm not asking you to reinvent the wheel; I'm happy that you're already doing this! I'm asking you to ensure everyone has access to that wheel. Continue what you're doing, just make sure to include leaders in those efforts. If you're not discussing employee mental health but you're reading this book, I hope these efforts for your leaders inspire you to extend the same acknowledgment and critical care to the rest of your organization—because everyone needs it.

There are many ways for a company to create change here. Staying true to our Paradox of Choice core principle, let's focus on five areas:

1. Collecting and actioning leadership mental health data
2. Explaining the importance of mental health resources for leaders
3. Shifting the organizational narrative around leadership mental health
4. Building leadership peer support groups
5. Integrating mental health education and training into leadership development

We'll examine the importance of utilizing these methods and discuss some general strategies for engaging with them. I don't want to be too prescriptive here, as each organization has its own unique structure, systems, and operating methods. For the methods I'm about to share, how you apply them is your decision. It depends on what's possible at your organization, who you involve for support, and people's willingness to contribute. What I will tell you is this:

- **Enlist advocates:**
  o Get the right people involved.
- **Plan your approach, methods, and goals:**
  o Plan short-, medium-, and long-term goals, and revise them when needed. The plan should be dynamic, not static.
- **Understand your leadership population and their concerns:**
  o Be prepared for pushback because it's likely you will encounter it. The EAST and SCARF models can help you plan for this. Remember, you're not just trying to change the minds of leaders in your organization, but hopefully everyone else too.

- **Consistency matters:**
  - o Changing ideas takes time and consistent effort. Keep the Recency Effect in mind (i.e., people are more likely to remember things presented to them more recently than those presented a while ago).[19] You can't expect people to change their minds and behaviors if you discuss something only once or twice a year and without a hell of a big "why." This message needs to be communicated as frequently as other key ideas you want to establish in your organization, which means talking about it consistently and clearly. Most importantly, make sure your tone conveys importance, urgency when necessary, and normalcy—not forcefulness, control, or whininess. That approach fails to gain support and won't work.
- **Allow for choice and flexibility based on individual needs:**
  - o Apply key lessons from Chapter 5: the systemic and identity influences people have will shape how they perceive and experience this change. This means factoring in these influences in different ways, at various times. You won't be able to cover *every* aspect, just as I couldn't. Recognizing it is still valuable, such as understanding that people's unique experiences should be acknowledged and heard, and that the organization has a role and responsibility to be educated on how to be inclusive by considering systemic and individual identity factors in leadership mental health.

Get a Pulse on Your Leaders' Needs

How do you encourage leaders to participate? Here's a great way to start: ask what their needs are so you can tailor changes to meet them, explain why, and have them feel involved in the process so they don't feel like it's being imposed upon them without their input. Sending out an (actually) anonymous survey can be helpful to gather this data. Please, please, please: don't just send a survey with no explanation! Your survey responses will be either scant, or unhelpful, at best. Keep the SCARF model in mind, and also ensure that your survey description clearly states that it's truly anonymous, acknowledging that sharing might be uncomfortable, and emphasizing that it's truly safe to do so. Offering people the chance to have a stake in the process can increase the likelihood of participation, even though some may choose not to engage, regardless of what is offered. Some sample questions to consider:

- What are some of your top mental or emotional stressors in leadership?
- What kind of support would you find most effective or helpful for your mental health at work as a leader?
- Would connecting with other leaders in a confidential space help you feel supported? Why or why not?
- If you'd like to meet with fellow leaders, how often would you want to meet?
- Would you like to receive education on leadership mental health? If so, which topics would be helpful to learn?

You have the opportunity to break the patterns you've seen in Part I of this book—such as leaders being evaluated but overlooked in data recommendations. Ensure that your leaders understand that this data will not simply sit in a digital void, collecting virtual dust, but will be acted upon in clear, visible ways. Also, sending out these surveys isn't a one-time effort. In my opinion, it would ideally be sent out at least twice a year. Quarterly would be even better, but some people might find that a little invasive and too frequent.

For Policy, Program, & Practice Shifters

Reflection—Leadership Mental Health Strategic Planning

- Does your company's internal anonymous engagement survey include questions about leadership mental health?
- If you do not currently track leadership mental health in surveys, what questions can you add to start collecting that data?
- For longer-term strategic planning, how will you incorporate this data to take steps to strategically support your leaders' mental health?

Explain Why Mental Health Resources Need to Be Used—Not Just Their Availability

Companies usually focus on telling their workforce that resources are available, and rarely take the time to explain why (or who) should use them. Just because we say a resource is available doesn't necessarily increase people's understanding of what it is, or their willingness or comfort to use it. These resources and systems are useless if people don't use them. Whether it's using behavioral health insurance coverage, taking mental health days, or calling the employee assistance program (EAP), leaders need specific encouragement to engage with these resources rather than just referring their team members to them. This encouragement can take many forms: prescheduled digital messages, live interactions, and more. This messaging could be as simple as,

> *"Don't forget these resources are available to everyone, not just your team members. They exist for you, too."*

I wouldn't be saying this if it weren't a consistent trend I've observed. This is about normalizing resource usage, not just awareness, amongst leaders. Leaders need to understand the numerous reasons why using these resources *themselves* is beneficial and essential for their mental health, overall well-being, and effective leadership. Not just focusing on referring team members to them in their efforts to be a supportive manager. Strong leadership includes seeking help when needed. A helpful way to do that? Ensuring that leaders are addressed explicitly in the same public message that's sent to employees whenever a company reminds its workforce of these resources throughout the year. Then leaders can witness these public moments of the organization doing its part to continue dismantling the stigma around leaders discussing their mental health at work. Ensuring that leaders also get the validation, acceptance, and the care they need.

Clarity in messaging is important; don't assume people will automatically understand. They might not until they're encouraged to, for various reasons discussed in Part I. I hosted a large virtual event while writing this book, and even though I clearly stated that leaders need to utilize mental health resources for themselves and model this behavior for their team, the other panelists I spoke with essentially glossed over it and focused on how leaders should predominantly prioritize serving others. Thank you for proving my point, even though it was frustrating at the time.

Shifting Organizational Narrative—A Slow (and Paramount) Burn

In Chapter 1, we discussed the power of narrative. Reshaping a narrative requires strong, gradual, and consistent effort over time—even when facing pushback from unexpected sources. Whether it's from fellow leaders or those who have never held leadership roles and may struggle or resist relating, it's crucial to rely on logic, reason, purpose, and intended outcomes in those moments.

When we think about shifting narratives, it's more than just changing words. It involves changing ideas, mindsets, biases, and expectations. Achieving this requires *considerable* modeling, visibility, and sustained effort. Use the power of storytelling in numbers whenever feasible and practical. It will take many voices consistently working together to drive this change, not just a soloist, no matter how loud and compelling. Often, what we see in organizations regarding leaders' role modeling around mental health is meant to create social permission for *others* to speak up. This is positive; keep doing it—and don't stop. But in *this* case, leaders need to speak up for themselves. It's a concurrent need.

If we're going to change the story about leadership mental health, we need to avoid the same trap of saying it's vital and missing the opportunity to explain *why* and *how* leaders need support from others, and what they'll do to care for their own mental health, too. The goal is to humanize leaders by showing who they are, not just what we expect them to be. Here are five key messages to consider focusing on in your organizational messaging:

- *Dismantle the organizational mental health hierarchy:*
  - There must be open conversations about emotional health in the workplace at all levels. Leaders deserve to feel psychologically safe and to have their own psychological contracts to discuss their mental health at work. Psychological contracts are honored for all, including leaders.

- *Crush leadership mental health stigma:*
  - o Leadership mental health must be free from stigma, judgment, and pressure. This is precisely what employees ask to have for themselves.
- *Normalize bi-directional care:*
  - o To normalize individual contributors asking how their leaders are doing, too. Remember in Chapter 3 when I said that team members need opportunities to support their leaders, too? They do. Everyone, regardless of job title, is a chronologically aged adult and can and should be able to show up for each other. Period.
- *Remove the leadership veil:*
  - o To clarify what leaders are responsible for daily (i.e., helping people understand what's really at stake each day).
- *Include mental health management as part of leadership development:*
  - o Leaders are responsible for managing their mental health, as a crucial component of healthy, strong, and effective leadership.

There are several channels you can use to do this (focus on what is most likely to succeed at your company based on proven past, or most likely to succeed, patterns):

- *Internal Newsletters and Intranets:*
  - o Do people at your company actually read internal newsletters and engage with your intranet? Highlight thought leadership pieces, including quotes from your leaders. Try to create opportunities for employees to interact with the content, connect with colleagues, and discuss these topics with their leaders.
- *All-Hands Meetings:*
  - o Would you like to give time and space to leaders who volunteer to share at an all-hands meeting? Do it there, as a featured segment at the beginning or end of a call. Mental health is important all year round, so if you really want to make a difference, do this at any time other than World Mental Health Day in October, Stress Awareness Month in April, or during Mental Health Awareness Month in May.

If that's not feasible, that's okay; you can still do it during those times when more people are likely to pay attention, during these publicized and designated periods.

- *Email:*
  - o Do you have a strong email open rate in your company? This is a good medium where you can send messages with data and updates about how mental health will be integrated into leadership development and executive onboarding processes as part of leadership competency models. Establish a quarterly routine of sharing leadership stories, highlighting struggles alongside successes at work. Sometimes, personalized emails that are separate from "regularly scheduled programming" can resonate more, especially when it's an honest stand-alone story, rather than being placed in an email marketing template lost amongst other updates.
- *Social Media:*
  - o Does your company have a social media platform that genuinely engages and shows real change, and doesn't just post for the sake of an algorithm and social optics? If you're going to do this, it better be authentic, not just "what looks good" clickbait. That approach will backfire faster than you can imagine, trust me. The impact of video can be helpful here, particularly for an increasingly visual workforce that needs to see other humans talking, instead of just reading more content. People want to hear and see stories, to see leaders as real people, not just posed photos with carefully calculated captions.
- *Company Website:*
  - o Do you want to put your money where your mouth is and hold your company to a publicly available standard? Your company's website can be a platform for that. Too often, companies list values on their websites that they fail to follow through on. Be the change. If you want bold visibility, transparency, and accountability, your website is the perfect place to showcase how you're *actually* getting the work done through tangible actions being taken in the organization, with proof of examples and explanations of how that effort is sustained.

For **Policy, Program, & Practice Shifters**

Action Planning—Shifting Your Company's Messaging

- Does your company's internal messaging emphasize the importance of supporting leadership mental health for sustainable leadership? If not, how can you change this?
- Does your company's internal messaging share stories of leaders who used the company's mental health resources, explaining why and how they benefited from them? Do these stories showcase the strength and courage it took for these leaders to speak up? If not, how can you incorporate this?
- Can you develop targeted, segmented messaging for both your leadership team and the entire organization? If so, what would you include in both campaigns and why? What intended outcomes would you try to produce through this messaging?

Building Internal Peer Support for Leaders

"Support needs to come from people who've actually sat in the chair. That means more peer-level spaces, more protected time for leader reflection. . .If you want to support leaders, start by letting them speak to each other—without fear, without optics, and without having to make it digestible for everyone else. . .it's about safety, understanding, and shared context. Leaders need space to speak honestly, without fear of being misunderstood, judged, or having their words used against them. And that kind of space only exists when you're talking to someone who's lived it too, who's had to make the same calls, carry the same weight, and manage the same internal conflicts."

Interviewee: male, Millennial, Black, C-Suite, consulting industry

"Peer support networks and leadership communities play a huge role in promoting better mental health for leaders. For me, being part of communities with other HR leaders has been incredibly energizing. These are people who truly get it—they're facing the same challenges, juggling the

> *same emotional weight, and navigating similar organizational dynamics. What makes these spaces so valuable is the validation. You feel seen, heard, and understood. There's no need to explain the 'why' behind your stress or decisions—they just know. And that mutual support, whether it's through sharing resources, venting, or just offering encouragement, helps you feel less isolated and more grounded. These communities have become a lifeline."*
>
> Interviewee: female, Asian, Millennial, Vice President, SaaS industry

When we actively work to create change, regardless of its nature, community plays a crucial role by creating dedicated time and space for the people who need to process that change. It's essential that those affected by the change feel psychologically safe discussing their experiences with others who understand—their peers.

Developing leadership peer support networks is a vital tool to support leadership mental health at work. While many leaders recognize this, some don't or underestimate it's importance. They need to understand that their participation in such a community will be beneficial (and essential) for sustainable leadership development through leader-to-leader support, extending beyond traditional spaces for upskilling cohorts in Base Tasks and Bonus Tasks. Leadership is challenging, and having someone alongside you to discuss it and offer encouragement can make all the difference. Connecting with others and receiving support for systemic pressures, expectations, stressors, and mental health struggles can mitigate the risk of leaders feeling disconnected, suffering silently, or burning out. This peer support structure is not a form of therapy, counseling, or any other clinical service. It does not cross any inappropriate boundaries. Leadership peer support networks are dedicated spaces for mutual support, accountability, personal and group reflection, sharing coping strategies, discussing challenges, and exchanging experiences. If you're going to build this support structure for your leaders, you have the responsibility to be clear about its framework, purpose, expected outcomes, and what it is not intended to be.

It's also important to offer various group options that reflect the diverse background needs of leaders (i.e., intersectionality needs, as discussed in Chapter 5). Recognizing the unique support each leader may require, based on their identity as well as their role, can help create more tailored spaces for leadership groups within your organization. Building these communities rooted in equity also involves considering who in your leadership population might be more hesitant to participate and understanding the reasons behind their hesitation. Understanding who feels safe entering these spaces and who does not. Addressing these concerns is crucial to fostering a culture where all leaders feel psychologically safe and empowered to participate in ways that are most necessary and effective for them.

Here are some examples of key starting elements to help you plan the development of your leadership mental health peer support network:

- *Identify the group's purpose & practices:*
  - o A mission statement or shared purpose might be: "The purpose of this leadership peer support group is to give leaders the space to normalize talking about their mental health in a supportive, nonjudgmental environment of their peers."
  - o Co-created norms: i.e., confidentiality, respect, trust, open-mindedness, etc.
  - o Topics: leading through fatigue, managing burnout, Imposter Syndrome, etc.
- *Talk about participation:*
  - o Clarify that participation is voluntary and encouraged due to its demonstrable benefits. Emphasize that leaders will not face judgment or criticism for choosing not to participate. Building psychological safety and linking purpose with outcomes are essential.
- *Establish a meeting cadence:*
  - o Quarterly, monthly, etc.
- *Offer variety:*
  - o Giving leaders the option to self-assign to various groups (i.e., female leaders, BIPOC leaders, etc.)

- *Recruit internal champions to help with group maintenance and visibility:*
  o Treat this group like any other employee resource group (ERG). It shows organizational recognition, investment, and will need advocates to promote the group's efforts and visibility within the larger organization.
- *Identify group facilitators if needed:*
  o Decide whether to have a group facilitator (i.e., an internal leader willing to volunteer and receive training to lead the group, or hiring an external facilitator if the organizational budget allows for it) to guide these discussions. Alternatively, the group could have an unstructured discussion. I understand that the latter might go off topic more easily. However, not having a designated facilitator may also help the group feel more comfortable, making it seem less formal and more like a casual meeting. Regardless of the approach, the group will need to agree on rules of conduct and stick to them.
  o There are pros and cons to using both internal and external facilitators for this purpose. Regardless of whether you choose an internal or external facilitator, *someone* will have an emotional reaction to that decision. If you select an internal leader, it might provide comfort for some leaders because it's a familiar face, while others might find it invasive. If you decide to hire an external, trained facilitator with a background in psychology and group facilitation, some individuals may feel even more comfortable and willing to open up because that external person may feel "safer" being outside the organization's dynamics. That's why using a well-explained and well-designed anonymous survey to gauge overall preferences is a crucial step, as it allows you to gather data on your leaders' preferences, while understanding that you can't satisfy everyone completely.
  o If you decide to train some of your leaders to be group facilitators, remember that while it might provide those leaders with a sense of enjoyment, this will be on top of their overall workload. Additionally, you need to consider the potential for compassion fatigue that they might experience from acting as

facilitators. We often see this when individuals are trained as peer support specialists, outside of helping professions, as the emotional impact is frequently underestimated. Any high-quality training will account for and should include strategies to recognize and manage compassion fatigue.

- *How the groups will be promoted:*
  - Consider which mediums to use, such as town halls, Slack channels, Teams announcements, newsletters, or email chains. Remember the importance of social proof in this context. This is an opportunity to highlight the purpose of the group and its champions, who can share testimonials about why it matters, why they are involved, and what they hope to achieve. Doing so can increase participation, gain support, and reduce stigma.

For Policy, Program, & Practice Shifters

Action Planning—Building Your Leadership Support Network

- Which existing structures can be used to establish these leadership peer support networks?
- What kind of concerns might prevent leaders from wanting to participate?
- Who can we ask to champion this group? Why will people listen to them specifically?
- How can we ensure that the group's values and rules are maintained?
- How can we ensure the group's ongoing upkeep and consistency?

Integrating Mental Health into Leadership Development

"Training. That's not a dirty word. Ensuring there is a protocol for new leaders to run through with HR so they are aligned on company offerings and expectations of them in their new role is essential

and often missed. . .Embedding mental well-being into leadership development programs and company policies can reinforce that it's a strength, not a liability."

Interviewee: male, Millennial, Caucasian, Director, software industry

"Dispel myths and promote understanding through education."

Interviewee: female, Millennial, Black, C-Suite, heavy civil construction industry

In Part I, we discussed how most leadership development programs prioritize performance, execution, and capability, with occasional attention to maintaining overall well-being through aspects such as mindfulness, nutrition, and sleep. Integrating mental health education and practices into leadership development means making it a core element, not an optional add-on. It demonstrates that mental health is fundamental to effective, sustainable leadership, and should include clear, data-backed messaging on why it's integrated. As we've established, much of that information is already available.

This doesn't mean just training leaders to build "mental fitness." It involves teaching them critical, practical self-management methods, emphasizing the importance of acknowledging and addressing individual mental health needs, and learning how to share about their mental health at work. This can be done in leadership onboarding and in ongoing leadership development through several approaches. To keep it simple, I've highlighted two main categories to help you get started:

1. Focusing on mental health self-management as a core leadership skill
2. Developing Mental Health at Work Conversational Literacy® so they can understand the importance of asking for help, how to do that effectively, and why (more on what this is shortly)

When it comes to integrating mental health self-management as a core element of leadership development, here are some examples of what this skills training should include and why. Some helpful topics to incorporate through the leadership perspective are: the importance of emotional self-care, recognizing personal needs for psychological safety, identifying and managing stress triggers, managing Imposter Syndrome, building discomfort tolerance (a personal favorite of mine that I was on endless harangues while I wrote this book), emotional self-regulation, navigating change and uncertainty, and practical stress management—just to name a few. At their core, these skills must be maintained individually and encouraged collectively. They should not only be integrated into leadership training, but also into organizational culture as indicators of healthy leadership, emotional intelligence, maturity, and capability. Positioned as fundamental leadership competencies, these skills shape how leaders engage with themselves, their work, and those they lead. They should be regarded as equally important as every other tactical, strategic, and foundational leadership skill. The key shift is this: managing mental health as a leader is not merely an acknowledgment of personal and human needs but also an investment in a professional imperative for your career. This approach allows leaders to be effective, adaptable, and trustworthy—qualities that are already expected of them.

Let's look at the second bucket: developing Mental Health at Work Conversational Literacy®, a term I trademarked in recent years to validate the necessity and skills-based nature of this form of communication at work. Throughout my career, hundreds—if not thousands—of leaders have consistently told me that they don't know how to navigate talking about their mental health or where the boundaries are. This motivated me to create a practical, actionable educational program built on this concept to teach them: Mental Health at Work Conversational Literacy®—For Leaders.[20] I'm not sharing this program to promote it; I'm sharing it because it's designed to meet this need. If I'm going to recommend that leaders receive specific training on discussing their mental health at work, supporting their peers, and supporting their teams, then I better follow my own advice and create that education. I was tired of this program not existing, so I made it.

The customizable program emphasizes realism, personalization, and professionalism (whatever "professionalism" means these days), designed as a trainable multidirectional leadership skill to use for themselves, with their peers, and toward those they lead. Leaders learn to advocate for themselves, while helping others. The program is also built around the leadership peer model, allowing groups of leaders to undergo training together, learning and processing in a psychologically safe space among their peers. Here are the six key educational areas of the program, based on leadership skill necessity at work:

- Understanding mental health at work
- How to overcome obstacles to conversations
- How to talk about your mental health as a leader
- How to support your leadership peers
- How to support your team's mental health
- Talking about mental health during times of systemic and social change (the intersectionality lens)

From making the case, setting boundaries, to providing useful scripts for giving and receiving help for themselves and others, and offering clear signs of what productive, helpful conversations look like, the program covers it all. Any comprehensive program teaching leaders how to develop this vital conversational skill should include these elements. Side note—we'll explore in detail how individual leaders can choose to talk about their mental health with others in Chapter 8.

For Policy, Program, & Practice Shifters

Planning Leadership Mental Health Education

- Do we currently have an internal leadership development program? If yes, does it include any mental health content? If not, what modules can we add to pilot?
- If we don't have a program in place, can we implement one? How do we secure the budget? Who do I need to engage to do this?
- Who can we consult or collaborate with to ensure our leaders receive the most effective education?

We've Started Building Our Leadership Mental Health Support Solution

In Chapter 3, we discussed the data-proven negative impact on leaders' mental health, leadership capacity, and even their careers. High stress levels, burnout, and emotional exhaustion—all impacting or even impairing leaders' decision-making abilities and overall effectiveness. Recognizing these issues means addressing them. Through education, resources, and supportive peer spaces built on top of a new narrative, leaders can mitigate these risks and adverse effects by being equipped with the necessary tools and support systems to manage stress and operate healthfully in their roles. These interventions aim not only to mitigate current strain but also to promote long-term mental well-being through sustainable leadership practices. Below are the first elements added to our Leadership Mental Health Support Solution, highlighted in **bold**.

Organizational Acknowledgment of Leadership Mental Health Needs

+

Organizational Acknowledgment of the Imperative to Support Leadership Mental Health

+

Organizational Dedication to a Strategic Approach to Support Leadership Mental Health

+

Organizational Focus on Leadership Usage of Resources

+

Organizational Dedication to Shifting the Narrative About Leadership Mental Health

+

Organizational Creation of Leadership Mental Health Peer Support Networks

+

Organizational Incorporation of Mental Health Education and Upskilling into Core Leadership Development Training

We Understand the Organizational Responsibility—What About Individual Leaders?

As I mentioned earlier, change must be systemic and multidirectional. We've discussed what organizations can do, especially the individuals in key roles who have the power to influence policy, programming, and the organizational narrative. We also need to focus on the changes that individual leaders need to make, too. If an organization facilitates change and establishes structures to support leaders, then leaders need to participate actively. Now that we've covered the bigger company picture, let's focus on *you*.

In the next chapter, we'll explore the internal narrative that may influence your thoughts and behaviors related to your mental health as a leader, whether you're aware of it or not. To intentionally engage in broader changes at your company, first, you need to achieve a deeper understanding of yourself. Later in Part II, this deeper understanding will guide how you design your mental health self-care plan to address your specific needs through personalization, planning, and action.

Chapter Key Takeaways

- Organizations have a Duty of Care to support their leaders' mental health at work.
- There are organizational strategic benefits to prioritizing leadership mental health.
- Leaders need community for their mental health—companies can create these spaces.
- Companies can support leadership mental health in several ways, including shifting the organizational narrative, establishing leadership peer support networks, and incorporating mental health education into leadership development training.
- Leaders need to develop Mental Health at Work Conversational Literacy® as a leadership skill, for themselves, their peers, and their teams.

7

Understanding Your Internal Narrative and Leadership Mental Health Archetype

> *"Somewhere along the way, we decided that the best leaders are the ones who feel the least or the ones who grind the hardest. . .and never show pain. That myth has become our measuring stick. And it's killing us. . .When we treat our pain like weakness, we pass that belief down the ladder. But when we own it, honor it, and grow from it—we give everyone permission to do the same."*
>
> Interviewee: male, Gen X, Caucasian, senior leadership, construction industry

IN CHAPTER 6, WE talked about how organizations can and should build structures, support systems, and shift the narrative to promote leadership mental health. If you're going to take part in that change process, whether for the first time or in a new way, you need to check in with yourself about how you feel about this new kind of participation. In this chapter, I want you to look inward. To gather internal insights before making external decisions for yourself and others. There are three ways you can do this:

1. Understand how you feel about your mental health as a leader
2. How these feelings and beliefs might manifest through your Leadership Mental Health Archetype
3. Use these new insights to guide how you discuss your mental health at work as a leader (up next in Chapter 8)

Shifting Your Internal Narrative

Your approach to this will be very personal. I'm not asking you to go from 0 to 60 right away, or to completely change how you see yourself, who you are, or how you talk about mental health. It's entirely your choice how, or even if, you want to change the way you think about your mental health in the context of your leadership, how you handle it, and if you ask for help.

Here's my ask: do the reflection work. Be willing to engage in a very honest conversation with yourself. That may be tough or uncomfortable, but the most important things that usually help us in the long run are. I'm asking you to actively participate in your own growth so that your mental health and career trajectory can withstand your leadership journey. This will require you to examine, and in some cases, confront and replace the habits, myths, fears, and beliefs you hold if you want to shift how they impact your behaviors.

Remember, we're working to repair a potentially damaged foundation, so you don't continue to sink into the cracks. You deserve a more self-compassionate internal framework for your mental health as a leader. To begin, let's ensure you're operating with a healthy and reasonable set of internal assumptions and determine if those need updating. When it comes to holistic big-feeling changes like these, that process needs structure. Humans aren't naturally built to look at things this way—that's why an approach steeped in targeted reflection with a planned strategy for change is needed.

Assess and Rebuilding Your Internal Narrative About Leadership Mental Health

Your first step is to complete the following reflection exercise, built on some of your reflections from Chapter 1, and determine if your beliefs about your mental health as a leader need to be revised. These "rules" and myths are deeply ingrained in leaders, for all the reasons we discussed in Part I. You must acknowledge these perceived truths and *your* story as you shift your narrative. Who you are is layered. Take the time to understand how you arrived at your "operating system" because you can't update it if you don't first see what you're working with and how it currently functions for you.

Reflection Exercise—Where Am I Now?

Reflect on the following questions and document your answers:

Building on my reflection answers from Chapter 1 and the Part I Individual Reflection Exercise,

- How have the beliefs and experiences I've identified influence my current internal narrative about my mental health as a leader?

- What does my internal narrative sound like? What thoughts does it produce? (i.e. "Struggling means I'm failing," or "Strong leaders shouldn't need this kind of help.")

- Based on my Statement of Intention and Declaration to Myself from the Part I Individual Reflection Exercise, why do I feel I currently maintain this internal narrative? Healthy or not, what function does that "serve" and why?

You wouldn't believe what you just reflected on unless you were taught or motivated to believe it for a reason. There's always a reason. Whether to protect your professional reputation, career, ego, or how others perceive you at work; don't feel bad if you've felt this way. Remember, you are a collection of moments, parts of your identity, and the various systems in which you operate. You didn't become this way on your own. However, you also have the responsibility to recognize these messages, how they affect your mental health at work, how you show up as a leader, and to decide if you want to update them—and why. Here's the hard truth: these assumptions and beliefs may serve to protect you in some way as a leader, but they may ultimately hurt and isolate you as a person. These behaviors and assumptions don't make you "stronger"; they may just be helping you get by. Now, it's time to ask yourself where you want to take your beliefs and why, building on your reflections from Chapter 2, and again, on your Part I Individual Reflection Exercise.

Reflection Exercise—Where Do I Want to Go?

Based on my reflections so far about my beliefs and behaviors surround-ing my mental health as a leader, and the Statement of Intention and Declaration to Myself that I created:

- Should I be more self-compassionate about my mental health as a leader? Why?

- Do I believe that my mental health as a leader should matter to those I lead? Why?

- Do I see supporting my mental health as part of effective leadership? Why?

- Do I think prioritizing my mental health is part of being a "good" leader? Why?

- What is my ultimate "why" for changing my internal narra-tive about my mental health as a leader?

Now that you've identified how your current narrative about your mental health as a leader compares to the Statement of Intention you set for yourself earlier in this book—let's look at your current workplace behaviors, how they affect you, and a different path forward using the Leadership Mental Health Archetypes. This approach will help you see your current behaviors related to your mental health as a leader, why they exist, and the contrast of what the healthier goal looks like for you instead.

Understanding Your Leadership Mental Health Archetype

> *"I would rather deal with the predictable pain of suffering in silence than the unpredictable and often worse pain of trying to be understood. . .My explicit strategy now is to lie. I'm always okay. I'm always good. There are no problems. Because I've found that self-sufficiency—however isolating—is a more reliable source of stability and peace than hoping for support that never really comes"*
>
> Interviewee: male, Millennial, Black, C-suite, consulting industry

Whenever I teach workshops on practical stress management, I encourage participants to identify the "stress story" they tell themselves—the reasons or even excuses they repeat and internalize about why they can't or shouldn't manage their stress consistently. I've heard some real doozies that are so self-destructive and deeply ingrained that I genuinely worry about how these people function. This is such a common occurrence that I ensure participants—especially leaders—take the time to slow down, recognize the story, understand why it needs to change, and have clear reasons for doing so. Drawing from experiences throughout my career, I've developed these Leadership Mental Health Archetypes to give leaders a "complete picture" they can connect those stories to, helping them see the full scope of where they are and why.

These archetypes offer a straightforward way to visualize your internal narrative about leadership mental health through specific, relatable examples. I encourage you to see this framework as the story you tell yourself, based on the common default behaviors and thoughts you most often engage in. These thoughts and behaviors reveal how you view and present yourself at work, particularly in relation to your mental health as a leader, whether consciously or unconsciously. Ultimately, influencing how you relate to others, talk about, or seek help for your mental health, or why you may avoid doing so.

Just as you can recognize your archetype, you also have the power and responsibility to challenge and change it if needed. We become attached to identities based on the ongoing stories we tell ourselves, those others tell us, or a mix of both. However, these archetypes aren't fixed identities; they are learned beliefs and behaviors that you have developed. Over time, you can rewrite your story in ways that support your mental health at work. If you became one archetype, you can become another.

Identifying Your Leadership Mental Health Archetype

I thought carefully about how I wanted to construct these. I gathered countless moments from throughout my career when I've worked with leaders, even while writing this book. Here are the seven I've selected, including their meanings, how they manifest at work, their benefits, and their challenges. The last archetype on this list is the "healthy goal."

- The Ostrich
- The Grain Mill
- The Insecurity Masker
- The Mother Hen or Father Goose
- The Frustrated Martyr
- The Porcupine
- The Sea Otter (the healthy goal)

Each of these archetypes, even the Sea Otter, can pose risks if not actively managed, such as poor mental health, social misunderstandings, impaired leadership skills, or overall decreased functioning. Remember: your archetype not only affects you, but can also impact those around you, both at work and outside of it.

You might see yourself in several of these archetypes, with some overlap depending on your circumstances at work. I encourage you to choose the archetype that feels most accurate to you, instinctively. Intuition is one of our greatest, yet often overlooked, strengths; trust it. These are meant to be broad, conceptual types. If none of them seem to fit, that's okay! If you find that you consistently embody two types, or none seem appropriate, that's also fine. Then I encourage you to create your own using the same template. The point is not to "self-diagnose" or cling to a profile. Like any other form of self-assessment, the purpose of it is to show you a set of behaviors that have developed, why, how they may help you sometimes, and how they may potentially set you back. Ultimately, enabling you to determine if you want or need to shift those behaviors, and why.

The Ostrich

What This May Mean: You tend to overlook mental health struggles overall, hoping they'll pass or disappear without help. You may acknowledge that you have them, but it's uncomfortable to face or discuss with others, for various reasons. You might avoid taking the time to recognize your mental health needs. You may dislike the discomfort that comes with struggle and often hope it will go away on its own if you distract yourself enough with other things.

How This Can Show Up at Work: Even when you're obviously struggling, whether to yourself or others, you pretend everything is F.I.N.E. (remember from Chapter 1?). You might avoid discussing mental health at work altogether, either by casually brushing it off or quickly changing the subject when it comes up. You may steer clear of these conversations because they might make you uncomfortable, maybe because you feel like you're under a microscope or facing challenging emotions, including meeting your own needs, even if it means ignoring signs of burnout or staying in it.

The Positives: Even when times are tough at work or you're stressed out, you're probably quite resilient and good at compartmentalizing. You tend to keep moving forward, and your team does too, during crises as long as they aren't focused on how you're doing.

The Negatives: Even if resources are available, you might hesitate to use them. You are one of those people who may delay addressing their feelings until you explode. You might feel reluctant to speak up because, when you do, it often doesn't go well. This is not only unhealthy and stressful for you, but it can also create an emotionally unsafe environment for those you lead. An unintentional negative effect on your team is that they might also feel they can't express themselves to you, because you rarely (if ever) reveal your feelings. You may unintentionally model emotional avoidance related to mental health.

The Grain Mill

What This May Mean: You might think that your productivity protects you and that grinding through stress and struggle is the only way forward. Taking a moment to address your mental health or stress management needs might seem like a distraction and could slow you down, undermining your overall purpose at work. You may see your ability to grind as a sign of strength and capability, making you feel worthy of handling the pressures of leadership. You are likely to equate the amount you produce and achieve with your self-worth, believing that your mental health in a leadership role isn't essential.

How This Can Show Up at Work: You may display high performance levels to hide your emotional struggles and tend to immerse yourself even more in work when overwhelmed (i.e., to channel your internal struggle). You might even ask for additional tasks and hide in your work, using your increased output as a badge of honor for pushing yourself further. You may rely on these accomplishments to comfort yourself, believing you are capable of achieving more even when you're not feeling good inside. You might avoid participating in mental health conversations because, in your view, they are "not part" of productivity or what's "necessary" at work.

The Positives: Your team and organization see you as the emotionally impenetrable—the way history intended. You're likely known for being "that leader" who, regardless of what's happening, *always* gets things done without a peep. You are viewed as consistently dependable and highly committed, always exceeding and never missing deadlines, regardless of what's happening in your personal life.

The Negatives: You may dehumanize yourself and make it seem like your mental health needs don't exist and shouldn't need to. You unintentionally glamorize self-sacrifice and burnout, creating unhealthy, unrealistic standards for productivity without prioritizing mental health self-management—setting a potentially unhealthy example for those you lead. Your hidden internal struggles are likely often met with admiration and praise for your relentless hustle. You might avoid using mental health resources because you may believe you don't need them, and you shouldn't feel you do. Your mindset risks leading you down a slippery slope into burnout or potentially altering your career path in ways you didn't intend, as your nervous system and mental health will ultimately make that decision for you.

The Insecurity Masker

What This May Mean: You might already feel uncertain about your role as a leader and worry that talking about your mental health struggles could give others more reasons to doubt you. You may underestimate how much effort you put into becoming a leader. You might think that sharing your mental health issues could lead others to see you as weak, incapable, or unqualified. This could seem familiar if you already deal with feelings of Imposter Syndrome (i.e., doubting your abilities despite clear evidence of your success that you've worked for).[1]

How This Can Show Up at Work: Depending on your personality type, you might resort to unhealthy coping behaviors to hide your internal struggles. This can include outright lying to others about how you're doing or overcompensating with positive emotions when you're feeling like s**t inside. You might use high levels of perfectionism or overperformance to mask your struggles so others "won't find you out." Additionally, you may avoid being transparent about your mental health because you see doing so as too risky a disclosure.

The Positives: You prioritize maintaining your credibility within your organization and actively engage in Impression Management. You're likely a high performer and are recognized for your consistent "can-do" attitude. Given your private struggles related to self-doubt, you may also utilize mental health support services to help you explore and navigate them.

The Negatives: You may feel uncomfortable if others question whether your optimism is authentic. You may not disclose to anyone that you seek mental health support as a leader, which could unintentionally reinforce a culture of silence in leadership—teaching others that admitting to mental health struggles makes a leader an "impostor," even if that's not your intention. Those you lead might also feel they need to wear that same mask because they see you doing it.

The Mother Hen or Father Goose

What This May Mean: You may believe that the most important use of your energy is to care for and look out for others' well-being. You are likely to often focus on genuinely supporting others' mental health and helping them manage their stress. You may see yourself as the emotional savior and protector of others because you believe they need you and may not be able to do it without you. You may even subscribe to Servant Leadership, or believe that part of being a leader is serving as a shield for those you lead.

How This Can Show Up at Work: You might be viewed as the "parental" type within your team, division, or even organization. As a parent-like protector, you're likely the go-to person for emotional support or shielding for others at work. You ensure that those you lead don't face emotional discomfort if you can help them avoid it, and you typically don't check in on yourself or ask others for support. When people check on you, you may respond politely with something like, *"Oh gosh, I'm fine, let's talk about what you need!"* You tend to be a caring fixer-type, trying to lift the burden off others because, if you can, you feel you've done your part for the day.

The Positives: You are likely very compassionate and empathetic, making great efforts to ensure those you lead feel psychologically safe with you. You ensure that everyone who works for you knows they can always approach you with anything happening in their lives, so you can determine how to support them best or help them access the necessary resources. You're recognized as one of the "good" ones—someone who goes above and beyond in the Base Tasks and Bonus Tasks when it comes to acknowledging mental health, encouraging self-care, and using emotional intelligence.

The Negatives: You may live an inch away from burnout but convince yourself that's what being in the service of others looks like. You might teach those you lead that only their mental health matters, even if it means that they keep standing on your shoulders while you sink. You may show them that you are, and will only be, their supporter, and that you never need support in return. You may experience compassion fatigue and struggle to acknowledge it. You might unintentionally create an emotional dependency on you from others at work, but you may also enjoy being needed that way. You may deprioritize your needs because your primary driver is to be needed by others.

The Frustrated Martyr

What This May Mean: You may believe that self-sacrifice is a natural aspect of leadership, but feel conflicted about it. You dedicate yourself fully to being a leader and supporting your team, while potentially secretly resenting this sacrifice. You may think your suffering demonstrates your commitment to leadership. Consistently putting your needs last gives you a sense of pride, even if it hurts.

How This Can Show Up at Work: When other leaders healthfully set boundaries to protect their well-being, or even people on your team, you might verbally tell them it's okay, but there's often an undertone of, *"But what about me?"* (i.e., passive-aggressive guilting) since you don't openly express your needs like they do. You may frequently decline help from others, push yourself to exhaustion, burnout, and high stress levels, yet you wear those signs of emotional suffering as a badge of honor, feeling others expect you to. Because if not you, then who? You may quietly wish that things were different, but you are afraid of what that could mean or what it would look like. You may make your team and others feel like you'll always be there for them, but likely with a "poor me" attitude undertone, sending mixed signals of support and manipulation.

The Positives: You are likely very loyal, dedicated, selfless, and supportive. You are committed to your team's success. Your team and leadership colleagues usually acknowledge your unwavering dedication to your work, the company's mission, and those you lead, often commenting on how deeply you care and show up for others. You may or may not be open to seeking emotional health support through counseling or other mental health resources because of the hard truths you may need to face. Still, you might resist feedback on the importance of letting go of self-sacrificing behaviors because it could be too painful or uncomfortable to explore.

The Negatives: You might handle emotional struggles in an unhealthy way. You may neglect your own emotional needs, signs of burnout, and ongoing stress in ways that are unintentionally harmful to yourself. A key risk with this archetype is that ignoring your emotional needs could eventually lead to emotional problems, resentment toward those you lead, and frustration from peers who choose not to follow your example. You might also create a dependency from others that you don't want or need. Additionally, you may unintentionally set a tone of unhealthy self-sacrifice, which others may interpret differently, and you might inadvertently set an example you don't intend to. Lastly, you might cause hesitation in others about trusting you, especially if there are strings attached, such as supporting someone when they open up, but then guilt-tripping them later, which defeats the purpose of them turning to you in the first place.

The Porcupine

What This May Mean: You might feel that being open and honest about struggles, or discussing your mental health, runs the risk of having misunderstandings or complications. As a result, you might keep others at a distance in many parts of your life—not just at work. You may have learned at some point in your life that trusting others doesn't go well, so you choose to utilize avoidance, even if you're suffering in silence.

How This Can Show Up at Work: You might keep your colleagues and team members at a distance because you don't want to discuss something so personal like mental health with anyone at work. You might use stonewalling[2] (i.e., shutting down) or defensiveness to avoid being honest about how you feel, to prevent the feeling of vulnerability that comes with that process. You may emotionally protect yourself with withdrawal, sarcasm, or even snippy anger if someone asks how you're doing. You might resist or rebuff offers of supportive conversations in a rude or snappy way, verbally stinging others when you feel under pressure from work, making people ultimately regret trying to support you. You may feel more psychologically safe when others don't get too close to you, and they probably think the same way, based on how you treat them.

The Positives: You are likely known for being independent and self-sufficient, and you tend to perform best when left to your own devices. Most people at work are clear about your boundaries and expect you not to discuss your mental health as a leader. Sometimes, you may feel resentful about this topic and hesitate to support others because you weren't given the same courtesy in your life, which may lead you to avoid the topic altogether. In other cases, you might be willing to care for others when they struggle with their mental health, but you may also be hesitant in case that conversation shifts toward you.

The Negatives: You may unintentionally damage professional relationships at work and alienate those who might want to support you. You might block opportunities for supportive conversations from all directions. Others may develop a narrative about you that sounds like, "don't ask how they are, you'll regret it." Additionally, you might give off the impression of active emotional suppression and stuck in a cycle you're unwilling to change. You may also be hesitant to seek counseling or mental health support because, based on previous lessons that taught you it's unsafe, you feel uncomfortable asking for help.

The Sea Otter (The Healthy Goal)

What This May Mean: You likely value emotional connection, honesty, and vulnerability with others both in general and at work. You recognize the importance of feeling psychologically safe and see the benefits of community; you tend to create and pursue opportunities for both. You understand that, as a functioning adult and leader, it's essential to be emotionally and cognitively adaptable through consistent mental health self-care practices.

How This Can Show Up at Work: You are likely recognized as someone who understands that sustainable leadership relies on mental health self-management and honesty about that process. You probably openly communicate that self-sacrifice in leadership is unhealthy. Colleagues can easily understand your values, perceive you as resilient, and know you take breaks when necessary. You're likely to set clear boundaries but are also willing to be flexible when needed. You usually act in a clear, communicative, and transparent manner. You likely demonstrate to your team and other leaders that it's safe to be emotionally vulnerable and that doing so is a strength in leadership.

The Positives: You demonstrate what it means, and that it's okay, to be a mixed bag of a human at work, especially in a leadership role. You show what it looks like to have a healthy integration of emotional stability, struggles, and successes. You are likely to care for your team and expect that they understand you also need care and rest. You ensure your team shares and cultivates a culture of mutual care, encouraging other leaders to do the same. If someone makes you feel guilty for prioritizing your mental health at work, you have no problem telling them why that's unhealthy and unreasonable, and then encourage them to examine their own biases and beliefs that lead them to say such things. You are likely to engage in teachable moments when people speak about mental health in ways that are disrespectful or incorrect, making sure to help them see why their words can harm trust and psychological safety at work.

The Negatives: Some people might mistakenly view your comfort with talking about mental health or your vulnerability as a sign of weakness. If they treat you that way, you may quickly respond with a firm rebuttal for making that wrongful assumption. When someone challenges your perspective on the importance of mental health at work, both for yourself or others, you might become verbally aggressive or forceful in defending why you approach mental health this way, causing them to feel like you're always ready to debate rather than discuss differences of opinion. In simple terms, your honesty and values may be intense for people who don't share those feelings and who might be nervous or hesitant to act differently for various reasons.

Reflection Exercise—Your Leadership Mental Health Archetype

- Which archetype(s) feel like me? How does this show up at work?

- What messages, experiences, or people shaped me into this archetype at work?

- How does my archetype serve me at work, whether healthfully or not? Is this sustainable?

- Have I always fit this archetype? Did my archetype evolve at any point in my career? If so, when and why?

Does this archetype:

- Affect my willingness to seek support for my mental health as a leader?

- Impact my willingness or permission to use mental health resources or participate in broader discussions about leadership and mental health at work?

- Influence my readiness to support my team members' mental health at work?

- Affect my willingness to support fellow leaders with their mental health at work?

Use Your Insights to Move Toward Your Healthy Leadership Mental Health Archetype

What ultimately matters is this: finding healthy ways to talk about your mental health as a leader and engaging in healthy practices to maintain it, too. No one can tell you how and why to do that except yourself. It will remain unchanged if you don't try to shift it, especially if you know you should. Whatever those reasons are, they are valid, personal, and important to you. If you want to shift toward a healthy Leadership Mental Health Archetype, it will take time. It took a significant amount of time for you to become the person you are now, including your beliefs, feelings, and behaviors regarding your mental health as a leader. As a result, it will also take time to change it. In Part I, you already decided that you need to make some changes, why, and what potential success could look like for you. You've identified your Leadership Mental Health Archetype. Now, it's time to determine the archetype you want to become, why, and how you'll get there.

Reflection Exercise—Shifting to My "Goal" Archetype

- Why do I want to be more like the Sea Otter (or the archetype I've outlined)?

- What do I want to experience from this archetype change?

- What specific changes and actions will I need to take to achieve this on a day-to-day basis?

- How will I hold myself accountable for this change?

- How will I explain to the people I trust at work why I'm making this change? And how can they support me?

- How should I explain this change to my team members so they understand why I'm making it?

- Will this change affect how I show up for others at work?

- Will this change how I might ask for support for my mental health at work?

Let the answers you've discovered in this chapter guide and support you in how you navigate these changes over time. Knowing your current archetype and goals will help you shift how you view and treat your mental health as a leader—which will impact you and those around you. Let's do a check-in on our Leadership Mental Health Solution, with the new elements, added in **bold,** below:

Individual Leaders Shifting to a Healthy Internal Narrative About Their Mental Health

+

Individual Leaders Identifying Their Leadership Mental Health Archetype

+

Individual Leaders Using Their Leadership Mental Health Archetype to Shift Their Beliefs and Behaviors at Work

Discovering and potentially shifting your Leadership Mental Health Archetype isn't the end of the Leadership Mental Health Support Solution. We're not just aiming to change your internal monologue; that's just gaining insight without creating change. To make reading this book worthwhile, your answers in this chapter must translate into action. If you want to create ripple effects, it all depends on what these insights mean to you and how you act on them. You get to decide how you apply this information. To support your ongoing growth around this topic, a consistent commitment to your awareness, and recognition that it requires regular care and reflection, is critical. If you ever find yourself slipping back into old archetype patterns, that's ok. You can't undo old mental pathways, but you can create new ones by consistently and gently reminding yourself of your long-term goals. Next up, we'll explore how you can specifically do that, through the conversations you have and the actions you can take at work.

Chapter Key Takeaways

- Understanding your internal narrative about leadership mental health is essential.
- Your Leadership Mental Health Archetype can be dynamic, not static. It isn't a permanent identity.
- Understanding why you want to change your archetype will be connected to your success of being able to do so.
- Knowing your Leadership Mental Health Archetype can help you identify which leadership mental health behaviors you need to change at work.
- Becoming the Sea Otter (or archetype of your choosing) is a long-term endeavor that requires insight, maintenance, and commitment.

8

How Leaders Can Create Change for Themselves and Their Peers

"It wasn't until I made the call to my boss to share my own struggles that the miraculous flood gate opened, and real change happened in our organization. My openness impacted me so greatly that I felt empowered to share my story with all leaders across our organization in hopes they would also feel empowered to be open about their own mental health struggles."

Interviewee: female, Baby Boomer, Caucasian, Director, beauty industry

"When you're the glue, others have a hard time seeing you as a finite resource, so unless other leaders step in with a strategy to share that burden, the result is burnout, resentment, or leaving. . .while there are times when one may be a 'captain,' one cannot persist in that capacity without support."

Interviewee: male, Millennial, Caucasian, Director, technology industry

BUILDING ON YOUR new insights from Chapter 7, we'll now focus on transforming the conversations you have with others in various ways and highlight the essential role that individual leaders play in driving that change. We will focus on how you can help reshape the narrative around leadership mental health, participate in your leadership community, model these changes without compromising credibility, and shift how you discuss your mental health at work—using the approach that best suits you. If you want to be the Sea Otter, you're going to have to talk and act like it, too. Pretty fun imagery to think about, right?

Various reflection questions and action-based exercises are included in this chapter to help you personalize your journey, enabling you to become both the creator and the beneficiary of new conversational norms and practices around leadership mental health at work. But first, let's take a quick pit stop for a reality check.

Why Leaders Must Personally Participate in Creating This Change

> "Once you reach a certain level of success, people assume everything is good. . .That's the thing about being a leader—your challenges are never seen as your own. They're always refracted through other people's lenses."
>
> Interviewee: male, Millennial, Black, C-suite, consulting industry
>
> "We shift the narrative by telling the truth and elevating the leaders who are doing the hard, inner work and not defaulting to the hard, outer grind. We need to show unapologetically that courage doesn't mean pushing through at all costs. It's about pausing when necessary. Asking for help. Admitting, 'I don't have it all together right now.' And still showing up."
>
> Interviewee: male, Gen X, Caucasian, senior leadership, construction industry

I'll be honest with you: support systems designed for leaders will stay ineffective unless individual leaders actively participate and help sustain them. While some leaders will build and maintain these systems, others can't just sit back as passive or uninvolved recipients. That's like leaders leaving other leaders stranded in the ocean.

If It's Built, and No One Comes, It Will Fail

"Having vocal leadership sponsorship of company-wide mental health initiatives demonstrates the importance of them and can encourage other leaders to actively engage in the conversations around this topic."

Interviewee: female, Gen X, Black, Director, consulting industry

Each leader has the responsibility and opportunity to help co-create these changes within their community, building and sustaining this movement. Every leader can decide how and when they will participate, whatever that means and looks like for them. Ideas and outcomes won't change just because systems are in place. They will change when people act differently. Think of it this way: if the system is the proverbial stage, then leaders are the actors bringing the structure to life, supporting what they claim to stand for. Not as a performance, but as voices for those who need to be heard, watched, listened to, and included in their efforts. The goal? Ensuring that supporting leadership mental health isn't just a good practice but an expected one.

I realize that being more vocal and visible about your mental health as a leader can evoke strong feelings or concerns for you. We discussed copious reasons in Part I for why you might (rightfully) feel this way. Your fears and concerns are valid. Acknowledge them; they are trying to tell you something. And, don't let them prevent you from making a change. What's important is recognizing them, understanding their origins, and deciding what to do with them. You need to decide how, or if, you engage with the topic of leadership mental health in your company to challenge the unhealthy, outdated, and unsustainable norms that weigh on you as both a person and a leader. All I ask is that you reflect on whether what you're doing now is sustainable for you. If it's not, consider that a different approach might be needed. Let's start with why, before examining how.

Your Why Will Drive Your How

> *"I kept waiting for someone else to fill the gaps I saw. Someone to do what needed to be done. But they didn't show up. So I did."*
>
> Interviewee: male, Gen X, Caucasian, senior leadership, construction industry
>
> *"I am not afraid to go where others feel uncomfortable, to have fierce conversations, and to be a courageous leader. I encourage and empower others to voice their feelings, share their struggles, because life is not meant to be experienced alone. We are in it together, and I am there for the good and the bad."*
>
> Interviewee: female, Millennial, Mexican-American, Elementary Principal, public education industry

Back to Cialdini's Laws of Influence from Chapter 1, because they apply here. You have organizational visibility, and that will influence your decisions about how visible you are (or are willing to be) regarding leadership mental health. As a leader, you serve as a signal within your organization, not just a title. Your position affects how you influence others, not only through your decisions but also by how you present yourself. As discussed in Chapter 1, people are highly perceptive of leadership behavior. This includes how you help shape their perception of your humanity as a leader and the importance of leadership mental health.

Your behavior, words, and even silence speak louder than anything else ever could. Cialdini's Law of Social Proof tells us that people tend to look to others' actions and behaviors to determine their own, especially when they're uncertain.[1] If you want to have a chance at being humanized and want the rest of your organization to care about leadership mental health, they will need to see you advocating for it. And when you act "as if," (no, not from the film *Clueless*, I mean the concept from Dr. Alfred Adler[2]), the goal will be to act how you want to act based on how you want things to be as if you've already overcome this potential challenge, even if you aren't there internally or externally—yet. Let me explain.

Dr. Adler was just as influential as Sigmund Freud (he didn't get the same press). Adler was a pioneer in the fields of individual psychology and community psychology, coining many concepts that people use today without knowing who to cite or thank, such as the influence of birth order on behavior[3] and the concept of having a Napoleon Complex (i.e., an inferiority complex[4]), among others. I earned my master's degree at the then-Adler School of Professional Psychology, now known as Adler University. What I truly value about my former Adlerian training, which continues to support me in my industrial–organizational psychology work, is that Adler saw people within the systems they exist in, not as isolated beings in their own worlds. This perspective feels especially relevant when discussing how leaders present themselves in relation to their mental health within various systems, particularly at work. Part of Adler's theories were driven by the human desire to escape feelings of inferiority, pursue achievement, and seek social connection. If that isn't a valuable framework for understanding the internal and external conflicts leaders face for talking about their mental health, then I don't know what is.

If you want to establish a clear psychological permission structure for leadership mental health for yourself and other leaders in your company, you need to model it. As a new leadership strength, rooted in courage and resolve, demonstrating your humanity and self-awareness. There are several approaches to take, depending on the available resources and your level of comfort. This is a very personal journey for you, and you must decide when you're ready to start and how. We'll explore a variety of options in this chapter that you can choose from.

Reflection Exercise—Leadership Mental Health Role Modeling

If you had to choose one way to begin shifting the narrative around leadership mental health at your company, what would it be?

- Why would you feel comfortable with that method?

- What would you want to share and why?

- What do you hope people would learn from you speaking up?

- What would a small win or success look like after you've shared?

Set Realistic Expectations

Will your disclosures and efforts be immediately well-received? Maybe yes, maybe no. Will it require effort, repetition, and courage on your part? Absolutely. Just as it took a lot of time to reach our current position with this narrative, it will also take time and many voices, including yours, to normalize a new narrative about the leadership experience of mental health. How, when, and why you do this—when executed effectively—will increase the chances of achieving that outcome. A gentle reminder, as I explained to those who can influence policies, programs, and practices in Chapter 6, the same guidance applies to you: even if you're evolving in how you discuss your mental health as a leader, it doesn't mean others will keep the same pace as you. As you change how you share, others will need to adjust and shift their ideas about leadership mental health—whether they're a leader or individual contributor. Some people will be appreciative of what you share, others may be indifferent, and some may even get triggered. You can't control how it will land. All you can control is what you share, how, when, why, and your goals for opening up.

If You Want Support & To Create Change, You Need to Speak Up

It will be difficult to share what's going on with you, get the support you need, or change others' perceptions if you're not willing to do your part to facilitate that change. You can't do any of that well without sharing to some degree about your story, why it matters, and what you want people to take away from it. The more leaders who intentionally do their part, including you, the better. That's why it's helpful for as many leaders as possible to understand their Leadership Mental Health Archetype. So each person can recognize their behaviors, the messages they send at work, identify what they want to move away from, know what to aim for instead—and why.

Shifting How You Participate in Conversations

You can't keep waiting for the "right time, place, and circumstance." Sometimes, it's just about *beginning*. If you keep waiting, you may build up so much pressure that you lash out at the next person who may unintentionally push you over the edge. That isn't helpful for you, and it's certainly not beneficial for them (consider the Leadership Mental Health Archetypes; does this behavior sound familiar and is it something you want to stop?). As I mentioned in the Introduction, let's start by addressing any concerns or fears you might have and discussing ways to work through and overcome them.

Before You Open Up, Work Through Your Concerns First

Before you act, take a moment to assess your current situation. This will help you identify any concerns you may have and determine your readiness to get involved—regardless of the path you choose. Answering these questions beforehand will hopefully you feel more settled (as much as you can be, anyway) as you build your plan of how you'll intentionally change your conversations and behaviors at work around this topic. Preparation and self-reflection are essential, rather than cannon-balling into the unknown conversational abyss. Remember, you have more control and influence in this process than you might realize. Take a moment to honestly reflect on the questions below to gain a deeper understanding of your feelings about engaging in these new behaviors and conversations at work:

Reflection Exercise—Where Are You Now?

Do I feel ready to share about my mental health as a leader?

- Why do I want to discuss my mental health as a leader? What do I hope to achieve by doing this?

- What concerns do I have about this process, and where do they come from?

- Am I worried about any possible consequences? What are they?

- Who can I talk to about my concerns, and how should I ask for their support?

- What do I need to feel psychologically safe enough to move past these concerns?

Remember, as a leader, you also deserve and need psychological safety around your mental health at work, which sometimes means creating it for yourself and asking for it from others. This way, you can feel supported and receive the help you need before, during, and after these conversations—just as others probably ask of you. If you feel like you need to learn how to do this in a more structured manner, remember the Mental Health at Work Conversational Literacy® program I mentioned in Chapter 6 where I encouraged organizations to provide this education to leaders? They can provide that education, but it's your responsibility to learn it. In cases where organizations "don't know what they don't know," it's your responsibility to tell them what you need to learn.

Overcome the Leadership Mental Health Paradox: Learn to Receive Help

Just as seeking help is essential, it's equally vital to allow others to provide it to you. In Chapters 4 and 5, we explored several leadership mental health lessons from *The Pitt*. I'm revisiting the series, again, because it clearly illustrates aspects of a leadership mental health paradox, the successes, failures, everything in between, and shows how incredibly beneficial it is when help is received in a safe environment.

What I love most about this show, and there are many things, is that it highlights the importance of not experiencing leadership mental health struggles in isolation. It demonstrates how grueling it can be to navigate the intense tension and challenges of leadership, even during a personal crisis. There was a powerful scene where Noah Wyle's character was hysterically crying in a closed room and on the verge of a panic attack. One of his new interns saw him through the window and entered to check on him and offer comfort. Wyle's character was visibly embarrassed and uncomfortable, not wanting someone he leads to see him in such a state of emotional disarray. However, his intern stayed with him and held space for him, not as a leader, but as a person. Ultimately, the intern encouraged Wyle to center himself, get up off the floor, and return to the ER floor, because his team and patients needed him. This scene demonstrated how we can, and should, make space for leaders when they need support, showing that their leadership isn't questioned when they accept help.

In a later scene of the same episode, the show also did a phenomenal job of showcasing the complexities of the "where do we go from here?" moments that can follow situations like this at work. The same intern told Wyle's character, in front of another leader, that he didn't want to burden him by asking for help on a case because he knew Wyle had been having a tough day and he was trying to be considerate of that. What was clearly intended as an act of care by his team member was received by Wyle's character as a doubt in his emotional consistency, fearing that his disclosure was being held over his head, especially when this exchange then happened in front of another leader (who did not judge him either, by the way). In a later episode of the show, and without giving away any spoilers, Wyle's character also addressed the entire ER team after a particularly challenging situation occurred at the clinic, impacting the entire clinical staff. Wyle allowed himself to get emotional in front of everyone and encouraged them to acknowledge and honor whatever complicated feelings were coming up for them, too. This was role modeling at its best, not just in serving others, but also in serving to humanize himself to his team.

What do these two juxtaposed scenes show us? A leadership mental health paradox and the genuine dilemma it presents. How contradictory and complex it can feel to show that you need support as a leader in the moment and in the moments that follow. It takes courage to be honest as a struggling leader while trying to preserve your reputation and credibility. It takes bravery to accept help from others, even from those who aren't in leadership roles. All of this, though it sounds dichotomous, is portrayed with beautiful clarity in a way I sincerely hope the show's creators and actors recognize.

When leaders experience, and demonstrate, that it is safe to receive help, whether from other leaders or team members, it can inspire other leaders to accept support, too. This involves being open to conversations when someone checks in on you. It includes allowing other leaders or even team members to take things off your plate when they offer. It also means letting others know you appreciate their concern if they check in on you. It means acknowledging that you don't want to, and shouldn't have to, carry the emotional burdens of leadership or the challenges of life outside of work alone. This builds trust and demonstrates that mutual care directed toward leaders isn't only appreciated but also necessary and encouraged.

If people are checking in on you, whether they are leaders or team members, that's great! It means they're already ahead of the curve, see you as a human behind the role, not just the title. If you feel ready to accept help, do your part to make the other person feel appreciated for the care they're giving you, especially if they've never offered before or you previously turned them down. What could this sound like in the moment? Let's look at two common scenarios:

- *Scenario*: A team member checks on you because you seem stressed:
  o Your response:
    - *"Thank you for asking. It's been a really tough week. I don't know what I need yet, but you checking in on me is helpful. Can I get back to you later?"*
      • *What this approach accomplishes*: It shows that you acknowledge they've tried to support you, explains you're not ready to receive it, and ensures they know it has nothing to do with them. This creates an opportunity for

another conversation later, and you're letting them know you want to do that when you're in the right headspace and have the words for it.

- *"Thank you for being willing to support me. I realize it might feel a bit odd since I'm your manager, but I appreciate you checking on me. If you can do [insert a reasonable task for a team member] or [something light they can handle], it would be helpful to me. Sound good?"*

  • *What this approach accomplishes:* You're letting your team member know you appreciate them checking on you, while acknowledging power dynamics. You're also letting them show up for you in an appropriate way by taking some tasks off your plate, without necessarily disclosing what's emotionally going on for you, depending on the scenario.

- *Scenario:* A fellow leader offers to do some projects for you because you seem overwhelmed:

  o *Your response:*

    - Option 1: *"Thanks for supporting me. It's hard for me to say I need help. Would you mind taking on A and B?"*

      • *What this approach accomplishes:* It shows your appreciation for their support, lets them know it's a difficult thing for you to do, and your willingness to move past that so they can take some work weight off your shoulders.

    - Option 2: *"Thanks for the offer. I am stressed, but I think I'm okay. If that changes and I need help, I'll let you know and appreciate that I can lean on you if I need to."*

      • *What this approach accomplishes:* It shows acknowledgment of their offer of help, but kindly sets a boundary that you don't want it, for reasons that you don't need to disclose. It also shows appreciation that they are there for you and that you can ask for help in the future.

Reflection Questions—Are You Open to Receiving Help?

If leadership colleagues or team members have offered to support you in the past, were you receptive to their help? Why or why not?

- If you weren't, what specific fears or concerns came up for you?

- How did those fears shape your response to that person?

- How would learning to accept help support your mental health and leadership capabilities at work?

- If the offer of support were to come up again, how would you respond differently next time?

Drawing Boundaries with "No"

Just as I would tell you that you cannot and should not force a team member, colleague, or anyone else to speak up about their mental health (because they don't have to), the same applies to you. Just because someone asks about your mental health or shows care does not mean you have to share with them. No matter what you are going through, this is the workplace, and you have no obligation to share your personal information or mental health experiences with others in that setting. You decide if you share, how, when, and with whom. Pay attention to how you feel day to day, because over time and as circumstances change—whether within or outside of you—your willingness to discuss this topic may shift. Be mindful of why you may not want to (i.e., is it unnecessary fear, lack of trust in a specific person who asks, etc.), because the reason matters. But how you say *"no thanks"* or a flat-out *"no"* also matters. A respectful way to say no is, *"I appreciate you checking on me. I don't really want to talk about it, thank you, though."*

Share Your Confidentiality Concerns

It's completely understandable to feel nervous about discussing your mental health at work, regardless of your role, especially if you're a leader. So, if you're concerned, speak up! Your confidentiality matters; make it clear if it's important to you, regardless of who you're talking to. Opening up is beneficial; sharing your concerns about that process is essential, too, and you can tailor that message depending on the audience. When you share something with someone and want it to stay private, it's your responsibility to let them know. For example, you might say to a leadership peer,

> *"I want to talk to you about it, but I'm nervous. It's not about you; I have trust issues with this kind of thing. Can you please promise me that you won't share this with anyone? I need to be able to trust you, even though I haven't trusted others at work before."*

This gives the other person a chance to show you they can be trusted, or for your intuition to let you know if they can't.

If your gut tells you that you've picked the wrong person to talk to, trust it, because in that moment, it's time to change course. How do you do that? By saying something like,

> *"You know what, I appreciate the offer, but I don't think I'm ready yet. I'll let you know if and when I am. I appreciate that you took the time."*

This course correction shows the boundary you're setting, which is what's germane in that moment, not that you don't trust the recipient. Depending on your relationship and rapport with that person, it's entirely up to you if you choose to tell them why you've changed your mind. If you do, just be prepared that the receiving party may feel criticized. And people who feel criticized can demonstrate a smorgasbord of reactions. With honesty must come preparation to deal with people's reactions. If you choose to engage in that conversation and want to explain your boundary, a helpful, mature, and firm response could sound something like this:

> *"I appreciate that you want to help me, but it's my choice if I want to receive that help. It's reasonable for me to ask you to respect that."*

How (and Who) You Share with Matters

If you're going to share about your mental health, it also means sharing intentionally, with purpose, and clarity. Defining what you need and who you need it from, are essential. That means tailoring what you share based on your audience and your needs. What can that look like?

- Picking a good time and place (as best as you can)
- Tailoring your message to your audience (more on this shortly)
- Sharing what's critical
- Sharing what you need and why
- Being prepared to maturely address pushback or misunderstandings, if they occur
- Sharing what you're going to be accountable for coming out of that conversation, and what good help could look like from the other person

Here's my guidance: practice "boundaried honesty" by finding a balance that works for you. This is not about engaging in an endless endurance race of emotional suppression. It also doesn't mean sharing your 25-year mental health history with people, sending your therapy notes in an email blast, or discussing your mental health every moment of business hours. It's about building your fence, the kind that has spaces between the slats. The in-between of an open playing field and an iron-clad door. Deciding what you'll let out and in. How you share something can have a different impact depending on the person receiving it, for various reasons. What you perceive as reasonable vulnerability might be interpreted differently by the person receiving it, depending on their position, life experiences, and professional relationship to you. This does not mean you should stay silent or filter your thoughts to the point that it completely stifles your sharing. It simply means you need to be self-aware, strategic, and intentional about how, to whom, and why you share.

I will share some helpful pointers here to help you get started on initiating these conversations. You don't want to be too reliant on specific scripts anyway, because you want to sound like *you*. All you need is the formula of what's important to cover, in a way that feels right for your role, life, and circumstances. I'll give you the highlights to hit—you will decide what they should (and need) to sound like. If you would like even more scripts, scenario-specific guidance, and a far deeper dive than what I'm providing here, I encourage you to read my first book, which has three entire chapters dedicated to discussing mental health at work as an individual, how to support colleagues, and supporting your team—addressing every granular aspect of those conversations (with nifty exercises too!).

Each conversation is an opportunity. You'll see a range of outcomes, some positive and some less so. For the latter, when it comes to your conversational contributions, it doesn't mean you're necessarily getting it wrong; it just means you're practicing and even making mistakes like everyone else. Just as you, as a leader, are expected to practice and improve different skills at work, the same expectation applies here. Improving in this area requires intention, practice, and ongoing reflection. Let's explore how you can set yourself up for success by examining common scenarios, the purpose of sharing certain conversations with specific audiences, and the reasons behind it. As with the rest of the content in this book, please note that these are high-level recommendations based on common scenarios, and you need to apply this information and the approaches based on your own individual circumstances.

Sharing with Fellow Leaders

- *Purpose:* To normalize mutual support among leaders for mental health at work. Focused on sharing with someone who understands and can discuss the ups and downs of leadership. This is a powerful space that isn't always available when a leader shares with their team, boss, or the wider organization. These are the conversations where leaders can take off their leadership masks and be real, recognizing that they are people, who happen to be leaders. This space builds trust, fosters community connection, and helps normalize these essential conversations among leaders.
- *What asking for help could sound like:*
  - *"I feel like I'm about to pop. I feel like you can relate based on what we talked about last week. I know you have a lot going on too, but do you have 30 minutes to catch up at the end of the day? I feel like we both need it."*
  - *What this approach accomplishes:* It gives you space to open up to someone who you know is a safe container, while acknowledging their challenges, and offering an opportunity for bidirectional support.

Sharing with Your Boss

- *Purpose:* To share what you're experiencing with the purpose of letting your manager know the support or resources you may need so you can effectively perform in your role as a leader. These conversations can sometimes focus more on performance, leadership responsibilities, and how your manager can support your success. Sharing what's going on with you, what you're struggling with, and how they can help is a great way to enable them to do that for you. Remember, your boss is also a leader. This can be a chance for them to support you, as they may have faced similar struggles.
- *What asking for help could sound like:*
  - *"I'm feeling spread thin right now and I'm having a hard time. I want to ensure that I'm accomplishing the most important strategic priorities, but I also want to give you a heads-up about my capacity and stress levels. Can we discuss this during our next 1:1? I know we haven't spoken about the latter before, but I'm feeling stretched thin and trying not to silo how I deal with it anymore. Thanks in advance for chatting with me about this."*
  - *What this approach accomplishes*: It lets your manager know that you're struggling, and that you're responsible to acknowledge it, so things don't get out of control. You are being proactive by showing your manager that you are self-aware enough to discuss your priorities and capacity with them, allowing for collaborative prioritization and adjustments. You're also highlighting understandable reservations about opening up, which enables your manager to demonstrate that they can (hopefully) be a safe container, while acknowledging that you may be nervous about getting in with them.

Sharing with Your Team

- *Purpose:* To humanize yourself as a leader so your team can realistically understand your capacity, and how you're trying to take care of yourself so you can show up for them. Highlight that you can struggle and lead effectively simultaneously, while discussing the challenges that come with achieving this balance. This also allows your team members to support you when appropriate. It demonstrates that you are role modeling the psychological safety you hope to receive, similar to how you create psychological safety for them to open up to you. And, regardless of title, anyone who is struggling has the responsibility to acknowledge it, manage it, and not take it out on others. This is a collective team value that everyone can and should practice to some degree.

- *What asking for help could sound like:*
  - *"Hey everyone, I know I haven't seemed like myself recently. I'm going through some personal stuff at home. And with our Q4 deadline coming up, it's a lot for me right now. I'm doing what I need to do to take care of myself. I just wanted to let you know that if I seem off, it's not because of you. Thank you all for your hard work. I know we can get to our goal—let's do this!"*
  - *What this approach accomplishes:* You demonstrate that you can struggle and lead at the same time, provide high-level information to let your team know you're struggling, and at a level of detail you're comfortable with. As a leader, you're being accountable to your team for explaining why your behavior has changed and, most importantly, what you're doing to manage it. And lastly, you're creating opportunities for them to step up and support you as appropriate.

Sharing with Human Resources

- *Purpose:* To receive assistance with making practical decisions about your workload, capacity, and other aspects related to your leadership performance and mental health. This may include addressing potential needs for accommodations, getting further information or being connected to mental health resources, or seeking guidance on options to take regarding getting the support you need. People who work in HR can manage these conversations in a more structured and solution-oriented manner, based on established support systems, company policies, and compliance requirements. HR professionals are generally trained to handle complex and sensitive situations, including mental health struggles, particularly from a compliance and legality perspective. They can help connect you to available resources without some of the complexities that can arise in relationship dynamics with your boss, colleagues, or team members.

- *What asking for help could sound like:*
  - o *"I was just diagnosed with an anxiety disorder and need to get an accommodation to work from home. I know I probably need to give you some kind of documentation, and there are probably certain processes we need to follow. How do we get this started?"*
  - o *What this approach accomplishes:* It shares relevant new health information that you're asking the company to formally consider regarding how, when, and where you work. You are indicating that you have new work needs based on individual mental health needs, and you want to collaborate with the company using their processes to help you succeed in your role. Please note that, depending on your location globally, each country (and sometimes even a state or province) has its own specific laws and procedures related to getting accommodations at work for mental health. Before disclosing this at work, ensure you understand how protected health information is legally handled in your country in the workplace, what employer responsibilities are (and aren't) regarding these disclosures, and what your legal rights are.

Taking Action—Starting a Conversation

Is there someone I want to open up to about my mental health at work? Who is it?

- Why do I feel comfortable sharing with them? What's our professional relationship like?

- Are they the right person for this conversation?

- What are my intended outcomes for this conversation, and what will I share?

- How will I ask them for help? What do I need from them?

What to Do If the Conversation Doesn't Go as Planned

Realism is essential for success here, and that means accepting that not every conversation will go smoothly. That's to be expected, and it's okay! Just because some conversations might be a bit tough doesn't mean they won't have positive outcomes ultimately, or that other conversations won't go smoothly. Remember when I mentioned earlier that everyone will be on a learning curve, including you and those who will be hearing from you? Just because they may not respond as you hoped doesn't mean the conversation is doomed for hellfire. It might simply be a misunderstanding, discomfort, or something else that can be addressed. There are opportunities here to share what you need, clarify if they're confused, help them understand what good support looks like for you (instead of what they might assume it should be), and so on. In some cases, they may not be able to support you in the way you're expecting. And that's okay too; it just means they may not know how or might be afraid to mess up the process.

However, in some cases, if a conversation doesn't go well in more malicious situations, you must know your rights and when to advocate for yourself even more. This means standing up for yourself and possibly escalating matters if you feel you can't get what you need, or, in worst cases, when those conversations go in a nefarious direction. I understand that the latter can be stressful, but here's why we need to address it. Sometimes, this involves letting someone know that their comments were hurtful and biased, inviting a conversation about why they made those statements, and giving them a chance to apologize and make amends. In other cases, depending on what transpired (i.e., if your disclosure was used as office gossip or used against you), that could mean escalating to legal action through a trusted HR representative at your company, other legal channels available to you at your company, or in other situations, seeking outside legal advice. Depending on your location, mental health disclosures in a professional setting have different legal protections, particularly regarding how that information is handled and work environment behaviors surrounding it. If that information is misused, understand your rights, and act accordingly based on the scenario and who's involved. Knowing how to communicate effectively about your mental health, especially as a leader, is your responsibility. Being aware of and acting on your rights is just as critical. When it comes to these situations, knowledge is power; I recommend that you research and stay informed about your rights relevant to your location.

Reflection Exercise—Does My Company Support My Mental Health as a Leader?

Do I feel like I can talk about my mental health at this company?

- If I can't, what does that mean for me?

- If I want to stay at this company, but feel I can't talk about my mental health, where else can I get that support?

- If I want to leave this company because I can't discuss my mental health as a leader, what "healthy signs" should I look for at the next company I apply to? What would a culture that supports mental health at that organization look like, including how leaders participate?

This set of reflection questions above may feel unnerving to answer. Just like we discussed earlier in this book, some companies and leaders will continue to choose not to support this endeavor. When people are telling you who they are and what they will and won't give you, listen to them. If that means you can't get the acknowledgment or support you need at your current company, and you're able to go elsewhere, I hope your answers to these reflection questions will aid your decision-making in finding healthier leadership pastures.

Having Community Can Help Your Mental Health at Work

"Peer support is everything. Full stop. Leadership can be brutally lonely, especially when you're the one trying to change the culture from the inside out. Having a space where you can talk with others who get it; the workload, the weight of responsibility, the internal battles, the fear of

being seen as weak. That space can be lifesaving. . .I believe leadership peer support will be one of the most transformative tools of the next decade. Not another corporate workshop. Not another performative campaign. But real, human, grounded connection forged in the fires we've all been through."

Interviewee: male, Gen X, Caucasian, senior leadership, construction industry

"Peer support groups are vital for giving leaders a confidential space to uncover and unpack their challenges. I belong to such groups, and it has been invaluable not only to share and learn from each other's experiences, but it has also given me much-needed perspectives on similar challenges that others are experiencing and potential solutions."

Interviewee: female, Gen X, Black, Director, consulting industry

Here, we'll explore how you can engage with, give, and receive support from your leadership peers. Have you wanted this support at different points in your career? Or even now? Then decide how you want to participate so you can receive, and hopefully give, that support too.

Having a community focused on leadership mental health isn't just "another support system"; it's a crucial means of having this conversation in a psychologically safe and meaningful way. It's an opportunity to create a noticeable shift in leadership culture, encouraging current and future leaders to prioritize and connect on leadership mental health in ways your predecessors may not have felt they could. Your peers are observing you, just as you are observing them. You all might wonder, at some point, if you can "step outside" your roles to connect with who you are and what you need from a mental health support perspective at work. This is where displays of honesty create social permission. How does this happen? In addition to organizational buy-in, support, and resources, individual leaders need to be involved in helping to maintain that supportive space.

Decide What Your Participation Will Look Like—and Why It Matters to You

"Peer support networks and leadership communities provide a safe space for leaders to share challenges, exchange strategies, and normalize discussions around mental health. They help break the isolation that often comes with leadership roles, offering perspective and reducing the stigma of vulnerability."

Interviewee: male, Millennial, Caucasian, Director, software industry

"I believe everyone is on their own journey. For me, it has not necessarily been about sharing my experiences, but rather about creating and fostering a supportive culture and providing appropriate outlets."

Interviewee: female, Millennial, Black, C-Suite, heavy civil construction industry

If your company has or is open to creating an internal leadership mental health peer support network, or even an ERG dedicated to it, they are ahead of the curve. As someone in a leadership role, you can already demonstrate your visible support by participating, even if you don't hold a formal facilitation or leadership position in that group. Your involvement, regardless of how you participate, affirms the need for this group's existence to the broader organization. The primary goal of this community is to provide leaders with the conversation and support they need for their mental health at work, and to address the emotional challenges of leadership. The second goal? Sending a message to the broader company that these conversations deserve time, space, and attention—and are essential for "good" leadership.

To do this purposefully and effectively, figure out why and how you want to be involved in a way that works for you, your comfort level, and your goals. What individuals need from each other in a community, regardless of the topic, is deeply personal. Everyone's approach is unique. Some will benefit simply from listening and being close to others who share their challenges. Others will find value in speaking up, helping manage the group, or even leading sessions. The key point is this: your level of participation in this community is entirely up to you, and no approach is more important than another. You need to show up and decide how you want to engage in a way that benefits both yourself and, in some way, your fellow leaders. I mention the latter because, in community, it's a give and take; so, don't just take. Before you (hopefully) dive in, consider the following questions.

Reflection & Taking Action

What Kind of Leadership Mental Health Community Do I Need?

- *Assess Your Needs & Readiness:*
  - Do I need community for my mental health at work as a leader? Why or why not?
  - Throughout my career, what kind of leadership mental health support do I wish I had? What would good support have looked like?
  - In my opinion, what do I think prevented previous organizations I've worked at from providing that support? If that support was available, why didn't I use it?
  - Do I feel ready to engage in this type of group now?
  - If I could have this community at my current company, what would I want to share and why?
- *Assess Your Beliefs:*
  - Do any of my leadership beliefs make me feel like I can't or shouldn't join this type of community? If so, what are they?
  - What new beliefs do I want to adopt? (i.e., "I deserve mental health support and community as a leader")
- *Assess Your Contribution Plan:*
  - How will I share my needs with other participants?
  - How do I plan to show up for others?
  - How can I make peers feel psychologically safe to talk about mental health at work, even if we don't have the same experiences or background?

(continued)

(*continued*)

- *Assess Your Logistics:*
  - o Who will I speak to about joining?
  - o How will I ensure that I make time in my schedule to participate?
- *Assess Your Path Forward:*
  - o If my company won't start this type of group, should I try to create this community with other leaders?
  - o Do I want to have a leadership role within this group?
  - o Who can I contact for assistance with this?
  - o Who can I speak with in my HR or People function for support on this?

Going deeper, consider the kind of role you may want to fulfill, understanding that this may change over time. Consider the following types of participation and which one feels right for you based on what you would want from this type of community:

- *Observer:* You want to listen to see how the group feels, but you know you want to be there.
- *Contributor:* You feel ready to share your experiences, learn from your fellow leaders, and support to them, too.
- *Advocate:* You want to ensure the organization understands the purpose of this group and help build ongoing support and resources for it.
- *Recruiter:* You want to encourage other leaders to join the group and help them understand why they need this space as well.
- *Facilitator:* You would like to receive formal facilitation training, either within or outside your organization, to help lead this group.

As I mentioned in Chapter 6, those who need this support will be the ones driving the change to get it. In this case, having an internal leadership mental health peer support community, to a degree, will need to be driven by leaders themselves. There are plenty of organizations that encourage the creation of communities and ERGs, while other companies don't care, and even in some cases, resist their creation. Depending on where you work and the company's culture, you and other leaders may need to drive the creation of this type of community if those in your organization who have the visibility and power to do so don't or won't.

Depending on your organization's culture, you might not need a formal group at all. You can take the initiative with some of your closest leadership peers by scheduling regular check-ins at a mutually agreed-upon cadence to see how everyone is doing, discuss challenges, and support one another. Any opportunity to create and participate in a community centered on leadership mental health is valuable, regardless of its format. It doesn't have to be an overly emotional appeal or anything like that; just something like,

> *"Hey everyone, from our conversations, I know we've all been struggling a lot recently. I had a thought: How would you all feel meeting virtually once a month for 45 minutes for a check-in? I'm open to your thoughts and suggestions. We do need something, so let's create it ourselves."*

A quick hot take here: in some cases, companies take issue with their workforce (at any level) self-organizing meet-up groups, perceiving the potential liabilities or threats they pose. However, if you're meeting resistance about trying to create spaces for leadership mental health, and you take those matters into your own hands to a degree that garners some attention from the company, it's *technically* a good thing. Because then the conversation with the organization becomes,

> *"We asked you for this, and you said no, so we did it ourselves. We want organizational support; would you be willing to provide that now?"*

Yes, I know it's direct and bold. Yes, it poses some risk to you. I meant what I said by referencing Phil Knight earlier in the book— you're remembered for the rules you break. Obviously, I'm not encouraging you to put your job at risk by acting with reckless abandon without taking your environment into account. Use reason, diplomacy, and sensible thinking, based on your specific company's setup and what is feasible, without scorching the earth, if you choose to go this route.

A word of caution to you: if your organization flat-out turns down the idea of having a specific support space for leaders' mental health, that's a red flag. I know that people choose to (or have to) stay at jobs for many reasons. Some are elective, and others are not. But if you're at an organization that shows it doesn't care about mental health as a leader—run, do not walk, to another company that does. The company is showing you who they are and will likely continue to be.

Accounting for Your Intersectionality Needs

"Representation matters, therefore, community matters. Witnessing others who look like you being vulnerable about their own mental health has been helpful."

Interviewee: female, Gen X, Black, Director, human resources industry

"There's a historical and cultural expectation—both external and internal—that Black professionals, especially in leadership, need to be strong at all times. Any admission of stress, exhaustion, or mental health challenges can be misinterpreted as a weakness rather than a reality of the job. I've seen how vulnerability can be weaponized against people who look like me, so I've been cautious about how much I share and with whom. At the same time, I recognize that breaking this cycle is important. The more leaders of color are open about mental health, the more we can push back against unrealistic expectations and create space for real conversations."

Interviewee: male, Gen X, Black, first-time manager, technology industry

Building on the concept of intersectionality from Chapter 5, this is a vital aspect of community support, particularly for a topic as personal and complex as mental health in leadership. Not only do individual leaders have specific needs for their own community, but we also need to recognize that each leader approaches these communities from a unique set of experiences, including their feelings of psychological safety and the potential stakes of disclosure depending on who they share with. Some may enter these communities feeling open and ready, while others may join (rightfully) with their proverbial armor on, having learned from past experiences that they can't take it off, even in spaces where they are encouraged to do so.

Some spaces can't be shared in the same way with others as with those from your own community, who understand those experiences better than anyone else. If you feel you have specific needs in this area, please honor them when deciding how to participate in these communities and conversations. This isn't about being overly cautious, politically correct, exclusive, or secluding leaders from each other. It's about respecting people's individual experiences and creating spaces where they feel comfortable sharing them. The last thing we want is for people to feel as if they're taking on extra risks in spaces where they shouldn't have to.

Reflection Exercise—Finding the Right Community for Me

Do any parts of my identity affect my sense of psychological safety when participating in conversations about my mental health with other leaders?

- In general, do I believe my experiences will be respected and heard by other leaders?

- Which past experiences make me feel this way, and what did I learn from them?

- Do I need support from others who share these parts of my identity within leadership? Or can I join a wider group? Why or why not?

- How can my awareness of these factors help me become a more active participant and advocate in this community?

Reflecting on these answers can help you become more aware of your intersectionality needs within these leadership communities and hopefully better understand the needs of others, too. This reflection will not only help you be intentional with your participation but also potentially strengthen your role as an advocate in these spaces.

Moving from Reflection to Action

> *"The key to balancing transparency and authority is intentionality. Share honestly, but with clarity and composure. Model self-awareness and healthy coping—not crisis. That way, you're showing strength through vulnerability, not in spite of it."*
>
> Interviewee: female, Millennial, Asian, Vice President, SaaS industry

If you want things to change for yourself and your fellow leaders regarding leadership mental health at work, each person's reflection must translate into action in some way. Regardless of your comfort level or readiness to join the leadership mental health conversation, here are three things that *every* leader can start doing now to help create individual change, and hopefully, cumulative change overall:

- *Use available mental health resources:* Everyone needs support at some point in their lives; no one is exempt from this. Decide how you will utilize support, what types, and when. Make use of what is accessible to you. If you feel ready or so bold, share with others which resources you're using and how they're helping you as a leader. Your usage of these resources can help destigmatize their use among other leaders too. It also sets an example for your team, showing that you're not just telling them to prioritize their mental health; you're doing it, too.
  - *Example:* If you're not already getting mental health support, a good way to dip your toe in is by calling your employee assistance program (EAP). Decide when you'll contact the EAP, one topic you want to discuss, and tell the counselor what you'd like to accomplish in that conversation—even if it's just to address any concerns you have about potentially going to therapy.

- *Reflect on how you'll shift the narrative:* If you're ready to help change the conversation about leadership mental health on a larger scale, consider how you'll approach it. There are different ways to approach this, some of which we covered in Chapter 6. So choose what you're prepared for, when you'll take action, through which channel, the message you want to share about leadership mental health, and why.
  - o *Example:* If you don't feel ready to share your mental health story at a broader level, consider where else you might begin. Is there a leader you're close to who seems hesitant to discuss their mental health? Start by gently sharing some of your struggles when the moment feels right (I know, somewhat easier said than done), with no expectation of reciprocity, and observe if it changes how they engage in that conversation with you. Or share some of the stressors you're experiencing in a one-on-one with a team member you have a strong rapport with, who you know will respond supportively to you.
- *Decide how you'd like to engage with your leadership community:* Reflect on whether you're ready to participate in, help create, or support a leadership mental health peer support community. Once you've made that decision, seek out or help establish those spaces.
  - o *Example:* If a leadership mental health peer support space doesn't exist in your organization, consider talking to one or two of your closest leadership friends at your company. Do a temperature check to see how they feel about having your own independent check-ins or working together to start a leadership mental health ERG.

Let's do a quick check-in on how our Leadership Mental Health Support Solution is stacking up, with the new elements added below in **bold**:

Individual Leader Acknowledgement to Participate in Creating Broader Change

+

Individual Leader Participation in Support Systems and Usage of Resources

+

Individual Leader Participation in Organizational Narrative
Shifting

+

Individual Leaders Having Conversations About Their Mental
Health at Work (Both Receiving and Starting)

+

Individual Leader Participation in and Fostering of a
Leadership Peer Support Mental Health Community

This chapter focused on how you can participate in conversations
to receive support for your mental health, support your peers, and contribute to changing the larger leadership mental health narrative
within your organization. Now, we reach the final part of the solution:
what you can do to care for your mental health as a leader, for the time
in between the conversations you have at work.

Chapter Key Takeaways

- Leaders should personalize how they discuss their mental
  health at work based on what works best for their individual
  circumstances.
- Leaders need to speak up if they need support for their mental
  health at work. Practicing "boundaried honesty" and "building
  your fence" will help you get the support you need, based on
  your comfort level, without losing credibility.
- Know your individual "why"; it will motivate the actions you
  take overall.
- Individual leaders can support one another, to foster honesty,
  boost trust, and build stronger connections.
- Leadership mental health peer support communities are psychologically safe and supportive environments where leaders
  can connect and support one another about mental health
  struggles at work and the emotional challenges of leadership.

9

Create Your Leadership Mental Health Self-Care Plan

> *"There's only one of me, and if I don't take care of myself, then I won't get to continue doing the work that fuels my passion. I can't possibly be there for others if I am not there for me. I listen to my body and mind and reflect on what I need."*
>
> Interviewee: female, Millennial, Mexican-American, Elementary Principal, public education industry

TALKING ABOUT YOUR mental health is one thing; consistently managing it is another. For all of the moments dedicated to creating impact and change that we discussed throughout Chapters 6, 7, and 8, your mental health self-care will need to be consistently present for the moments in between. The goal is to prevent death by a thousand cuts; instead, we aim for a thousand small moments that can collectively reinforce support for your mental health, manage leadership capacity, and take the edge off (as much as possible, anyway) of the emotional burdens of leadership and mental health struggles in general. In Part I, we discussed how neglecting leadership mental health can negatively impact your overall functioning, how you lead, and even your career path. Consistently managing your mental health will help reduce these risks. That's the primary focus in this home stretch.

The Importance of Personalization

> *"The most important coping strategy I use is metacognitive journaling. . .This practice has allowed me to identify my triggers, observe the patterns in my thinking, and reevaluate decisions through a more strategic lens. It's helped me build a life that feels more aligned and intentional . . . It's become a never-ending conversation with someone who's endlessly empathetic: myself . . . In doing this, I've learned how to be my own best friend. And that's helped me feel less alone in the weight of leadership."*
>
> Interviewee: male, Millennial, Black, C-Suite, consulting industry

Personalization is a valuable ally when creating an effective strategy to manage your mental health as a leader. How you approach it or who you choose to talk to about it is entirely your decision.

Using Existing Leadership Theory to Find What Works for You

Just like we discussed in Part I, "good" leadership is heavily influenced by context and individual circumstances. You will need to identify and understand what works for your mental health, preferences, and situation. Using sociological and leadership theories can support this personal process. Think of them as flexible tools to shape your mindset, not fixed blueprints. There's no single correct or ideal way—what matters is what feels right, is necessary, and is achievable for you. Not by copying others without doing your back-end prep and discovering what you need, when, and why.

Contingency Theory tells us that leaders need to understand themselves internally and what works best for them to be an effective leader.[1]

This logical approach suggests that creating and managing your mental health as a leader through a mental health self-care plan will need to involve recognizing that what works for one person may not work for another, which is completely normal given our diverse situations. In practice, this means choosing actions that feel right and enjoyable rather than burdensome. The goal is to develop a plan that aligns with your reality, values, willingness to act, and even potential limitations. Your ability to lead others starts with understanding the support you need to function, not just the skills you need to perform. A *Mercer* piece put it really well,[2]

> *"If you're chronically stressed at work, it's time to stop buying into the myth that leaders and managers must be selfless martyrs. You're putting your own health and well-being, along with your team's effectiveness and engagement, at risk. Instead of working yourself to exhaustion, start developing a self-care strategy to manage the demands of your job."*

In addition to individual preferences and rightness of fit, consider how you fit into the larger systems within your particular environment (another nod back to intersectionality in Chapter 5). Take sociologist C. Wright Mills's theory of sociological imagination. This theory encourages you to connect your personal situation to the structural context and larger systems in which you live.[3] Reflect on your systems, the challenges they bring, your interactions with these challenges, and the mental health struggles they may cause you as a leader. This will help you identify your specific stressors and possible solutions. With this insight, you can develop a realistic plan to mitigate the impacts on your mental health and maintain consistent emotional self-care as a leader. Good news: you already did some of this work in the Part 1 Individual Reflection Exercise - use it!

The Importance of Assessment, Planning, and Consistency

Develop your leadership mental health self-care plan as a regular habit, just like any other essential leadership skill. Starting new habits can be challenging, especially when they are important. As a leader, you're (hopefully) already aware of the value of discipline and consistent follow-through; apply the same principles to your mental health self-care. Here are some self-assessment questions to increase your chances of success in that process.

- *Assessing My Needs:*
  - o What are my top three mental health needs as a leader?
  - o Why are these needs important?
  - o What are the top three behaviors I need to engage in to meet these needs?

- *Making My Plan:*
  - o What do I want to do to take care of my mental health?
  - o Why do I want to do these things?
  - o How will these practices effectively support my mental health as a leader?

- *Quality Assurance Check-Ins:*
  - o How will I determine what progress looks like?
  - o How often will I check in with myself?
  - o Do I need to enlist a "buddy" in this process to help keep me accountable or give feedback on whether it seems like I've improved?

If you want to become stronger in this skill over time, you need to build a plan to actually use it.

Three Concrete Mental Health Self-Care Tools That Work

"I continue to go to therapy once a week, and I work out 5 days a week. I also travel and spend time with my family to cope with work and life."

Interviewee: male, Gen X, Black, Director, entertainment industry

"One of the most important lessons I've learned as a leader is that self-care isn't optional—it's essential. . .I've had to actively manage with self-care practices—taking breaks, setting boundaries, seeking sup-port—so I can continue to show up fully. . .The emotional demands of leadership can be heavy, and I've had to be intentional about how

> *I protect my energy and mental well-being. . . These practices are simple but powerful. They allow me to stay grounded in high-stress environments and model what healthy boundaries and emotional regulation can look like for my team."*
>
> Interviewee: female, Millennial, Asian, Vice President, SaaS industry

You already have a lot on your plate, I mean, in your trough (remember the uncomfortable imagery from Chapter 4?). The last thing I want to do is overwhelm you with 12 options for managing your mental health, especially given the constant barrage of messages from social media, other media sources, and people telling you what should work for you—because opinions are like a**holes, and everyone has one. That's why I'm offering just three. However, if none of these options work for you, that's okay; you can choose to find something else. I want to provide a choice in each category because each can help ease the mental strain of leadership and general mental health struggles, with input from different important sources:

- Practicing mental health maintenance habits
- Communicating capacity to others
- Maintaining a holistic perspective

Identify and Practice Your Mental Wellbeing Non-Negotiables™

Years ago, I trademarked a concept called the Mental Wellbeing Non-Negotiables™. I'm sharing it not because I created it, but because people tell me it works, as it incorporates personalization, execution, and realism when it comes to managing mental health. This model came from my frustration with the wellness industry overall, where endless solutions were advertised as "this works for everyone," when that's just not true. And that should be okay. The wellness industry sometimes sacrifices personalization for the sake of scalability and sound bites.

For example, I'm a former therapist, and meditation doesn't work for me. Yoga doesn't relax me. So, why should I do those things for my mental health? Just because the wellness industry tells me to? If those activities don't produce the results I need, I should do something different. So, here's what I suggest instead.

When it comes to identifying your own Mental Wellbeing Non-Negotiables™, find something that makes you feel good, positively impacts your mental health (without causing harm to yourself or others), and practice it consistently—barring death, dismemberment, hell, high water, or illness—and I'm not kidding. Managing mental health is just as essential as sleeping, eating, bathing, and breathing. That means identifying and consistently practicing at least one Mental Wellbeing Non-Negotiable™ and adapting it when necessary. My top Mental Wellbeing Non-Negotiables™ are being in nature at least once a week, playing with my dog every night, even when she doesn't want to (she's a Red Heeler mix, so she's a spicy, opinionated fur baby), and salsa dancing. The last one is *my* form of meditation.

When I'm dancing, my mind literally goes blank because I'm in a flow state, while my body follows a (hopefully) good lead. When I tore my ACL in a spectacular fashion while feeding reindeer during a snowstorm in Norway (yes, it happened, no, my orthopedic surgeon didn't believe me), that made dancing difficult. So, what did I do? I shuffled around to music on crutches in our flat (we lived in London at the time). The pandemic also made dancing difficult—dancing isn't exactly a social-distancing-friendly activity. After healing from my surgery, I thought to myself, "*Well, I have hardwood floors, salsa music, and a mostly willing husband—this will have to do.*" And it did. My point is this: find what works for you, be accountable to do it, and do it consistently—with the exceptions above in mind. Here are the five things you can reflect on to identify your Mental Wellbeing Non-Negotiables™.

- *Acknowledge:*
  o The importance of having a Mental Wellbeing Non-Negotiable™ for your leadership mental health, and why.
- *Pick:*
  o What you truly like doing—not what the wellness industry dictates you should like to do. Whether it's listening to the

wind in the evenings, buying a unicorn costume and dancing around in it to Metallica in your living room, or doing
some deep belly breathing in the shower, pick what works,
and DO IT.

- *Decide on a Schedule:*
  o If you only have one hour a week, then that's what you have
    to do. Do you want to do five minutes a day instead? Great,
    do that. Being realistic based on your schedule is what matters.
- *Be Consistent:*
  o Adapt circumstantially as needed.
- *Share with Others:*
  o Create accountability to others. It may even inspire them to
    discover and practice their own Mental Wellbeing Non-
    Negotiables™ too.

For all you recovering perfectionists out there—please know that
the goal here is practice, not perfection.

Communicating Capacity as a Mental Well-being Management Tool

I drew inspiration for this from when Brené Brown was on Tim Ferriss's
podcast, where she discussed why romantic partners must communicate their capacity to each other when they're stressed.[4] This relates to
mental health at work, I promise, stay with me for a minute. Here's
why: sometimes partners have to carry each other, and they don't know
what they each need unless they tell each other in an easily understandable, quantifiable way. What Brené recommended is that each
partner communicate their emotional states on a scale from 0 to 100
(0 being "I'm practically comatose" to 100 being "I'm firing on all cyl-
inders"), to say what they are and are not capable of that day, and how
they can show kindness to each other. For those of you in committed
long-term relationships, you might be snickering as you read this and
possibly thinking, "HA! *Right, we could say that to each other, but. . .*"
It's okay—I'm fully aware that "The Greatest Hits Marriage Fights" are
a challenging recurring obstacle to overcome. Anyway, my adaptation
of what Brené shared is applicable at work, no romantic relationship required.

I'm expanding on this idea based on how you evaluate your own level of functioning and communicate that to others at work, which relates back to humanizing you as a leader, rather than the machine that people often personify you to be. Remember to respect that scale with exceptions (of course). While Brené's reference is about how partners support each other, my take is centered on how you acknowledge, manage, and communicate your capacity at work, to those you collaborate with and rely on, and vice versa. I discuss this often in my practical stress management workshops, and I'm sharing it here because I've been told it's a crowd favorite, so we must be onto something. There are two ways you can approach this self-assessment exercise:

1. When you're calm (i.e., here's what I think I'll need and how I'll feel at that level). Or,
2. Pause when you're in the moment and notice your capacity. Over time, when you have self-ranked a variety of levels, you can collate and realign them.

There's no "right way" to do this, because you'll need to do what's right for you and potentially experiment by trying it both ways for accuracy. Please, please keep this documented and update it iteratively as needed; this isn't just meant to be a static one-time mental exercise. Whether you go digital or stick with old-school analog with a paper and pen, when s**t hits the fan, you're not going to remember reading what I've written or what you thought about when you marinated on this exercise the week before when your body is in survival mode on any given Thursday. In those moments, your nervous system is trying to respond and fight the perceived saber-tooth tiger in your environment, wanting to make you its amuse-bouche, when it can't tell the difference between that and you just trying to get through the day at work as a leader.

Here's how to do this self-reflection exercise. Define what your specific capacity scale looks like, with intervals that feel right for you. For some people, that might be every 10 points, 25 points, or even every 5—it's up to you. You should choose the number of intervals that seems reasonable to keep track of, but I recommend doing at least four. For each level of the scale, here's an example of what you'll need to fill out:

- Ex: In the 0–100 scale, at the 45-point marker:
  - o *I Feel This:*
    - What specific emotions am I feeling?
    - What are they trying to tell me?
  - o *I Need These Things:*
    - What are my corresponding needs?
    - Do I need support?
    - How can I support myself? Do I need support from anyone else?
  - o *I Can't Do These Things:*
    - What are my reasonable limitations?
    - What do I *actually* need to accomplish, and what can wait?
    - How do I effectively communicate this to others and when?
  - o *How I'll Manage Where I Am:*
    - How will I communicate my capacity to others?
    - What will I say if I receive pushback?
    - What am I going to do to take care of myself? Which of my Mental Wellbeing Non-Negotiables™ can I use to help take the edge off?
  - o *Why I Will Accept Where I Am Today:*
    - Why I will logically and reasonably accept that this self-advocacy practice is a healthy, mature responsible practice that I'm implementing.

The goal is consistent self-assessment, making adjustments as needed, and following through. Remember, role modeling this behavior benefits not only your mental health but also demonstrates communicating about capacity as a mental health support tool to your team and fellow leaders, hopefully encouraging them to adopt a similar practice. It also creates opportunities for team members and leadership peers to support you and share some of your mental or cognitive load when appropriate, possible, or needed. Additionally, if you encourage others to engage in this capacity communication practice, it may give you the chance to support them and help share their mental load when they need assistance, too.

Yes, doing this through the lens of leadership might face some resistance. I've worked with companies that would literally cackle at me for even suggesting that their leaders do this. Obviously, I believe they are wrong to behave like this. But that's just the way of the world sometimes, you can't win 'em all. But that doesn't make this practice any less valuable, essential, or legitimate. That's why being transparent about your reasons for sharing about your capacity and how you manage it is crucial for your functioning and mental health as a leader, allowing you to continue leading effectively. There's no valid opposition to that. Remember what I said in Chapter 8: if your company pushes back against this, you may need to consider some tough decisions to change your circumstances.

Use the PERMA Model to Support Your Mental Health as a Leader

Sometimes, individual mental health self-care practices and sharing your capacity with others isn't enough. Sometimes, getting through the day as a leader requires zooming out to gain perspective—taking the 30,000-foot view when other strategies aren't effective. As humans, we're equipped (and perhaps cursed?) with self-awareness and self-reflection, yet we often get so caught up in daily life that we forget these tools are available to us—especially if we haven't heard of them in the circles we hang out in. Some days, zooming out may not even feel possible or helpful. I've been there myself, trust me. Even on the days when we can't see the purpose of help or zooming out to gain perspective, it's essential to remember that intentionally seeking and creating opportunities to broaden our perspectives can and often do have a positive, cumulative impact over time.

Let's look at psychologist Martin Seligman's PERMA model. It might sound crunchy, but it does help. This model can help you identify the broader strokes of your life and circumstances, enabling you to step away from the leadership trough when you really need to or if you're stuck in Atlas mode. Seligman created this model to help people find internal happiness, fulfillment, and meaning in life by discovering these core elements of well-being,[5] including:

- *Positive Emotion:* nurturing joy, hope, pride
- *Engagement:* making sure you "get in the flow" in experiences
- *Relationships:* lean on support and connection from others
- *Meaning:* engage in actions with purpose, beyond yourself
- *Accomplishment:* experience your sense of mastery and growth in your skills

What are some ways you can apply the PERMA model as a leader to help support your mental health at work?

- *Positive Emotions:*
  - o Take a moment to enjoy good vibes. Ask yourself how you're feeling today.
  - o If it's not a positive feeling, what can you do to reach that place so you can feel it? Or is there another "stop over" emotion that would still feel good? (i.e., I can't make it to joy today, but I can feel content).
- *Engagement:*
  - o Stay connected to what you're doing instead of just going through the motions. Ask yourself what you're connecting to in your work and why, so you can hopefully appreciate it more.
  - o If you're feeling overwhelmed, consider whether you need to communicate your capacity to others or delegate tasks, so you can feel more engaged overall. I know, this is easier said than done.
- *Relationships:*
  - o Reflect on who genuinely supports you at work and allow yourself to feel gratitude for them.
  - o Let these people know that you appreciate their support—it can make them feel appreciated, too.
- *Meaning:*
  - o Ask yourself what you believe your larger purpose is at work. Is it ensuring your team has a good leader? Are you mission-driven? Do you want to be able to put food on the table for your family? Any answer is correct—because it's meaning derived by you.

o Take a moment to connect with this to help lift you out of the daily grind. Stay grounded in *your* why.

- *Accomplishment:*
  o Take a moment to acknowledge how much you've improved a skill and what it took to achieve that progress.
  o What small wins can you celebrate without second-guessing whether you deserve them?

Why will using the PERMA model help you? Think of yourself as a tree, with each element acting as a deep root that keeps you grounded during the ongoing storm of leadership. Reflecting on and nurturing each element will ensure they remain strong, helping you maintain perspective on tough days, allowing you to be more flexible, open, and clear with those you lead—and understand your fellow leaders' struggles, too.

Remember, this is another model that requires regular check-ins with yourself, so you can rely on it anytime you need it, rather than hoping it will work reactively and occasionally. You don't just use this resource when your resilience levels are in the gutter and you can't tolerate any more discomfort than you already have. Using it when things are going well can make it even more helpful to use when things aren't. Each of these areas is important, although some may feel more relevant than others on any given day. Think of this model as your leadership mental health dashboard with different sections to focus on, helping you recalibrate when needed. You decide how often to check in with yourself (psst—this could even be one of your Mental Wellbeing Non-Negotiables™ that you practice!).

Pick What Works for You—and Use It!

Using any of these three approaches can give you a greater sense of what you can control and influence on the days when you feel like you can't control or influence anything. We always have something in our control and influence, Stephen Covey taught us that in his book *The*

7 Habits Of Highly Effective People, through focusing on the 1st habit—Being Proactive—and his model of the Circle of Influence®, by sharing:

> *"When we're proactive, we focus our efforts on our Circle of Influence®. We work on the things we can do something about. This allows us to expand our influence over time and create more choices and opportunities. When we're reactive, we get stuck focusing on our Circle of Concern™—on things over which we have little or no control."*[6]

Part II—Conclusion

Tallying Up Our Leadership Mental Health Support Solution. What Do We Do Next?

Throughout Part II, we looked at the responsibilities of companies, from developing support systems for leaders to fostering psychological safety through narrative-shifting conversations to honoring the Duty of Care. We also explored what individual leaders are accountable for, including finding mental health self-care methods, understanding and adjusting internal self-talk, participating in community, and using the Leadership Mental Health Archetypes to understand and improve their mental health behaviors at work.

We've now reached the final elements of our solution that we've assembled throughout Part II as our proverbial "antidote" to the elements of the Weight on Leadership Mental Health Equation in Part I. Let's take a look at our final tally, with the new elements in **bold**:

Organizational Acknowledgment of Leadership
Mental Health Needs

+

Organizational Acknowledgment of the Imperative
to Support Leadership Mental Health

+

Organizational Dedication to a Strategic Approach
to Support Leadership Mental Health

+

Organizational Focus on Leadership Usage of Resources

+

Organizational Dedication to Shifting the Narrative
About Leadership Mental Health

+

Organizational Creation of Leadership Mental
Health Peer Support Networks

+

Organizational Incorporation of Mental Health Education and
Upskilling into Core Leadership Development Training

+

Individual Leaders Shifting to a Healthy Internal
Narrative About Their Mental Health

+

Individual Leaders Identifying Their Leadership
Mental Health Archetype

+

Individual Leaders Using Their Leadership Mental Health
Archetype to Shift Their Beliefs and Behaviors at Work

+

Individual Leader Acknowledgment to Participate
in Creating Broader Change

+

Individual Leader Participation in Support Systems
and Usage of Resources

+

Individual Leader Participation in Organizational Narrative Shifting

+

Individual Leaders Having Conversations About Their Mental
Health at Work (Both Receiving and Starting)

+

Individual Leader Participation in and Fostering of a Leadership
Peer Support Mental Health Community

+

Individual Leaders Creating a Mental Health Self-Care Plan

+

**Individual Leaders Creating Change for Their Mental Health
Through Personalization, Assessment, Planning, and Consistency**

+

**Individual Leaders Identifying and Practicing Mental
Wellbeing Non-Negotiables™**

+

**Individual Leaders Communicating Their Capacity as a
Leadership Mental Health Management Tool**

+

**Individual Leaders Using the PERMA Model to Maintain
Perspective To Support Their Mental Health at Work**

If I had to pick three themes from the solutions above, it
would be these:

1. Individual accountability for change
2. Rebuilding organizational structures
3. Shifting collective ideas

In Part II, we shifted from identifying the problem to developing solutions that address it from multiple perspectives of those involved and affected. I chose to call this the Leadership Mental Health Support Solution, not to suggest it is the only answer, but to demonstrate that different components can contribute to a solution, and that each person has access to various responsibilities, accountabilities, and methods. It's layered and multidirectional because no single person, company, or industry can handle this alone or in one way. Remember at the start of the book, when I said it would take as many villages, and the people in them, as possible? I wasn't kidding. With ongoing effort, strategic change, and a collective willingness, we *can* achieve this. Otherwise, the stage I mentioned in Chapter 8 will have a brief performance before fading away.

Now what? Let's bring everything together and use that metaphorical fire beneath your feet that you've been walking over to survive leadership to instead spark change to help you better manage its impact on you and your mental health, through your new perspective and the individual actions you will take. So, let's finish the same way we started: with a compelling case, honesty, and a dash of hope.

PART II: INDIVIDUAL REFLECTION EXERCISE

Create Your Leadership Mental Health Action Plan

Purpose

In the Individual Reflection Exercise at the end of Part I, you wrote your Statement of Intention & Declaration to Yourself. Building on that, and your reflections from throughout Part I, you will now identify and consolidate your reflection insights from throughout Part II so you can create a personalized, practical, action-oriented plan that you can use and adapt as needed over time. This is where the rubber meets the road.

Step 1: List Your Priorities

Returning to the Paradox of Choice, please apply it here. Don't create a list of 10 priorities! While I love the enthusiasm, that isn't just another to-do list for you. List the three most important changes that you want to make, whether that's for your mental health as a leader, how you show up for other leaders, or how you shift the narrative around this topic at your organization. For example,

1. *"I want to start actively managing my mental well-being."*
2. *"I want to start supporting my leadership peers."*
3. *"I want to help shift the leadership mental health narrative at my company."*

Step 2: Find (and Use) Your Resources

Trust me when I say this, the type of mental health resources your organization (hopefully) has are listed somewhere. Whether it's from your onboarding documents, emails from HR, or even a newsletter—they exist. Go find them! And guess what, you have other resources too, outside and inside of work. Colleagues you're close to at work, healthcare professionals outside of work, friends, family, etc. Identify the top three resources that you want to utilize to support your mental health as a leader and engage with them. For example,

1. *"I've never been to therapy, so let me start by calling our EAP."*
2. *"My best friend keeps asking how I'm doing. I'm going to accept her help, start being honest, and stop being a hero."*
3. *"I don't know what resources we have—I will commit to finding and using at least 1-2 of them."*

Step 3: Decide What Actions You'll Take, When You'll Start, and How You'll Measure Them

For the priorities that you listed above, highlight specific actions you will take to address them, when you can realistically start, and how you'll monitor your progress. For example,

1. *"I will choose and practice one Mental Wellbeing Non-Negotiable™ twice a month. I will start doing this next month. I will check-in with myself in three months to see how this is going and if I need to make changes."*
2. *"I will ask how my leadership peers are doing at least once a month. I will start doing this next week. After a couple of months, I'll ask my peers if my check-ins have been helpful, and if there's anything else I could do instead to better help them."*
3. *"I will share my mental health story in our internal company newsletter for World Mental Health Day. I will reach out to*

(continued)

(continued)

> *my colleague next week that manages this content to let them know I'm interested. Depending on peoples' response to what I share, the month after, I will find one more way to support the leadership mental health efforts at my company."*

Step 4: Plan How You'll Overcome Potential Obstacles

As we have discussed throughout this book, changing behaviors, ideas, and conversations often involves encountering obstacles along the way. Whether from yourself or others. Highlight what the most likely three obstacles are that you may encounter, and how you plan to overcome them. For example,

1. *"I struggle with self-sabotaging behaviors. I'll need to be aware of this, so I don't get in my own way."*
2. *"I tend to think things aren't possible when I listen to negative people who don't either—I'll need to make sure I don't let them influence my decision-making for my mental health self-management."*
3. *"I often think I don't have the time to take care of myself, but that's just perception. I will need to make the time."*

Step 5: Create Your Leadership Mental Health Accountability & Commitment Statement

Building on your Statement of Intention & Declaration To Yourself from Part I, now create your Leadership Mental Health Accountability & Commitment Statement to take you forward into action. For example,

"My mental health is important to me, and it should be to my team and the company. I will do what's in my control by managing and supporting my mental health and choose to view this as a critical part of leadership. I will ask for help from others when I need it. I will show up for my leadership peers when they need help, too. I have the tools I need—now it's time to use them."

Part II: Key Takeaways

- Leadership mental health should be viewed, treated, and prioritized as a **strategic, ethical, and logical organizational priority.**
- Systemic change for leadership mental health **needs to be co-created.**
- **Leaders need to examine and adjust their internal beliefs,** values, and behaviors about their mental health at work.
- **Leaders are responsible for developing their own personalized mental health self-care plan** and must see it as a critical leadership development endeavor.
- **Recognizing the humanity of leaders** is not only necessary, but it's good for business, too.

10

Go Action What You've Learned

WE'VE COVERED A *lot* of ground. From the mildewed archives of history to the modern-day vice grip on leaders' heads, to the logical, sustainable, and actionable ways, we *need to* and *can create* change. Let me be the first to congratulate you. We climbed a mental Everest-level mountain together. Not only did you not give up, but you reached the top, oxygen mask strapped to your face, wobbly legs—and all. Now, it's time to go down the mountain and share with others what you've learned at the summit.

Now *you* get to decide what you'll do next. Every reader will. That's amazing to me; every decision, conversation, and moment can (and will) lead to collective change. So please, do it, because your mental health, and this change at large, can't wait any longer.

I'm a sucker for a good quote. I'm not a politico by any means, but according to the *International Churchill Society*, while these words have been popularly attributed to Winston Churchill and he never actually said them,[1] the intention of the sentiment remains the same: to persevere when times are tough.

"If you're going through hell—keep going."

I know you may be tired, frustrated, or even hopeless. You wouldn't have read this book if you weren't. But incremental change is possible, and necessary, for you and your leadership peers. So, if you're going through hell, keep going, and consider this book your fire-resistant suit so you don't keep getting burned. Or if you're often hungry like me, your snack sustenance for the journey, so you don't starve along the way.

This is where your unhealthy self-sacrifice ends and your persever-ance with support begins. Now ask for it, because you have a book's worth of valid proof. You can do this; I know you can. If anyone disa-grees with the changes you're trying to make for your leadership men-tal health, please send them my way. Because in the lyrical words of the beloved singer and rapper T-Pain, I'll say to them, *"Talk to me, I talk back."*[2]

Notes

Introduction

1. Edelman. (2025). "2025 Edelman Trust Barometer Global Report Trust and the Crisis of Grievance." https://www.edelman.com/sites/g/files/aatuss191/files/2025-01/2025%20Edelman%20Trust%20Barometer%20Global%20Report_01.23.25.pdf (accessed July 29, 2025.)
2. LaMotte, S. (2023). "Why Swearing Is a Sign of Intelligence, Helps Manage Pain and More." *CNN*, last updated June 1, 2023. https://www.cnn.com/2021/01/26/health/swearing-benefits-wellness/index.html.
3. Jay, K. and Jay, T. (2015). "Taboo Word Fluency and Knowledge of Slurs and General Pejoratives: Deconstructing the Poverty-of-Vocabulary Myth." *Language Sciences* 52: 251–259. https://www.sciencedirect.com/science/article/abs/pii/S038800011400151X.
4. Schwartz, B. (2004). *The Paradox of Choice*. Harper Perennial.
5. Eckert, T. (2023). "Managers Impact Our Mental Health More Than Doctors, Therapists—and Same as Spouses." UKG news release, January 24, 2023. https://www.ukg.com/about-us/newsroom/managers-impact-our-mental-health-more-doctors-therapists-and-same-spouses.
6. Bustamante, N. (2023). "What Is Gestalt Psychology? Theory, Principles, & Examples." *Simply Psychology*, updated September 7, 2023. https://www.simplypsychology.org/what-is-gestalt-psychology.html#Gestalt-principles.

Preface

1. Feigofsky, S. (2022). "Imposter Syndrome." *National Library of Medicine National Center for Biotechnology Information, PMC PubMed Central, HeartRhythm Case Reports* 8 (12): 861–862. https://pmc.ncbi.nlm.nih.gov/articles/PMC9811106/.
2. Greenleaf, R.E. (2025). *What Is Servant Leadership?* Center for Servant Leadership. https://www.greenleaf.org/what-is-servant-leadership (accessed February 8, 2025).

Chapter 1: Leadership Mental Health: The History of Being Screwed

1. IMDB. "Air – Quotes." https://www.imdb.com/title/tt16419074/quotes/?item=qt6863912 (accessed August 25, 2025).
2. King, A., Johnson, D., and Van Vugt, M. (2009). "The Origins and Evolution of Leadership." *Current Biology* 19 (19): R911–R916. https://www.sciencedirect.com/science/article/pii/S0960982209014122.
3. UNICEF. (2021). "Defining Social Norms and Related Concepts." https://www.unicef.org/media/111061/file/Social-norms-definitions-2021.pdf.
4. Cherry, K. (2025). What Are Heuristics? *VeryWell Mind*, last updated November 12, 2025. https://www.verywellmind.com/what-is-a-heuristic-2795235.
5. Howard, L. and Travis, J. (2022). "The Social Cognitive Model of Leadership Perceptions: Proposing a Dynamic, Integrated Theory of Leadership Identification and Appraisal." *University of South Carolina Upstate Student Research Journal* 15:7. https://scholarcommons.sc.edu/cgi/viewcontent.cgi?article=1026&context=uscusrj.
6. Travers, M. (2023). "Why Are We Attracted to Strongman Leaders?" *Psychology Today*. January 19, 2023. https://www.psychologytoday.com/us/blog/social-instincts/202301/why-are-we-attracted-to-strongman-leaders.
7. Toader, A.F. and Martin, R. (2023). "Bringing the Cognitive Revolution Forward: What Can Team Cognition Contribute to Our Understanding of Leadership?". *The Leadership Quarterly* 34 (1): 101619. https://www.sciencedirect.com/science/article/abs/pii/S1048984322000224.
8. Maccoby, M. (2004). "Why People Follow the Leader: The Power of Transference." *Harvard Business Review*. September 2004 Magazine. https://hbr.org/2004/09/why-people-follow-the-leader-the-power-of-transference.

9. Cook, A., Zill, A., Meyer, B. et al. (2020). "Perceiving Leadership Structures in Teams: Effects of Cognitive Schemas and Perceived Communication." *Small Group Research* 52 (3): 251–287. https://journals.sagepub.com/doi/full/10.1177/1046496420950480.

10. Dooley, R. (2024). "Robert Cialdini's Principles of Influence Have Held Up for 40 Years. Here's Why." *Forbes*, May 14, 2024. https://www.forbes.com/sites/rogerdooley/2024/05/14/robert-cialdinis-principles-of-influence-have-held-up-for-40-years-heres-why.

11. Hogg, M. (2001). "A Social Identity Theory of Leadership." *Society for Personality and Social Psychology, Personality and Social Psychology Review* 5 (3): 184–200. https://journals.sagepub.com/doi/10.1207/S15327957PSPR0503_1.

12. Nickerson, C. (2024). "Impression Management: Erving Goffman Theory." *Simply Psychology*, updated January 29, 2024. https://www.simplypsychology.org/impression-management.html.

13. IMDB. "*Barbie – Sharon Rooney: Barbie.*" https://www.imdb.com/title/tt1517268/characters/nm5287110/ (accessed August 25, 2025).

14. Laker, B., Weisz, N., Pereira, V., and De Massis, A. (2023). "The Emotional Landscape of Leadership." *MIT Sloan Management Review*, December 7, 2023, https://sloanreview.mit.edu/article/the-emotional-landscape-of-leadership/.

Chapter 2: The Dehumanization of Leaders: VPs Don't Have Panic Attacks . . . Right? (Wrong)

1. "Understanding Motivational Interviewing." *Motivational Interviewing Network of Trainers*. https://motivationalinterviewing.org/understanding-motivational-interviewing (accessed February 10, 2025).

2. Berman, L. (2012). *Behind the 8-Ball: A Recovery Guide for the Families of Gamblers*. iUniverse.

3. Maccoby, M. "Why People Follow the Leader: The Power of Transference." *Harvard Business Review*. September 2004 Magazine. https://hbr.org/2004/09/why-people-follow-the-leader-the-power-of-transference.

4. Cloutier, A. and Barling, J. (2023). "Expectations of Leaders' Mental Health." *Journal of Leadership and Organizational Studies* 30 (3): https://journals.sagepub.com/doi/full/10.1177/15480518231178637.

5. Queensland Brain Institute. (2023). "Half of World's Population Will Experience a Mental Health Disorder." *Harvard Medical School.* July 31, 2023. https://hms.harvard.edu/news/half-worlds-population-will-experience-mental-health-disorder.

6. Bryan, R. (2024). "36% of Managers Report Alarming Levels of Stress and Burnout in 2024." *Forbes*. https://www.forbes.com/sites/bryanrobinson/2024/09/26/managers-report-stress-and-burnout-in-2024/.

7. Harms, P.D., Crede, M. et al. (2017). "Leadership and Stress: A Meta-Analytic Review." *Science Direct, A Leadership Quarterly* 28 (1): 178–194. https://www.sciencedirect.com/science/article/abs/pii/S1048984316300923.

8. Peiro, J. and Rodriguez, I. "Work Stress, Leadership and Organizational Health." *Research Gate*, Papeles del Psicólogo – Psychologist Papers. (January – 2008). https://www.researchgate.net/publication/287466404_Work_stress_leadership_and_organizational_health.

9. Coyle-Shapiro, J. "Psychological Contracts." *The London School of Economics and Political Science*. https://eprints.lse.ac.uk/26866/1/Psychological_contracts_(LSERO).pdf (accessed March 3, 2025).

10. Freyd, J. "Research." https://www.jjfreyd.com/about-research (accessed February 17, 2025).

11. *BiteSize Learning*. "The Five Dysfunctions of a Team (And How to Overcome Them)." https://www.bitesizelearning.co.uk/resources/five-dysfunctions-of-a-team-summary-pyramid (accessed February 17, 2025).

12. Schopfer, Q. and Eshmawey, M. (2022). "Shared Psychotic Disorder in Old Age: Syndrome of Folie à Deux." *National Library of Medicine National Center for Biotechnology*, PubMed Central, *Case Reports in Psychiatry* 2022:8811140. https://pmc.ncbi.nlm.nih.gov/articles/PMC9085334/.

13. *Psychology Today*. "Illusory Truth Effect." https://www.psychologytoday.com/us/basics/illusory-truth-effect (accessed February 17, 2025).

14. Fazio, L., Brashier, N., Payne, B., and Marsh, E. (2015). "Knowledge Does Not Protect Against Illusory Truth." *American Psychological Association*. *Journal of Experimental Psychological: General* 144 (5): 993–1002. https://www.apa.org/pubs/journals/features/xge-0000098.pdf.

Chapter 3: The Impact: Leadership Well-Being, Career Path, and Performance

1. Bryan, R. (2024). "36% of Managers Report Alarming Levels of Stress and Burnout in 2024." *Forbes*. https://www.forbes.com/sites/bryanrobinson/2024/09/26/managers-report-stress-and-burnout-in-2024/.

2. Patrick, H. (2025). "Leadership, Stress and the Importance of Self-Care." *Mercer*. https://www.mercer.com/en-ca/insights/total-rewards/employee-wellbeing/leadership-stress-and-the-importance-of-self-care/ (accessed February 15, 2025).

3. *Lyra Health.* (2024). "2024 State of Workforce Mental Health Report." https://www.lyrahealth.com/2024-state-of-workforce-mental-health-report/ (accessed February 10, 2025).
4. Fernández-Jiménez, E. and Maran, D. (2024). "Editorial: Break the Mental Health Stigma: Mental Health in the Workplace." *National Library of Medicine*, National Center for Biotechnology Information, PMC PubMed Central. *Frontiers in Psychiatry* 15: 1427097. https://pmc.ncbi.nlm.nih.gov/articles/PMC11150767/.
5. Laker, B., Weisz, N., Pereira, V., and De Massis, A. (2023). "The Emotional Landscape of Leadership." *MITSloan Management Review.* December 7, 2023. https://sloanreview.mit.edu/article/the-emotional-landscape-of-leadership/.
6. Lyra Health. (2025). "2025 Workforce Mental Health Trends." https://www.lyrahealth.com/blog/workforce-mental-health-trends-2025/ (accessed February 17, 2025).
7. Maccoby, M. (2004). "Why People Follow the Leader: The Power of Transference." *Harvard Business Review.* Magazine. https://hbr.org/2004/09/why-people-follow-the-leader-the-power-of-transference.
8. Bertollo, A., Puntel, C., Varela da Silva, B. et al. (2025). "Neurobiological Relationships Between Neurodevelopmental Disorders and Mood Disorders." *National Library of Medicine National Center for Biotechnology Information. Brain Sciences* 15 (3): 307. https://pmc.ncbi.nlm.nih.gov/articles/PMC11940368/.
9. Baumer, N. and Freueh, J. (2021). "What Is Neurodiversity?" *Harvard Medical School-Harvard Health Publishing*, November 23, 2021. https://www.health.harvard.edu/blog/what-is-neurodiversity-202111232645.
10. Dennison, K. (2024). "The Benefits of Neurodiversity in Leadership." *Forbes.* November 14, 2024. https://www.forbes.com/sites/karadennison/2024/11/14/the-benefits-of-neurodiversity-in-leadership/.
11. World Economic Forum. (2023). "Neurodiversity and Leadership: How to Create a Diverse and Inclusive Executive Team," August 22, 2023. https://www.weforum.org/stories/2023/08/neurodiversity-how-to-create-inclusive-leadership-team/.
12. Malchiodi, C. (2021). "Understanding Fight, Flight, Freeze, and the Feign Response." *Psychology Today*, June 13, 2021. https://www.psychologytoday.com/us/blog/arts-and-health/202106understanding-fight-flight-freeze-and-the-feign-response.
13. Budiarto, Y. and Helmi, A.F. (2021). "Shame and Self-Esteem: A Meta-Analysis." *National Library of Medicine*, National Center for Biotechnology Information. *Europe's Journal of Psychology* 17 (2): 131–145. https://pmc.ncbi.nlm.nih.gov/articles/PMC8768475/.

14. Cleveland Clinic (2022). "What Is Burnout?" https://health.clevelandclinic.org/signs-of-burnout.
15. Gleeson, B. (2023). "Burden of Command: How Leaders Identify and Reduce Burnout in Themselves and Their Teams." *Forbes*. https://www.forbes.com/sites/brentgleeson/2023/06/21/burden-of-command-how-leaders-identify-and-reduce-burnout-in-themselves-and-their-teams/.
16. "The Morning Show on 7." *Instagram*. https://www.instagram.com/reel/DMG-yuXiudK/?igsh=NDN1b3cxZDJxbnV2 (accessed July 31, 2025).
17. Tangalakis-Lippert, K. (2025). "Gen Z's 'Conscious Unbossing' Should Be a Wake-Up Call for Businesses." *Business Insider*. https://www.businessinsider.com/gen-z-consciously-unbossing-avoid-management-roles-preserve-mental-health-2025-4.

Chapter 4: The Leadership "Plate" Has Become a Deep Trough—and Leaders Are Strapped to It

1. Stanford University. "Growth Mindset and Enhanced Learning." https://teachingcommons.stanford.edu/teaching-guides/foundations-course-design/learning-activities/growth-mindset-and-enhanced-learning (accessed August 26, 2025).
2. Lauren Landry. (2019). "Why Emotional Intelligence Is Important in Leadership." *Harvard Business School Online*. April 3, 2019. https://online.hbs.edu/blog/post/emotional-intelligence-in-leadership.
3. American Psychological Association. (2024). "What is psychological safety at work? Here's how to start creating it." Last updated March 4, 2024. https://www.apa.org/topics/healthy-workplaces/psychological-safety.
4. *Radical Candor LLC*. "Video Tip: What Is Radical Candor? Learn The Basic Principles In 6 Minutes." https://www.radicalcandor.com/blog/what-is-radical-candor (accessed August 28, 2025).
5. Reese, H. (2023). "What Is Emotional Labor, and Why Does It Matter?" *Greater Good Magazine*. April 4, 2023. https://greatergood.berkeley.edu/article/item/what_is_emotional_labor_and_why_does_it_matter.
6. Wittmers, A. and Maier, G. (2023). "Leaders' Mental Health in Times of Crisis: Work Intensification, Emotional Demands and the Moderating Role of Organizational Support and Self-Efficacy." *Frontiers in Psychology* 14: 1122881. https://pmc.ncbi.nlm.nih.gov/articles/PMC10186101/.
7. Mackenzie, J. (2025). "The Unravelling of Yoon Suk Yeol: South Korea's 'Stubborn and Hot-Tempered' Martial Law President." *BBC*. April 3, 2025. https://www.bbc.com/news/articles/c86py30qezvo.
8. Haq, S. (2025). "UK Supreme Court Says Legal Definition of 'Woman' Excludes Trans Women, in Landmark Ruling." *CNN*. April 16, 2025.

https://www.cnn.com/2025/04/16/uk/uk-supreme-court-ruling-definition-woman-intl.

9. Quirox-Gutierrez, M. (2024). "Disgruntled Boeing Investors Take Aim at $33 Million Pay for Ex-CEO Amid Ongoing Safety Issues." *Fortune.* May 14, 2024. https://fortune.com/2024/05/17/what-is-going-on-at-boeing-disgruntled-investors-ceo-pay-millions/.

10. *SAP.* (2020). "How Crisis Changes the Role of a Leader." *Forbes.* September 30, 2020. https://www.forbes.com/sites/sap/2025/04/01/5-tips-for-effective-liquidity-management/.

11. Wright, G. "VUCA (Volatility, Uncertainty, Complexity and Ambiguity)" *TechTarget.* https://www.techtarget.com/whatis/definition/VUCA-volatility-uncertainty-complexity-and-ambiguity (accessed April 1, 2025).

12. Edelman. "2025 Edelman Trust Barometer Global Report on Trust and the Crisis of Grievance." https://www.edelman.com/trust/2025/trust-barometer (accessed April 2, 2025).

13. Fandom. "4:00 P.M. (Season 1)/Transcript." https://thepitt.fandom.com/wiki/4:00_P.M._(Season_1)/Transcript (accessed August 26, 2025).

14. University of Hawai'i. "Camus: The Myth of Sisyphus." https://www2.hawaii.edu/~freeman/courses/phil360/16.%20Myth%20of%20Sisyphus.pdf (accessed August 27, 2025).

15. Brenner, B. (2024). "The Psychology of Cancel Culture: Impacts on Mental Health." *Therapy Group of DC.* October 29, 2024. https://therapygroupdc.com/therapist-dc-blog/the-psychology-of-cancel-culture-impacts-on-mental-health/.

16. *LinkedIn.* "Post from Braden Wallake Personal Profile." https://www.linkedin.com/posts/bradenwallake_this-will-be-the-most-vulnerable-thing-ill-activity-6962886723617910784-_L4w/?utm_source=linkedin_share&utm_medium=member_desktop_web (accessed August 26, 2025).

17. Toler, L. (2022). "The Mental Health Effects of Cancel Culture." *VeryWellMind.* April 14, 2022. https://www.verywellmind.com/the-mental-health-effects-of-cancel-culture-5119201.

Chapter 5: Leadership Mental Health Is Also Shaped by Context and Identity

1. Calm. "2023 Workplace Mental Health Trends Report: The Future of Work." https://info.calm.com/rs/541-LYF-023/images/Calm-Business-2023-Workplace-Mental-Health-Trends-Report.pdf (accessed August 7, 2025).

2. United Way of the National Capital Area. (2024). "What Is Intersectionality Theory? Definitions and Examples." November 20, 2024. https://unitedwaynca.org/what-is-intersectionality/.

3. Crenshaw, K. (1989). "Demarginalizing the Intersection of Race and Sex: A Black Feminist Critique of Antidiscrimination Doctrine, Feminist Theory and Antiracist Politics." *University of Chicago Legal Forum* 1989 (1): 8. https://chicagounbound.uchicago.edu/cgi/viewcontent.cgi?article =1052&context=uclf.

4. Kaur, H. (2023). "The Differences Between Race and Ethnicity - And Why They're So Hard to Define." *CNN.* May 30, 2023. https://www. cnn.com/2023/05/30/us/race-ethnicity-difference-explainer-cec/ index.html.

5. American Psychological Association. "Culture." https://dictionary.apa. org/culture (accessed April 8, 2025).

6. Faye, G. (2005). "Stigma: Barrier to Mental Health Care Among Ethnic Minorities." *Taylor and Francis Online. Issues in Mental Health Nursing* 26 (10): https://www.tandfonline.com/doi/full/10.1080/0161284050028 0638.

7. Jocelyn Apodaca Scholssberg. (2023). "Confronting Mental Health Barriers in the Asian American and Pacific Islander Community." *UCLA Health.* May 9, 2023. https://www.uclahealth.org/news/article/confronting- mental-health-barriers-asian-american-and-2.

8. Hogan. "Leadership Emergence in Japan: Insights from Hogan Personality Data." https://www.hoganassessments.com/news-events/updates/ leadership-emergence-in-japan-insights-from-hogan-personality-data/ (accessed April 9, 2025).

9. Ascend Global Leaders. (2024). "Ascend Releases New Landmark Report About Asian and Pacific Islander Professionals' Mental Health Challenges." November 12, 2024. https://www.ascendleadership.org/press release/api-mental-health-3-cultivating-well-being.

10. Galoustian, G. (2021). "Study Aims to (Re)Define Latino Manhood and Masculinity." *Florida Atlantic University.* March 22, 2021. https://www .fau.edu/newsdesk/articles/latino-leadership-study.php.

11. Ibanez, F. (2023). "Latinas in Leadership Positions in the United States: Theories, Characteristics, and Recommendations." *DePaul University,* College of Science and Health Theses and Dissertations, Summer, June 9, 2023. https://via.library.depaul.edu/cgi/viewcontent.cgi?article=1497& context=csh_etd.

12. David, R.E., Lee, S, Johnson, T.P., and Rothschild, S.K. (2019). "Measuring the Elusive Construct of Personalismo Among Mexican American, Puerto Rican, and Cuban American Adults." *National Library of Medicine National Center for Biotechnology Information,* PubMed

Central, *Hispanic Journal of Behavioural Sciences* 41 (1): 103–121. https:// pmc.ncbi.nlm.nih.gov/articles/PMC8205428/.

13. Bruneau, M. (2024). "Voices of Latina Leadership: How These 7 Founders Strategically Leveraged Community to Scale." *Forbes*. September 24, 2024. https://www.forbes.com/sites/meganbruneau/2024/09/24/voices-of-latina-leadership-how-these-7-founders-strategically-leveraged-community-to-scale/.

14. Human Resources Professional Association. (2024). "Creating Psychological Safety for Black Leaders: In Conversation with Chivon John." February 1, 2024. https://www.hrpa.ca/hr-insights/creating-psychological-safety-for-black-leaders-in-conversation-with-chivon-john/.

15. VandenBosch, T. (2024). "How Black Leaders Can Protect Their Well-Being from Microaggressions." *Forbes*. June 24, 2024. https://www.forbes.com/sites/topsievandenbosch/2024/06/24/how-black-leaders-can-protect-their-well-being-from-microaggressions/.

16. The Hartford. "Mental Health at Work for Black Americans." https:// assets.thehartford.com/image/upload/mental_health_at_work_black_americans.pdf (accessed August 27, 2025).

17. Doman, M. (2021). *Yes, You Can Talk About Mental Health at Work (Here's Why And How To Do It Really Well)*. Trigger Publishing.

18. Bailey, A. (2023). "Here's Every Word of America Ferrara's Big Barbie Monologue." *Elle*. July 25, 2023. https://www.elle.com/culture/movies-tv/a44640422/america-ferrera-full-barbie-monologue/.

19. *The Myers Briggs Company*. (2020). "Stress, Gender, and Leadership: A Research Study from The Myers-Briggs Company." https://www.themyersbriggs.com/-/media/Myers-Briggs/Files/GLOBAL/Company/Research/Stress_gender_and_leadership_Report.pdf.

20. Brassey, J. and Bharwaga, R. (2024). "Prioritizing the health of Female Employees Is a Strategic Imperative. Here Are 4 Ways To Do It." *World Economic Forum*. March 8, 2024. https://www.weforum.org/stories/2024/03/womens-mental-health-is-a-strategic-imperative-heres-how-employers-can-bolster-it-today/.

21. Yakali, D. (2024). "'He is just Ken:' Deconstructing Hegemonic Masculinity in Barbie (2023 Movie)." *National Library of Medicine*, National Center for Biotechnical Information, Frontiers in Sociology, April 5, 2024. https:// pmc.ncbi.nlm.nih.gov/articles/PMC11026851/.

22. Herron, A. (2024). "How to Provide Support for Mental Health Across the Generations." *WebMD*. August 27, 2024. https://www.webmdhealthservices.com/blog/how-to-provide-support-for-mental-health-across-the-generations/.

23. Sokoler, S. (2023). "Breaking the Stigma: Addressing Mental Health in the C-Suite." *Forbes*. June 16, 2023. https://www.forbes.com/councils/forbesbusinesscouncil/2023/06/16/breaking-the-stigma-addressing-mental-health-in-the-c-suite/.

24. Klinghoffer, D. and Kirkpatrick-Husk, K. (2023). "More Than 50% of Managers Feel Burned Out." *Harvard Business Review*. May 18, 2023. https://hbr.org/2023/05/more-than-50-of-managers-feel-burned-out.

25. "Great Expectations: Making Hybrid Work Work." *Microsoft Work Trend Index*, March 16, 2022. https://www.microsoft.com/en-us/worklab/work-trend-index/great-expectations-making-hybrid-work-work.

26. Mass General Brigham McLean Hospital. (2025). "The Silent Strain at the Top: Mental Health Among Executive Leadership." June 12, 2025. https://www.mcleanhospital.org/news/silent-strain-top-mental-health-among-executive-leadership.

27. Sherman, G., Lee, J., Cuddy, A. et al. (2012). "Leadership Is Associated with Lower Levels of Stress." *National Library of Medicine National Center for Biotechnology Information. Proceedings of the National Academy of Sciences (PNAS)*. September 24, 109 (44): 17903–17907. https://pmc.ncbi.nlm.nih.gov/articles/PMC3497788/.

28. *Last Week Tonight With John Oliver*. "Air Traffic Control." *HBO*. Uploaded June 2, 2025. YouTube. https://www.youtube.com/watch?v=YeABJbvcJ_k&ab_channel=LastWeekTonight.

29. Lee, Y. and Kim, H. (2023). "Performance Pressure and Mental Health Among Finance Workers in Korea: A Cross-Sectional Study." *National Library of Medicine – National Center for Biotechnology Information. Epidemiology and Health*. November 7, 2023. https://pmc.ncbi.nlm.nih.gov/articles/PMC10876446/.

30. U.S. Centers for Disease Control and Prevention. (2024). "Risk Factors for Stress and Burnout." April 23, 2024. National Institute for Occupational Safety and Health. Healthcare Workers. https://www.cdc.gov/niosh/healthcare/risk-factors/stress-burnout.html.

31. Davis, P. (2023). "How Teams Can Help Address Burnout in the Legal Profession." *The National Association for Law Placement*. January 2023. https://www.nalp.org/how-teams-can-help-address-burnout.

32. Dennis, P. (2023). "98% of HR Professionals Are Feeling Burned Out – What Can They Do?" *SelectSoftware Reviews* (28 June). https://www.selectsoftwarereviews.com/blog/98-of-hr-professionals-are-feeling-burned-out-what-can-they-do.

33. Shumway, E. (2022). "Survey: Almost All HR Pros Are Burned Out—And Many Are Thinking of Leaving." *HRDive*. April 22, 2022. https://www.hrdive.com/news/survey-almost-all-hr-pros-are-burned-out-and-many-are-thinking-of-leavin/622488/.

34. National Academy of Engineering. (2024). "Suicide and Mental Health Challenges in the Construction Industry." May 30, 2024. https://www.nationalacademies.org/news/2024/05/suicide-and-mental-health-challenges-in-the-construction-industry.

35. *Spring Health*. "How Manufacturers Are Reducing the Mental Health Stigma." https://www.springhealth.com/customers/manufacturing (accessed May 2, 2025).

36. *IMDB*. "The Last of Us – Through the Valley – Quotes." https://m.imdb.com/title/tt31804612/quotes/?ref_=tt_dyk_qu (accessed August 26, 2025).

Chapter 6: How Organizations Can Support Leadership Mental Health

1. Indeed.com. "A Guide to Employer Duty of Care." https://uk.indeed.com/hire/c/info/duty-of-care (accessed December 16, 2025).

2. *The National Health Service*. "The Care Certificate Duty of Care." https://www.hee.nhs.uk/sites/default/files/documents/Standard-3%20Duty%20of%20care%2013.06.16.pdf (accessed August 8, 2025).

3. *Canadian Human Rights Commission*. "Workplace Accommodation: A Guide for Federally Regulated Employers." https://www.chrc-ccdp.gc.ca/resources/publications/workplace-accommodation-guide (accessed May 30, 2025).

4. Ilke, I., Thomas, G., Chu, C. et al. (2018). "Leadership Behavior and Employee Well-Being: An Integrated Review and a Future Research Agenda." *The Leadership Quarterly*. 29 (1): 179–202. https://www.researchgate.net/publication/345682369_Leadership_behavior_and_employee_well-being_An_integrated_review_and_a_future_research_agenda.

5. Julie Dextras-Gauthier, Marie-Hélène Gilbert, Justine Dma, and Laetitia Bomoya Adou. (2023). "Organizational Culture and Leadership Behaviors: Is Manager's Psychological Health the Missing Piece?" *Frontiers in Psychology*, September 27, 2023. Organizational Psychology. https://www.frontiersin.org/journals/psychology/articles/10.3389/fpsyg.2023.1237775/full.

6. Ginger. "2021 Third Annual Workforce Attitudes Toward Mental Health Report." https://f.hubspotusercontent40.net/hubfs/5327495/Ginger_WFA2021.pdf (accessed August 8, 2025).

7. MacKenzie, M. (2018). "Why CEOs Need to Talk About Mental Health." *Forbes*. May 15, 2018. https://www.forbes.com/sites/macaelamackenzie/2018/05/15/mental-health-awareness-month-why-ceos-need-to-talk-about-mental-health/.

8. Maclellan, L. (2025). "Board Burnout Is a Major Risk to All Companies—Here's How They Can Protect Their Top Directors." *Fortune*. March 17, 2025. https://fortune.com/2025/03/17/board-burnout-risk-three-steps-to-avoid/.

9. Staglin, G. (2023). "Stress Management for Leaders, Improved Mental Health for the Workplace." *Forbes*. April 25, 2023. https://www.forbes.com/sites/onemind/2023/04/25/stress-management-for-leaders-improved-mental-health-for-the-workplace/.

10. Garrity, K. (2023). "Fetterman: I Assumed Speaking About Mental Health Challenges Would End My Career." *Politico*. December 31, 2023. https://www.politico.com/news/2023/12/31/john-fetterman-mental-health-00133359.

11. Turnbull, T. (2023). "Jacinda Ardern: New Zealand PM Quits Citing Burnout." *BBC*. January 17, 2023. https://www.bbc.com/news/world-asia-64327224.

12. Coyle, J. (2025). "'The Studio' Is the Defining Portrait or Modern Hollywood." *AP News*. March 26, 2025. https://apnews.com/article/studio-seth-rogen-tv-show-52762ef0f06d28099924fecb020eabb9.

13. Arzubi, E. LinkedIn post. May 20, 2025. Retrieved on May 20, 2025. https://www.linkedin.com/posts/drzoobs_our-greatest-president-battled-severe-depression-activity-7330559672208244736-Y7Gs/.

14. Gourani, S. (2023). "Humanize Leadership and Make Your Struggles Part of Your Story." *Forbes*. November 28, 2023. https://www.forbes.com/sites/soulaimagourani/2023/11/28/humanize-leadership-and-make-your-struggles-part-of-your-story/.

15. Hill, R. (2024). "How Showing Vulnerability Can Strengthen Your Leadership." *Association For Talent Development*. August 29, 2024. https://www.td.org/content/atd-blog/how-showing-vulnerability-can-strengthen-your-leadership.

16. Grabarek, P. and Sawyer, K. (2025). "'Struggling with Leadership?' That Might Be a Strength." *Psychology Today*, May 13, 2025. https://www.psychologytoday.com/us/blog/leading-for-wellness/202505/struggling-with-leadership-that-might-be-a-strength.

17. The NeuroLeadership Institute. (2023). "5 Ways to Spark (or Destroy) Your Employees' Motivation." October 17, 2023. https://neuroleadership.com/your-brain-at-work/scarf-model-motivate-your-employees.

18. The Behavioural Insights Team. "EAST-Four Simple Ways to Apply Behavioural Insights-Revised and Updated Edition." https://www.bi.team/wp-content/uploads/2014/04/BIT-EAST-1.pdf (accessed May 28, 2025).

19. American Psychological Association. "Recency Effect." APA Dictionary of Psychology. https://dictionary.apa.org/recency-effect (accessed August 8, 2025).

20. The Workplace Mental Health Method™ - Melissa Doman LLC. "Mental Health at Work Conversational Literacy® – For Leaders." https://www.melissadoman.com/leadership-certification-program (accessed August 10, 2025).

Chapter 7: Understanding Your Internal Narrative and Leadership Mental Health Archetype

1. Booth, S. (2025). "Imposter Syndrome: How to Overcome It." *WebMD*. February 11, 2025. https://www.webmd.com/balance/what-is-imposter-syndrome.

2. Gottman. "The Four Horsemen: Stonewalling." https://www.gottman.com/blog/the-four-horsemen-stonewalling/ (accessed December 6, 2025).

Chapter 8: How Leaders Create Change for Themselves and Their Peers

1. *Influence At Work.* "The Science of Persuasion - Seven Principles of Persuasion." https://www.influenceatwork.com/7-principles-of-persuasion/ (accessed June 6, 2025).

2. Hoffman, R. (2025). "Adlerian Therapy: Key Concepts & Techniques." *Simply Psychology*, April 4. https://www.simplypsychology.org/adlerian-therapy.html.

3. Foster, K. (2024). "Birth Order Theory: Insights into Your Personality." *BetterHelp*. October 10, 2024. https://www.betterhelp.com/advice/family/birth-order-theory-insights-into-your-personality/.

4. Knapen, J., Blaker, N., and Van Vugt, M. (2018). "The Napoleon Complex: When Shorter Men Take More." *National Library of Medicine National Center for Biotechnology Information. Psychological Sciences* 29 (7): 1134–1144. https://pmc.ncbi.nlm.nih.gov/articles/PMC6247438/.

Chapter 9: Creating Your Leadership Mental Health Self-Care Plan

1. Shonk, K. (2025). "The Contingency Theory of Leadership: A Focus on Fit." *Harvard Law School – Program On Negotiation*. June 12, 2025. https://www.pon.harvard.edu/daily/leadership-skills-daily/the-contingency-theory-of-leadership-a-focus-on-fit/.
2. Hyland, P. "Leadership, Stress and the Importance of Self-Care." *Mercer*. https://www.mercer.com/en-ca/insights/total-rewards/employee-wellbeing/leadership-stress-and-the-importance-of-self-care/ (accessed July 6, 2025).
3. National University. "What is Sociological Imagination?" https://www.nu.edu/blog/what-is-sociological-imagination/ (accessed July 6, 2025).
4. Brene Brown on The Tim Ferriss Show. "How To Save Your Marriage." *YouTube*. February 6, 2020. https://www.youtube.com/watch?v=Wh5SUF0gPWQ&ab_channel=TimFerriss (accessed July 6, 2025).
5. Madeson, M. (2017). "Seligman's PERMA+ Model Explained: A Theory of Wellbeing." *Positive Psychology*. February 24, 2017. https://positivepsychology.com/perma-model/.
6. *FranklinCovey*. "Habit 1: Be Proactive". https://www.franklincovey.com/courses/the-7-habits/habit-1/ (accessed August 12, 2025).

Chapter 10: Go Action What You've Learned

1. International Churchill Society. (2023). "Quotes Falsely Attributed to Winston Churchill." January 17, 2023. https://winstonchurchill.org/resources/quotes/quotes-falsely-attributed/.
2. AZLyrics. "T-Pain Lyrics." https://www.azlyrics.com/lyrics/tpain/buyuadrankshawtysnappin.html (accessed August 28, 2025).

Acknowledgments

This second book could not have come into existence without the following people.

To my husband, Matt, I love you. From pitch to publish, just like with my first book, I literally could not have made it through this process again without your continuous love, support, and encouragement. Thank you for always believing in me, my work, and what I'm trying to accomplish.

To my parents, David and Penny, my brother Mark, and my sister Sandy—for always cheering me on. Whenever I think I don't have the energy for another milestone, this family's strength reminds me I do. Thank you for continuing to be inspiring examples of purpose, achievement, and tenacity. I called on those skills endlessly as I wrote this second book.

To my commissioning editor, Brian, who boldly encouraged me to break big ideas, with big words, and a big voice. And to my developmental editor, Julie, for ensuring I did it in a coherent, logical, and succinct way—when I approached word count with reckless abandon.

To my friends, for always being there for me. You kept me going on the days when I felt I had nothing left to give. I felt your strength, care, and love as you proverbially held my head up as I crawled across the finish line.

To my team, I wouldn't have had the bandwidth or brain cells to write this book without you simultaneously supporting and keeping my business running. I appreciate all of you more than you know.

To my interviewees, for sharing your stories in such a raw and meaningful way. Your words brought this book to life more than my sentiments and any data ever could.

To the musician Sierra Hull, for helping me push through my initial writer's block when I saw your show at Mission Ballroom in Denver. Your otherworldly mandolin-playing abilities, voice, and timbre shifted me into a flow state, allowing me to start writing this book literally on my phone during your show.

To my therapist, Whitney, for helping me overcome my feelings of Imposter Syndrome about writing this book. You helped me see that my feelings weren't about my abilities, knowing what to say, or if I "should" say it. You helped me see that my feelings were a combination of passion, anticipation, and determination to get it *right*. When I told you why I was writing this book, you said it made you feel seen as a leader in a way you never had before. I'm appreciative that I could give something back to you.

To everyone who follows and implements my work to create change in your corners of the world, I will always do this work for you. Thank you for taking the time to tell me that my efforts are making a difference. It keeps me going on the days I worry when I'm not doing enough. You make me feel that I do, and I am forever grateful for that.

About the Author

MELISSA DOMAN, M.A. is an Organizational Psychologist, former mental health therapist, mental health at work specialist, and the Founder of The Workplace Mental Health Method™. She is also the author of *Yes, You Can Talk About Mental Health at Work (Here's Why and How to Do It Really Well)*.

After working as a mental health therapist in a variety of settings, Melissa left the clinical field and transitioned into industrial-organizational psychology, specifically workplace mental health, with one core goal: to equip companies, individuals, and leaders with the skills they need to have constructive conversations about mental health, team dynamics, and communication at work. Her work aims to accomplish just that. She uses her hybrid background of education and field experience to translate complex ideas into simple, practical, actionable knowledge, helping to bridge the workplace mental health skills gap in the World of Work.

Melissa has spoken, presented, and consulted for companies across sectors and around the world, including clients like Google, Estée Lauder, the MLS team—Orlando City Soccer Club, Microsoft, the National Health Service (NHS) of England, Salesforce, and more. She has spoken at international and national conferences, summits, and has spoken and mentored at SXSW. She has been featured as a subject matter expert in CNN, Vogue, NPR, Fast Company, the BBC, CNBC, Inc., and in LinkedIn's 2022 Top 10 Voices on Mental Health. Across every medium, Melissa is determined to bring the topic of mental health at work to as many industries and minds as possible. Having lived abroad in South Korea, England, and Australia, and traveled to 50+ countries (with surpassing 100 as her lifelong ambition), Melissa leverages these experiences to inform how she works with companies and audiences worldwide.

Melissa lives in Denver, Colorado, with her husband, Matt, and their dog, Lola. She loves salsa dancing, has an intense relationship with coffee, and does a pretty decent Chewbacca impression.

Index

A

accountability, xxix, 3, 7, 58, 73, 74, 77, 149, 151, 215, 223, 226

Achieving Business Excellence: Health, Well-Being and Performance, 27

Adler University, 183

Air (film), xx, 4

Ardern, Former Prime Minister Jacinda, 132

Arzubi, Dr. Eric, 135

Asian and Pacific Islander (API) cultures, 86

Association of Talent Development, 137

B

Baby Boomers, 100, 101

Barbie (film), 95, 96

Bennis, Warren, 69

Black community, 90

Black leader, 89, 90

book goals, xxv, xxvi, xxvii

Brown, Brené, 34, 137, 215

C

Calhoun, David, 65

Call-Out Culture, 76

Calm, 79–80, 109

Camus, Albert, 72

Cancel Culture, 73, 76

career trajectory impact and leadership effectiveness, 45–46

Cialdini, Robert, 11, 182

community, having, 198–199

compulsive gambling, 21

confidentiality, 190–196

construction industry, 114

Contingency Theory, 210–211

Crenshaw, Kimberlé, 81, 85

D
DePaul University, 88
diversity, equity, inclusion,
        and belonging (DEIB),
        xxii, 60, 70, 97–98
Duty of Care (law), 129–130
Duty to Inquire (law), 130

E
The EAST model (Easy, Attractive,
        Social, and Timely),
        139, 141–142
Edelman, xx, 71
Elle (magazine), 95
Emotional Labor, 63, 98
The Emotional Landscape of
        Leadership (article), 16
emotional support structures,
        lack of, 41–43
Employee Assistance Program
        (EAP), 20, 21, 146, 206
The Encouraged Perspective, xxv
ethnicity, 80–92

F
Fetterman, Senator John, 132
Finance industry, 108–110
*The Five Dysfunctions of a Team:
        A Leadership Fable* (Patrick
        Lencioni), 29
Forbes, 25, 36, 39, 44, 50, 88,
        90, 104, 132
Fortune, 132
Freud, Sigmund, 183
Freyd, Jennifer, 28
Frontiers in Psychology, 64,
        67, 131
Frontiers in Sociology Journal, 96
Frontiers of Psychology, 67

G
Ganz, Marshall, 136
gender
    identity influences, 97–98
    identity spectrum, 94
    norms, 92–93, 97
    role, 92
    stigma, 93–96
Gender-Based Emotion
        Shaming, 93, 95, 115
generational identity, 100–104
Generation X, 100–101
Generation Z, 103–104
Gerwig, Greta, 95–97
Ginger 2021, 131
Goffman, Erving, 12

H
The Hartford, 91
Harvard Business Review (HBR),
        104–105, 132
Healthcare industry, 108–111
HRDive, 113
Human Resources (HR) industry,
        112–114, 195–196
*Human Resources Professional
        Association*, 90

I
Illusory Truth Effect, 31–32
Impression Management,
        12, 31
individual reflection exercise,
        120–122, 224–226
influence perceptions,
        8, 80–82
institutional betrayal, 26, 28, 29,
        39, 46
institutional blindness, 28–29

intergenerational tug-of-war of mental health and leadership, 98–104
internal narrative, 162
  assess and rebuilding, 163–164
  Leadership Mental Health Archetypes, 165–177
internet social scrutiny, 73–77
intersectionality, 79, 204–205
  complexity of, 115
  compounded effects of, 81–82

J
Japanese corporate culture, 86
Jordan, Michael, 4
Journal of Epidemiology and Health, 109

L
The Last of Us (TV show), 118
Last Week Tonight with John Oliver (TV show), 107
Latina female leaders, 88–89
Latinx community, 87
Legal industry, leadership mental health, 108, 110
Law of Consistency, 11–12
layoffs, 65–66, 113
leaders, xx, xix, xxi–xxii
  attribute meaning, 11
  dehumanization of, 19–35
  emotional composure and professionalism, 110
  interpret behavior, 10–11
  mental representations, 10
  pressure to make public statements, 71
leadership, 6
  archetypes, 5–8

Base Tasks, 57, 58
behaviors, 9–14
Bonus Tasks, 58–60
burden, 56–57
career trajectory, 48–51
from communities of color, 90
darker side of Bonus Tasks, 61–65
development, 154–157
effectiveness, 45–46
emotional capacity, 16–17, 47, 103
gender, 92–104
intensifying weight, 56–57
Magical Thinking, 21–23
mental health as a career liability, 46–48
mental illness prototypes, 23–26
meta-analysis study, 26
neurodiversity in, 43–45
plate to trough, 56
positions, 12
public opinion, 73–77
roles, xxii
self-sacrifice, 30–33
seniority, 104–106
support networks, 151–154
systemic folie à deux, 30–33
well-being prototypes, 23–26
leadership machine maintenance programs, 22
leadership mental health, xxi, xxvi–xxvii
  archetype, 165–177
  career trajectory impact, 45–46
  community, 198–199
  community participation, 200–204

leadership mental health
(*Continued*)
  compounded effects of
    intersectionality, 81–82
  confidentiality
    concerns, 190–193
  construction industry, 114–115
  culture, 82–84
  ethnic identity, 83–92
  experiences, 104–106
  false correlations, 15–17
  generational identity, 100–104
  ignoring data on, 38–40
  impact on, 38
  inaccurate perceptions of, 20–21
  industry lens, 108
  industry-specific
    challenges, 106–108
  influence perceptions, 8, 80–82
  intergenerational tug-of-
    war, 98–100
  intersectionality needs, 204–205
  lack of emotional support
    structures, 41–43
  law industry, 108–110
  learn to receive help, 186–189
  map, 120–122
  organizational role and
    responsibility, 125–159
  peer support network, 150–154
  reflection to action, 206–208
  self-care, 39, 209–224
  set up to fail, 14–15
  shame, 46–47
  social norms shape
    perceptions, 83
  social stigmas, 85
  sociological assignment of power,
    4–5
  storytelling, 8
  support solution, 127, 158, 177,
    207, 221–224
  team culture impact, 51–53
  younger generations, 51
Lencioni, Patrick, 29
Lincoln, Abraham, 135
LinkedIn, 74

M
Maccoby, Michael, 10
masculinity, 94
*Mass General Brigham McLean
  Hospital,* 105
McKinsey Health Institute, 95–96
medical industry, 108–112
men, mental health, 94
mental health, xxiv
Mental Health At Work
  Conversational
  Literacy®, 156–157
mental health self-care
  tools, 212–213
mental well-being management
  tool, 215–220
Mental Wellbeing Non-Negotiables™,
  213–215
Millennials, 102
Miller, William R., 20
MIT Sloan Management Review,
  16, 40
Motivational Interviewing (MI),
  20, 21
Myers-Briggs study, 95, 106

N
Nanus, Burt, 69
National Academy of Engineering,
  114

National Alliance on Mental Illness (NAMI), 91
National Association for Law Placement, 110
National Health Service (NHS) healthcare system, 130
National Library of Medicine (NLOM), 39
neurodivergent leaders, 43–45
Nike, xx, 4

O
The Old Idea Being Broken, xxv
organizations, 125–126
  all-hands meetings, 148–149
  build human behavior into your approach, 139–142
  company website, 149
  crushing leadership mental health stigma, 148
  dismantling mental health hierarchy, 147
  email, 149
  in entertainment, 133
  in government, 132–133
  imperative, 128–129
  including mental health management as part of leadership development, 148
  internal newsletters and intranets, 148
  leadership veil, removing, 148
  logical strategic case, 130–134
  mental health resources, 146–147
  methods of impact, 142–157
  moral case, 129–130
  narrative, 147–150
  normalization case, 134–137
  normalizing bi-directional care, 148
  practical ways, 138–142
  responsibility, 159
  social media, 149
  strategy, 138–139
  transformation, 128, 142

P
peer group, 142
PERMA Model, 218–220
2020 *Pew Research Center* study, 76
The Pitt (TV show), 72, 111, 133, 186
polarization-driven unrest, 68–70
policy, program, & practice shifters xxii, 134, 142, 145, 150, 154, 157
power
  dynamics, xxiv
  sociological assignment of, 4–5
psychological contracts, 27–28
Psychology Today, 9, 137

R
realism, 197
reader responsibilities, xxvii, xxviii, xxix
reflection exercise, 163–164, 175–176, 184, 186, 198, 205
Rock, David, 139
Rogen, Seth, 133
Rollnick, Stephen, 20
ruthless process, xxii

S
SCARF Model, 139–141
SelectSoftware Reviews, 113
self-assessment exercise, 216

self-care plan
  assessment, 211–212
  consistency, 211–212
  mental health self-care tools,
    212–213
  mental well-being management
    tool, 215–220
  *Mental Wellbeing Non-
    Negotiables™*, 213–215
  PERMA Model, 218–220
  personalization, 210–212
  planning, 211–212
self-reflection, 185
Seligman, Martin, 218
sharing about your mental health
    with HR, 195–196
sharing about your mental health
    with fellow leaders, 193
sharing about your mental health
    with your boss, 194
sharing about your mental
    health with your team,
    194–195
Social Cognitive Model of
    Leadership Perceptions, 9
Social Identity Theory, 12, 73
social influences, 84
social media, 66, 67, 73, 74
social stigmas, 85
social tribalism, 70
societal chaos, 67
Sonny Vaccaro, 4, 6
Spring Health, 114–115
2024 State of Workforce Mental
    Health Report, 39
storytelling, 8
The Strategies for Taking Charge
    (Bennis, Nanus), 69
The Studio (TV show), 133

suicide, 43, 76, 96, 109, 114, 115
supervisor-subordinate
    relationship, 28
sustainable leadership, 130–134
systemic volatility, 68–70

T
The Principles of Influence (book), 11
The Workforce Institute, xxiv
trigger-like reaction, xx
Trust Barometer Global Report on
    Trust and the Crisis of
    Grievance, xx, 71
tyrannical leaders, 9

U
University of Hawai'i, 72
*U.S. Centers for Disease Control
    and Prevention (CDC)*, 110
U.S. workers, 91–92

V
VeryWellMind, 76
vicious cycle, 14
volatility, uncertainty, complexity
    and ambiguity
    (VUCA) model, 69

W
WebMD, 100
Weight on Leadership Mental
    Health Equation, 17,
    33–34, 53, 57, 77, 116–118,
    126–127, 221–223
women
  emotional contortionism, 96
  experience exhaustion, 96
  leadership, 95
  mental health, 94

work, 13
    intensification, 64–65
work cultures, 110
Workforce Attitudes Toward
    Mental Health Report, 131
World Economic Forum, 44, 95

Y
*Yes, You Can Talk About Mental
    Health at Work (Here's
    Why and How to Do It
    Really Well)* (book), xii
Yoon Suk Yeol, 65